Good Housekeeping

COMPLETE
INDIAN AND FAR EASTERN
COOKBOOK

Good Housekeeping

COMPLETE
INDIAN AND FAR EASTERN
COOKBOOK

DEALERFIELD

First published in 1997

1 2 3 4 5 6 7 8 9 10

This edition published for Dealerfield Ltd, 1997

First published in the United Kingdom in 1997 by Ebury Press
Random House, 20 Vauxhall Bridge Road, London SW1V 2SA

Random House Australia (Pty) Limited
20 Alfred Street, Milsons Point, Sydney, New South Wales 2061, Australia

Random House New Zealand Limited
187 Poland Road, Glenfield, Auckland 10, New Zealand

Random House South Africa (Pty) Limited
Endulini, 5a Jubilee Road, Parktown 2193, South Africa

Random House UK Limited Reg. No. 954009

A CIP catalogue record for this book is available from the British Library.

ISBN 0 09 186074 1

Managing editor: Julia Canning
Design: Christine Wood
Cover design: The Senate
Additional recipes: Joanna Farrow
Introduction: Judy Bastyra
Colour illustrations: Madeleine David
Additional photography: Laurie Evans

Colour reproduction by Masterlith Ltd, Mitcham
Printed and bound in Portugal by Printer Portuguesa L.d.a.

Foreword

The *Good Housekeeping Complete Indian and Asian Cookbook* brings together a wonderful collection of recipes, drawn from some of the most exciting cuisines in the world. An inspiration for any cook, the authentic-tasting recipes range from deliciously piquant snacks and fiery curries to spice-flavoured grills and aromatic vegetarian dishes.

Presented in an easy-to-follow format, many of the recipes are quick and simple to cook, making them ideal for everyday cooking, while others are perfect for creating an exotic feast, offering a memorable meal for friends. All the recipes have been double-tested in the kitchens of the Good Housekeeping Institute so that you can cook with complete confidence and, in addition, each recipe has a calorie count, preparation and cooking times and freezing instructions to help you plan your meals.

To put you at ease with unfamiliar foodstuffs, at the beginning of the book there is a helpful guide to the ingredients featured in the recipes. Many of these are readily available, but where items may be difficult to find, substitutes are recommended. As a bonus, a section on techniques gives clear guidance on specific preparation skills, from dry-roasting spices to preparing fresh coconut.

An invaluable source of exciting ideas for all occasions, this book gives you the best of the flavours of India and Asia and, above all, offers a thoroughly enjoyable style of cooking.

Moyra Fraser
Cookery Editor, *Good Housekeeping*

Cookery notes

- Both metric and imperial measures are given for the recipes. Follow either metric or imperial throughout as they are not interchangeable.

- All spoon measures are level unless otherwise stated. Sets of measuring spoons are available in metric and imperial for accurate measurement of small quantities.

- Ovens should be preheated to the specified temperature. Grills should also be preheated. The cooking times given in the recipes assume that this has been done.

- Where a stage is specified in brackets under freezing, the dish should be frozen at the end of that stage.

- Size 2 eggs should be used, except where otherwise specified. Free-range eggs are recommended.

- Use freshly ground black pepper unless otherwise specified.

- Use fresh rather than dried herbs unless dried herbs are suggested in the recipe.

Contents

Introduction

Spiced Pork Wontons, Chilli Fried Chicken With Coconut Noodles, Spiced Tikka Kebabs and Oriental Tofu And Bean Salad are just a few of the tempting recipes that you will find in this book.

Nowadays, an eclectic approach to cooking is becoming increasingly popular – ideas are drawn from many different countries, resulting in an interesting combination of flavours and textures, all complementing one another. You no longer have to stick rigidly to one cuisine for a whole meal, you have the freedom to mix and match different dishes, choosing your favourite ingredients and cooking techniques to suit your mood.

Inspired by this new and exciting approach to meal planning, this book brings together a wonderfully exotic range of dishes from India, China, Thailand and other far-eastern regions of the world. Some of the recipes are traditional dishes; others are examples of 'fusion' cooking – using authentic recipes for inspiration to create something new.

Meal planning

Harmony and balance are the key words when planning a meal with Indian and Asian dishes. Colours, textures and flavours should blend and harmonise with each other to create a spread that is pleasing to all the senses. Whether you serve a meal in the Western-style three-course format, or opt for the traditional Asian way of serving a selection of dishes all at once, make sure that the dishes complement one another. Think in terms of spicy and subtle, sweet and sour, hot and mild, soft and crunchy.

Serve accompaniments such as rice or flat breads to soak up any sauce in curries; offer cooling raita with a fiery dish; serve noodles to give stir-fries substance; partner a brown-looking dish with colourful vegetables for a visual lift; offer chutneys and dipping sauces with drier grilled food to add flavour and moisture.

Mix and match dishes from different regions as you like. The accent is on flexibility, the only hard and fast rule being that the meal is intended to be enjoyed in a happy and relaxed manner.

Preparation

With Indian and Asian food, the secret of success is to plan ahead and take care in preparation. The actual cooking is often very simple and quick, but the preparation, although straightforward, needs forward planning. So much depends on flavour and allowing time for the spices and herbs to permeate the dish. Sometimes a dish may need to marinate for several hours, or even overnight, to allow the flavourings to seep into the ingredients before the actual cooking time, which may only take a few minutes. This marinating process is an important stage in the recipe and should not be reduced in time.

Attention to detail is also necessary in preparation. With quick cooking such as stir-frying, when the food is literally tossed in a wok for a few minutes, each ingredient must be cut in a uniform way, to ensure even cooking and attractive presentation. Before you begin stir-frying, it is essential that all the ingredients are fully prepared and arranged close to hand as, once you start the cooking process, you really cannot stop – it's over in minutes.

Grinding whole spices at home may seem time-consuming, but the resulting flavour is far superior to the ready-ground type. You can also make your own spice mixes, such as garam masala and Chinese five-spice powder (see page 12). Dry-roasting the whole spices (see page 19) before grinding helps to release more flavour from the spices. In many of the dishes, spicy pastes made from spices, onions, garlic and other flavourings are at the core of the dish, adding distinctive taste to the main ingredients.

It's worth building up a store-cupboard of non-perishable items, such as soy sauce, Thai fish sauce, sesame oil, chilli sauce, black bean sauce, rice vinegar and dried spices, so that you only need to buy fresh ingredients when following recipes. Cans of coconut milk and bamboo shoots are also a convenient standby, and dried noodles and rice are always useful as versatile accompaniments.

As with all cuisines, buy fresh ingredients that are in prime condition. This is especially important for dishes that require very short cooking methods.

Utensils

No elaborate utensils are needed to cook the recipes in this book, but a few specific items will prove invaluable.
- A wok is obviously the best pan to use for stir-frying, but a large, deep frying pan makes a good substitute.
- A roomy, heavy-based flameproof casserole dish, which can be used on the hob as well as in the oven, is a versatile and very useful piece of equipment, particularly when a lid is called for in the cooking process.
- If you have one good-quality sharp knife, this should stand you in stead for most chopping and slicing needs.
- For blending and puréeing, a blender or food processor is

vital. Traditionally, a pestle and mortar is used for grinding spices, but an electric spice grinder also does the job very efficiently. An electric spice grinder is also handy for making curry pastes and marinades.

- When you need to lift food from hot oil or from a marinade, a slotted spoon is a must.
- Wooden skewers are traditionally used in satay or kebabs and give an authentic look to the food. To prevent the skewers from scorching, it is advisable to soak the skewers in cold water for at least 30 minutes before use.

Cooking methods

In many of the dishes featured in this book, the cooking methods are quick and simple. Stir-frying is a popular Oriental method and takes a matter of moments. The important point about stir-frying is that you must keep the food moving around the pan at all times, so that the ingredients cook evenly (see page 25). Grilling is another quick method, widely used in India as well as Asia. A conventional grill can be used effectively for most grilled dishes, and in the summer, a barbecue makes an excellent alternative, particularly for kebabs and tandoori dishes. Basting with a marinade or oil is essential for adding flavour and keeping the ingredients moist (see page 25).

Deep-frying, braising and steaming are just a few more methods used throughout the regions, all of which are uncomplicated but vary slightly from country to country.

Presentation

Attractive presentation is an important aspect of Indian and Asian cooking. Attention to the way the food is arranged on the plate, garnishes and even the way that the table is laid are all part of the charm of this style of cooking.

But, as with the choice of dishes, allow yourself the freedom to feel relaxed and serve the food in the mood of the moment. Much of the food is informal in style and calls for a relaxed setting. However, when laying the table, there are certain items which are fun to use and also offer a practical use during the meal.

- Put out finger dipping bowls when you are serving food that is dipped into a sauce. Use delicate bowls and float a lemon slice on the water. Always provide napkins with the bowls.
- Chopsticks are fun to use with Oriental dishes and give the table setting a sense of atmosphere. For soup, Oriental bowls with matching spoons look attractive and are also

useful for many other dishes.

- Drinking utensils can add a decorative touch to the table, too. Saki cups and handleless Chinese tea cups are just two ideas. A crisp white wine is the perfect accompaniment to most spicy dishes – serve it chilled in tall tapering glasses. Add lime twists to tumblers of mineral water

With a well-balanced menu, the complementary colours and textures of the dishes automatically make the food look appealing, but garnishes often give that vital finishing touch. A deftly arranged sprig of fresh coriander or a few wedges of lime or lemon might make all the difference to the final effect. A few classic garnishing ideas include:

- Spring onion curls – thinly slice spring onions, then drop into cold water and leave until curled.
- Crisp fried onion rings – slice onion into rings and fry in a little oil until browned and crisp. Drain on kitchen paper.
- Toasted coconut – pare or grate some fresh coconut, spread out on a baking tray and toast in a medium oven for about 10 minutes. Desiccated coconut makes a quick alternative.
- Toasted sesame seeds – brown under a grill for a few minutes, shaking the pan regularly.
- Banana leaves – an attractive serving idea, as food can be presented on the leaves; particularly good for plain rice. They are available from Asian stores.
- Chilli flowers – slice along the length of the chilli, keeping the stalk end intact, then drop into ice cold water to allow the cut lengths to curl.

These finishing touches will make all the difference to your meal, but, above all, remember that in India and Asia mealtimes are the focus of family life and entertaining is a great joy and opportunity to show your generosity and hospitality. Abundance is the key word – a table laden with exotic dishes is a feast for the eyes as well as the stomach. Follow this creed, and you can't go wrong! Happy cooking and eating!

Ingredients

In the following pages you will find a helpful guide to the many different ingredients that feature in Indian and Asian cooking

These days, authentic ingredients are far easier to find. Supermarkets are becoming ever more cosmopolitan in their range of goods, and some stores now have an 'ethnic' section which is an invaluable source of inspiration. Scour too the fresh herb section where you may well find packs of Indian or Thai herbs and spices. Don't forget small specialist shops, market stalls and wholefood or healthfood shops – these often offer the best choice and need your custom.

SPICES AND HERBS

Essential to all Indian and Asian dishes are the pungent spices and herbs that give the food its distinctive and exotic flavour.

BUYING AND STORING TIPS
For depth of flavour and that authentic spicy 'zing', buy spices in small quantities from a shop with a fast turnover. A packet of dried spices should release a powerful aroma when opened. If you have the time, buy whole spices and grind them yourself at home – this gives the best flavour by far. When choosing fresh herbs, look for bright colours and avoid any with wilted, browning leaves.

Store both ground and whole spices in airtight containers in a cool, dark place for not more than 6 months. If you keep them for any longer, they will begin to lose their flavour. Fresh herbs will keep in the refrigerator for a few days.

HOW HOT?
The 'hotness' of a dish is very much a matter of personal taste. Remember that spicy does not necessarily equal hot. It is chillies, either fresh or dried, or in powder form, that add heat to curries. There is a wide range of chillies to choose from these days. Although generally the larger the chilli the milder the flavour, there are some dramatic exceptions. The only certain way to gauge potency is by taste. So, when using an unidentified batch for the first time proceed with caution, adding a little at a time. For a milder dish, remove the seeds before using.

USEFUL EQUIPMENT
There are a few items of kitchen equipment that will prove invaluable for preparing spices and herbs for Indian and Asian dishes. A food processor or blender is almost essential for making curry pastes, and for puréeing ginger and garlic. For crushing whole spices at home, a good, heavy pestle and mortar, or an electric spice grinder, will be extremely useful.

BASIL
Several different types of basil are used in Thai cooking, but ordinary basil works well. Sweet basil can be found in some Oriental stores and as the name implies this variety has a particularly sweet flavour.

CARDAMOM
Available both as tiny green pods and large black pods containing seeds, cardamom has a strong aromatic quality. Use the pods whole or, for a more intense flavour, take out the seeds and grind or use these whole, discarding the pods.

CASSIA BARK
A relative of cinnamon, cassia bark has a strong cinnamon flavour. Pieces are added to many Indian dishes. It has a coarser appearance than true cinnamon sticks.

CAYENNE PEPPER
Cayenne pepper is ground from the pods and seeds of a hot, red variety of the capsicum family. It should be used with caution as the strength varies from brand to brand.

CHILLIES
Fresh green and red chillies are used extensively in Indian and Asian cooking. Red chillies are simply ripe green chillies; their flavour usually differs although the intensity is often the same. In general, the smaller chillies tend to be hotter, but there are exceptions. Remove seeds for a milder flavour.

Dried chillies can be bought whole or crushed, as chilli flakes. Both include the seeds which are very fiery and are generally best removed.

Whether using dried or fresh chillies, remember that their seeds and flesh can 'burn'. Wear rubber gloves for protection or at least make sure that you wash your hands thoroughly after preparation. In particular, eyes sting painfully if you happen to touch them after preparing chillies.

Cinnamon

Whole cinnamon sticks have a stronger, more intense flavour and aroma than ground cinnamon and keep their flavour for longer. However, they are difficult to grind at home. Buy ground cinnamon in small quantities.

Cloves

Whole and ground cloves are used in Indian cooking to add an aromatic flavour to dishes. Cloves are also one of the ingredients in Chinese five-spice powder.

Coriander leaves

A really pungent, intensely flavoured fresh herb that looks a little like flat-leaf parsley, except that the leaves are more rounded and less spiky. Chop or tear into pieces or purée with spices.

Coriander roots are also used to flavour spice pastes. Some good greengrocers and ethnic stores sell large bunches of coriander with the roots still attached; scrub well before use. Coriander stalks can be used as a substitute.

Coriander seeds

Coriander seeds taste completely different from the fresh herb. They have a fairly mild flavour and are used in many Indian dishes. Dry-roasted seeds can be ground directly onto foods.

Cumin

A vital flavouring in curries, cumin has a strong slightly bitter flavour. Dry roasting gives it a milder flavour. Whole seeds keep their flavour better than ground cumin.

Curry paste

Thai red curry paste and green curry paste form the basis of many Thai curries. Recipes are given on page 18, but they are also available ready-made from Oriental stores and many supermarkets. Once opened, reseal and store in the refrigerator for up to 1 month.

Ready-made Indian curry pastes are widely available from supermarkets and come in mild, medium and hot strengths.

Tandoori and tikka pastes are also sold and are useful for quick cooking.

Fennel seeds

These tiny pale green seeds lend a delicate aniseed flavour to dishes. They are particularly good with fish and vegetables.

Fenugreek

Small hard seeds with a distinctive aroma, fenugreek seeds are traditionally ground and used as a component of curry powder. They have a rather bitter pungent flavour, so use judiciously in curries.

Five-spice powder

A ground spice mixture, usually containing star anise, cloves, fennel seeds, cinnamon and Chinese pepper. Blends do vary, however; some contain dried orange peel. Use sparingly to give a distinctive Chinese accent.

To make your own powder, grind together 25 ml (5 tsp) anise pepper, 25 ml (5 tsp) star anise, 12 cm (5 inch) cassia bark or cinnamon stick, 30 ml (2 tbsp) whole cloves and 35 ml (7 tsp) fennel seeds. Store in an airtight jar for up to 1 month.

Galangal

This is a member of the ginger family and is similar in appearance, but with a slightly transparent pink-tinged skin and dark rings. It has a milder but more aromatic flavour than root ginger and is commonly used in Thai cooking. It is now available from some larger supermarkets as well as Oriental food stores. Dried galangal can be used if the fresh root is unavailable.

Garam masala

An aromatic spice mixture used in Indian cooking, garam masala usually contains cardamoms, cumin and pepper but recipes vary greatly. The ready-made version is readily available, but if you have time, it is worth making your own for a better flavour.

To make your own garam masala, grind together 4 black cardamoms or 10 green cardamoms, 15 ml (1 tbsp) black peppercorns and 10 ml (2 tsp) cumin seeds. The amounts can be increased or decreased according to taste, and spices such as dried red chillies or whole coriander seeds may be added if wished. Only make small quantities at a time as the flavour does not stay fresh for long.

Ginger

Fresh root ginger comes from the root stems of a tropical plant and has a hot sweetish taste. A popular ingredient in Far Eastern cookery, fresh root ginger is now widely available from supermarkets. Before use, the skin is peeled off, then the ginger is sliced, chopped, grated or made into a paste. When grating ginger, use the finest blade.

Root ginger is also sold in dried form, or it may be dried and ground.

Stem (green) ginger is available preserved in syrup.

Kaffir lime leaves

The leaves of the kaffir lime tree have a very aromatic lime flavour and are used whole – like bay leaves – to flavour sauces, soups and stews, or chopped or shredded and used to flavour fish cakes, meat koftas, kebabs and marinades for fish and meat. There is no real substitute, although freshly grated lime rind may be used as a last resort. The fresh leaves are available from Oriental food stores and can be frozen for future use.

Lemon grass

A tall, hard grass, pale green in colour, available from some supermarkets and Oriental stores. The very tough outer leaves should be discarded. It is the thick bottom end that has the most flavour. Bruise or crush with a rolling pin, or slice, to release maximum flavour and aroma. Lemon grass can also be chopped and then ground with other spices to form a paste. The stalks can be frozen whole.

MINT
Fresh mint is used to add flavour to Indian dishes and is the classic ingredient of raita, the cooling yogurt-based accompaniment to curries. Mint-flavoured fresh chutney is also a popular partner to hot dishes.

MUSTARD SEEDS
Black, brown and white seeds are available. Frying the seeds extracts their delicious flavour.

SAFFRON
The dried stigma of the saffron crocus, saffron has a wonderful subtle flavour and aroma, and imparts a hint of yellow colour to a dish. The whole stigmas (strands) give superior results. Powdered saffron is also available but the flavour is not as good.

Although saffron is expensive, a little goes a long way. A large pinch is all that is needed in most dishes. The stigmas are usually soaked before use (see page 19).

SESAME SEEDS
These small, creamy-coloured spice seeds have a rich, sweet, slightly nutty flavour which is enhanced by toasting or frying. Black sesame seeds are also used.

STAR ANISE
This is the star-shaped fruit of an evergreen tree native to China. When dried it is a red-brown colour and the flavour is like pungent aniseed. It can be used whole to flavour a dish, but is also one of the ingredients of Chinese five-spice powder.

SZECHUAN PEPPERCORNS
These are reddish-brown peppercorns and are very aromatic. They are available from most supermarkets.

TAMARIND
This is the large pod of the tamarind tree. It is seeded, peeled and pressed into a dark-brown pulp which is sold dried in block form. Tamarind juice is used to add a sour flavour to curries and sauces. It is available ready-made from some supermarkets, or you can make your own juice at home.

To make tamarind juice, break 25 g (1 oz) off the block and blend in 45 ml (3 tbsp) hot water. Strain the liquid through a sieve, pressing down hard with a spoon to extract as much of the pulp as possible – the juice should be almost paste-like. Discard the pulp left in the sieve and use the juice according to the recipe. If tamarind pulp is unavailable, lemon juice can be used instead.

TURMERIC
Turmeric is the root of a plant related to the ginger family and is most commonly sold dried and ground. Like saffron, turmeric colours food that it is cooked with yellow, but that is where the similarity with saffron ends. Turmeric has a much harsher, almost earthy flavour and should be used sparingly in dishes.

FLAVOURING AGENTS

There are some flavourings that do not fall into the category of herbs or spices. Most of these are bottled sauces, but some oils, wines and vinegars also impart distinctive flavours.

BLACK BEAN SAUCE
This thick, dark brown, salty sauce is made from fermented soya beans. It is used to add flavour to sauces and stir-fries. Available from larger supermarkets, once opened black bean sauce should be stored, tightly closed, in the refrigerator for no longer than 1 month.

CHILLI SAUCE
Hot chilli sauce is used in many Far Eastern dishes. Sometimes sold under the Thai name of *sambal olek*, it is widely available, but ordinary chilli sauce can be used if preferred.

HOISIN SAUCE
A sweet, reddish-brown, rather spicy sauce made from garlic, soya beans, sugar and spices. Used in Chinese cooking.

OYSTER SAUCE
This is a thick Chinese sauce which is sweet and salty at the same time. It is used to flavour many dishes and is widely available from supermarkets.

RICE WINE
Rice wine is popular in Far Eastern cooking. Shaohsing wine,

from China, has a rich, sherry-like flavour and can be found in some larger supermarkets and Oriental stores. Use sherry as an alternative.

Saki is a Japanese rice wine, while mirin is a sweetened version of saki. Again, use sherry as an alternative.

RICE VINEGAR
Vinegar made from rice is a common ingredient in Chinese and Japanese dishes. It is available from good healthfood shops, some delicatessens and Oriental stores. Use sherry or white wine vinegar as an alternative.

SESAME OIL
A delicious, highly fragrant amber liquid, sesame oil is more seasoning than oil. Buy it in small bottles, as it slowly deteriorates.

SHRIMP PASTE
Shrimp paste, or *nam prik* as it is called in Thailand, is made from dried shrimps and used to flavour many Thai pastes and sauces. It is available commercially from Oriental stores. A recipe for a home-made version is given on page 52.

SOY SAUCE
Made from a mixture of fermented soya beans, flour and water, this is one of the essential ingredients of Chinese cooking, and is also used as a condiment. It is available in light and dark varieties. Light soy sauce is most frequently used in cooking; despite its lighter colour, it is full of flavour. Dark soy sauce has been fermented longer than light soy sauce and therefore has a fuller flavour and deeper colour.

In Thai cooking, a thick sweet soy sauce, called *kecap manis*, is used to add flavour. This is available commercially, but you can make a version at home – combine 100 ml (4 fl oz) dark soy sauce with 45 ml (3 tbsp) molasses and 22 ml (1½ tbsp) dark brown sugar in a saucepan. Heat gently, stirring, until the sugar has dissolved.

THAI FISH SAUCE
This is called *nam pla* in Thailand where it is used rather like soy sauce. A salty, brown liquid, it is made from fermented fish and is readily available from Oriental food stores and larger supermarkets. Light soy sauce or a mashed anchovy can be substituted if necessary.

VEGETABLES, FRUIT AND NUTS

With the increased availability of fresh Indian and Asian ingredients in this country, it is possible to create dishes that are truly authentic in character.

AUBERGINES
These range in colour from white and whitish green through dark green to yellowish purple to red purple or black. They are use extensively in Indian curries, and are often degorged (see page 20) before cooking, to remove the bitter juices.

BAMBOO SHOOTS
The tender shoots of the bamboo plant have an acceptable crunchy texture. Fresh bamboo shoots are available from Oriental stores, otherwise they are available sliced and halved in cans.

BEAN SPROUTS
These are the crisp shoots of the mung bean and are widely available from supermarkets and healthfood stores. They add a crisp texture to salads and stir-fries. Use bean sprouts as soon as possible after buying.

COCONUT
The coconut milk referred to in many recipes has nothing to do with the natural 'milk' or juice in the centre of the coconut, but is actually made using either fresh coconut or creamed coconut. It is used extensively in Indian and Asian dishes and is particularly good for thickening soups and curries, adding a subtle, creamy flavour. It is available in cans from most supermarkets and ethnic stores, but it is also simple to make at home by reconstituting powdered or creamed coconut.

Creamed coconut is sold in blocks from most supermarkets and only a small amount is needed to both flavour and thicken a sauce. To make thick coconut milk from creamed coconut, break a 200 g (7 oz) block into a bowl. Add 450 ml (¾ pint) warm water and stir until dissolved. Strain through muslin or a fine sieve before using. For a thinner milk, stir in an extra 150 ml (¼ pint) water and strain before use.

KAFFIR LIMES

Small wrinkly limes from a particular variety of lime tree, kaffir limes are not as juicy as their familiar smooth-skinned relation but they have a sweeter, more delicate flavour. Kaffir limes make an intriguing garnish. If unobtainable, use ordinary lime or lemon as a substitute.

LYCHEES

Originating in China, lychees are stone fruit the size of small plums. They have hard brittle skins, ranging from pink to brown, which encase fragrant, pearly white, juicy flesh. Peel and stone before use.

MANGOES

These are large stone fruit which can vary in shape from round to narrow and long to pear-shaped. Their juicy fibrous flesh has a distinctive, delicate flavour. The flesh clings to the stone – there is a technique to removing the flesh neatly from the fruit (see page 22).

MOOLI

These are Oriental white radishes which are long and conical in shape, usually with a thin white skin. They have a pungent aroma but the flavour is milder than conventional red radishes. Daikon is a Japanese variety of white radish.

MUSHROOMS

Several Oriental mushrooms are available fresh from supermarkets, including the pale fan-shaped oyster mushroom, and the tan coloured velvety shiitake mushroom.

Dried black mushrooms and shiitake mushrooms are often used in Far Eastern cooking, adding a wonderful flavour to dishes. These are available from Oriental stores. They need to be soaked in boiling water for 20-30 minutes before use.

NORI

Nori are sheets of seaweed and are popular in Japanese cooking. They are used extensively in the making of sushi.

Packets of nori are now available from larger supermarkets and can be obtained from specialist stores.

OKRA

These are dark green, podded vegetables which look rather like ribbed chillies. Both pods and seeds are eaten. Wipe clean and remove the stems before cooking.

PAK CHOI

A Chinese leaf vegetable, pak choi is often used in stir-fry dishes and is available from some supermarkets and Oriental shops. Chinese cabbage is a good alternative.

PAPAYAS

Smooth skinned with a delicate flavour, papayas have juicy orange-pink flesh with lots of black seeds in the centre. The seeds are usually removed because they have a peppery flavour.

PEANUTS

These nuts are particularly synonymous with Thai and Indonesian cooking and are added to sauces as well as used as a condiment for curries and salads. Buy raw unsalted nuts, with or without their reddish skins, and toast them at home: place the nuts on a baking sheet and roast in the oven at 200°C (400°F) Mark 6 for 8-10 minutes until golden.

WATER CHESTNUTS

Looking very similar to sweet chestnuts, these small tubers are sometimes available fresh, but canned water chestnuts make an excellent substitute. Water chestnuts have white flesh with a mild, sweet flavour and a crisp, crunchy texture.

YARD LONG BEANS

Available from ethnic stores, these long thin green beans are similar to French beans but three to four times longer. They often feature in Far Eastern cooking. Substitute French beans if necessary.

GRAINS AND PULSES

DAL

Dal is the collective name given to the great variety of pulses, dried peas and lentils cooked in India. Dal are rich in protein and play a crucial role in the diets of many vegetarians. Two examples of dal are chana dal (husked, split black chick peas) and masoor dal (split red lentils). Both are available from larger supermarkets or Indian grocers.

GRAM FLOUR

Also known as besan, gram flour is a very fine-textured flour made from ground chick peas and gives an authentic flavour to Indian dishes. It is available from Indian grocers, but if unobtainable, plain wholemeal flour makes a good substitute.

NOODLES

Egg noodles are enormously popular in China, and also Japan, where they are called ramen. They are made with wheat flour, water and eggs and come in various shapes and sizes, ranging from thin thread noodles to nest egg noodles. Most are available in dried form from major supermarkets, while the fresh variety are sold in Oriental stores. Some egg noodles are simply soaked to soften but most require some boiling. When cooked, rinse well under cold water to remove the starch.

Rice noodles, made with rice, flour and water, vary in shape from ribbon-like shapes to very fine noodles, which are usually called vermicelli. Whiter and more transparent in appearance than egg noodles, rice noodles are often made in long strands which are folded over for packaging. All dried rice noodles are just as starchy as the egg variety and need rinsing after boiling. They can also be deep-fried, when they puff up and become crisp and light.

Transparent of cellophane noodles are made from mung beans and are sold in long strands which are folded over for packaging.

For all noodles follow the cooking instructions on the packet, for best results.

RICE

Rice plays an important role in Indian and Asian cooking. Basmati rice, prized for its slender, delicately-perfumed grains, is the supreme rice of Indian cooking. It is widely available from supermarkets. For cooking technique see page 26.

Thai fragrant rice, again widely available, is also delicious and is an essential part of a Thai meal. Try steaming the rice for fluffy results, see page 26. For this method you will need 300 ml (½ pint) water to 225 g (8 oz) rice.

Glutinous rice cooks into a sticky mass and is particularly popular in Japanese and Chinese cuisines. It is now becoming more available in major supermarkets. Follow the packet instructions for cooking.

RICE FLOUR

Similar in texture and taste to cornflour, rice flour can be bought at most Oriental stores and good healthfood stores.

TOFU

Firm tofu, available in block form, is used in many Oriental vegetable dishes. It is made from fermented and pressed soya beans and has a texture rather like hard cheese. Although rather bland in flavour, it readily absorbs the flavours of foods that it is cooked with. Drain off the liquid from the packet and cut the tofu into cubes.

WONTON WRAPPERS

Small thin squares of dough, wonton wrappers are sold fresh or frozen in most Oriental food stores. If unobtainable, try making them yourself as they are simple to prepare.

For home-made wonton wrappers, sift 150 g (5 oz) plain flour with 2.5 ml (½ tsp) salt into a bowl. Gradually work in 1 egg and enough cold water to form a stiff dough. Knead for 5 minutes. Wrap and chill for 30 minutes. Roll out the dough in batches as thinly as possible, using a pasta machine if possible, then cut into 7.5 cm (3 inch) squares. Use immediately, or freeze for future use.

Techniques

Thai red curry paste

2 long thin fresh red chillies
8 dried red chillies
4 kaffir lime leaves
2.5 cm (1 inch) piece galangal
4 shallots
4 garlic cloves
2 lemon grass stalks
5 ml (1 tsp) ground black pepper
5 ml (1 tsp) ground turmeric
30 ml (2 tbsp) sunflower oil

1 Using a small sharp knife, halve and deseed the fresh and dried chillies, wearing rubber gloves to prevent skin irritation, then roughly chop the chillies and lime leaves.

3 Peel off and discard any tough outer layers from the lemon grass. Trim the thin end, then chop.

2 Peel the galangal, trim and discard any woody or shrivelled parts, then chop. Peel and chop the shallots and garlic.

4 Put these prepared ingredients in a spice grinder or blender with the black pepper, turmeric and sunflower oil and purée to form a smooth paste. Store in a screw-topped jar for up to 1 month

Thai green curry paste

4 long thin green chillies
2-4 small green chillies
4 garlic cloves
2.5 cm (1 inch) piece fresh root ginger
1 lemon grass stalk
6 spring onions, trimmed
4 coriander roots, scrubbed
4 kaffir lime leaves
15 ml (1 tbsp) chopped fresh coriander

1 Wearing rubber gloves to prevent skin irritation, deseed the chillies, then roughly chop. Peel and chop the garlic, ginger and lemon grass. Chop the spring onions and coriander roots. Shred the lime leaves.

2 Place all the ingredients in a spice grinder or mortar. Grind or pound to form a smooth paste, adding a little water if necessary. Store in a screw-topped jar for up to 1 month.

Dry-roasting spices

Heat a small heavy-based pan over medium heat. Add the whole spices, such as cumin and coriander seeds, and stir continually until they are evenly browned and release their aroma. Cool slightly before grinding.

Grinding whole spices

Crush seeds with a pestle and mortar, or with a rolling pin, until finely ground. Alternatively, use an electric spice grinder. Freshly ground spices produce a better flavour than spices that have been bought ready-ground.

Making tamarind juice

For homemade tamarind juice, break off a block of tamarind pulp and blend in hot water. Strain the mixture through a sieve, pressing down hard with a spoon to extract as much of the pulp as possible.

Soaking saffron strands

To extract the delicate yellow colour and aromatic flavour from saffron strands, place the strands in a bowl, pour over warm water and leave to soak for about 10 minutes.

Slicing fresh root ginger

Using a small sharp knife, thinly peel the skin from the root ginger. Cut the ginger into thick slices, then cut into thin strips. Chop into smaller pieces if necessary.

Bruising lemon grass

Strike the end of the lemon stalk firmly with the end of a rolling pin to release the flavour. Use whole to flavour sauces. Remember to remove the stalk before serving the dish.

Chopping fresh coriander

Trim off the stalks from the sprigs and chop the coriander leaves finely with a sharp knife. A small handful of fresh coriander will produce about 45 ml (3 tbsp) chopped coriander.

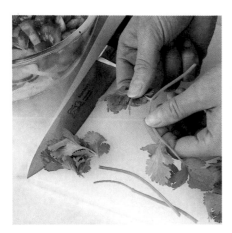

Slicing fresh chillies

Wearing rubber gloves to prevent skin irritation, cut the stalk from the chilli. Cut the chilli in half and remove the seeds if a milder flavour is preferred. Slice the chilli as required.

Preparing fresh okra

Wipe the okra with a damp cloth, then trim, removing a small piece from each end. Do not cut into the flesh or the dish will acquire an unpleasant glutinous texture during cooking.

Degorging aubergines

Put the aubergine slices in a colander set over a plate and sprinkle with salt. Leave for 30 minutes to extract the bitter juices. Rinse in cold water and pat dry with kitchen paper.

Cutting ribbon slices

To cut ribbon slices from vegetables such as carrots and courgettes, you will need a swivel peeler. Pressing firmly with the peeler, pare long thin ribbons from the vegetables.

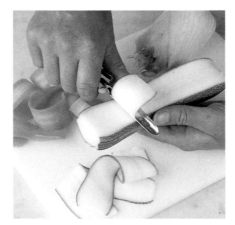

Shredding spring onions

Trim the spring onions at both ends, then halve each onion lengthways. Cut each spring onion into long, thin strips, then drop into cold water to create curls, ideal for garnishing.

Finely chopping onion

Peel the onion, leaving the root end intact. Cut in half lengthways and lay one half, cut-side down, on a board. Slice through the onion, keeping root end intact, then cut crosswise.

Cutting carrot strips

Peel the carrots, then trim off all rounded edges. Cut into 6 cm (2½ inch) lengths, then cut into 3 mm (⅛ inch) thick slices. Stack 4 or 5 slices on top of each other and cut into strips.

Removing skins from tomatoes

Mark a shallow cross on the bottom of each tomato, then put in a heatproof bowl and pour on boiling water to cover. Leave for about 30 seconds. Remove and peel away the skins.

Refreshing vegetables

To preserve the fresh colour of green vegetables and to stop the cooking process, drain the blanched vegetables in a colander, then refresh under cold running water.

Dry-frying nuts

Place nuts, such as blanched almonds or unsalted cashew nuts, in a dry, heavy-based frying pan and place over a low heat. Move the nuts around the pan until they are golden brown.

Preparing fresh coconut

Wrap the coconut in a tea-towel, grip it firmly and crack with a hammer – the 'milk' will spill out. Remove the coconut flesh and peel off the hard brown skin using a vegetable peeler.

Cutting the flesh neatly from a fresh mango

1 Cut the mango either side of (and close to) the stone to make 2 large pieces. Cut the flesh within these pieces into cubes, without breaking the skin.

2 Push the skin inside out to expose the cubes; peel off the skin. Peel the remaining centre section of flesh, still attached to the stone; slice the flesh from the stone.

Preparing fresh pineapple

Cut off the leaf crown, then slice off the skin, cutting downwards. Remove any remaining brown 'eyes' with the tip of a knife. Cut into slices and remove the central core.

Preparing fresh papaya

Using a sharp knife, peel and halve the papaya. Scoop out the seeds with a teaspoon and discard. Cut the flesh into wedges or slices, or serve simply with fresh lemon wedges.

Preparing fresh lychees

Peel off the brittle skin with your fingers to reveal the pearly flesh. Using a sharp knife, cut the flesh in half, cutting round the stone. Remove the stone and discard.

Preparing melon and watermelon

Cut the melon into quarters, then scoop out the seeds with a small spoon and discard. Using a large knife, cut the flesh away from the skin before slicing into chunks.

Cleaning fresh mussels

1 Put the mussels in the sink and under cold running water, scrape off any mud or barnacles with a sharp knife, or scrub with a small stiff brush. Pull away the hair-like beard that protrudes from the shell.

2 Tap any mussels that remain open with the back of the knife. If they refuse to close, throw them away as they will not be fit to eat. Rinse the mussels again in cold water until there is no trace of sand or grit.

Cleaning shelled scallops

Trim away and discard the soft fringe-like part of the scallop and remove the tough greyish 'connective' muscle from the side of the white meat. If required, separate the roe from the white flesh.

Preparing fresh squid

1 Holding the body of the squid in one hand, pull the squid 'pouch' and the tentacles apart. The soft contents of the body should emerge with the tentacles. Cut the tentacles away from the head just below the eyes. Discard the head.

2 Using your fingers, squeeze out the plastic-like 'quill' and any soft innards from the pouch. Discard. Peel off the thin layer of dark skin that covers the body and discard. Rinse the tentacles and the squid pouch thoroughly under cold running water.

3 The cleaned squid pouch may now be sliced into rings. Alternatively, cut open the pouch to give large pieces, then cut into squares and score using a small sharp knife. Follow cooking instructions closely, to avoid ruining the tender texture of the squid.

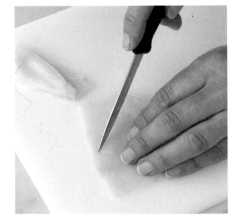

Preparing large raw or cooked prawns

1 Grip the head between thumb and forefinger; hold tail shell with other hand. Gently pull the head off. Peel away the shells, leaving the fan-like tail shell attached, if wished.

2 Using a small sharp knife, make a shallow slit along the outer curve of each prawn from the tail to the head end and remove the dark intestinal vein, which has a bitter taste.

Grilling large prawns

Place the prawns on the grill rack and grill as close to the heat as possible, turning and basting frequently with a marinade. For ease of turning, thread onto bamboo skewers.

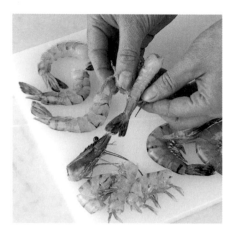

Preparing fresh crab meat

1 Twist off the legs and claws from the body. Break each claw in half, then crack with a rolling pin without crushing the flesh. Break the shell on the legs with your hands. Using a slender skewer, carefully extract the flesh.

2 Put the crab on its back and, holding the shell firmly, press the body section upwards and ease it away. With a teaspoon, scoop out the creamy meat from the shell. Discard the stomach bag which is between the eyes.

3 Pull away from the body and discard the inedible feathery gills or 'dead man's fingers'. Using a large heavy knife, cut the body in half. Using a skewer, remove the flesh from the tiny crevices.

Tucking chicken wings

To give roasted or grilled chicken wings an attractive finished shape, before cooking tuck the tip of each chicken wing under the thickest part of the wing, to form a triangle.

Slashing poultry pieces

Before marinating duck or chicken pieces, slash the flesh using a sharp knife, to allow the marinade to permeate through the meat. The skin is usually removed first.

Marinating poultry pieces

Turn the chicken or duck pieces in the marinade and rub the mixture well into the slashes to ensure flavours permeate. Remove from the marinade with a slotted spoon or two forks.

Preparing meat kebabs

For thin strips of meat, thread the strips onto skewers in a zig-zag fashion. When threading cubes of meat onto skewers, do not pack too tightly or they will not cook through.

Basting meat and poultry

Use a spoon to baste meat with pan juices or a marinade during roasting or grilling, to give the meat a golden glaze and ensure that the flesh remains moist during the cooking time.

Stir-frying technique

When stir-frying, make sure that the ingredients are cut into even-sized pieces so that they cook evenly, and always keep the food moving around the pan during cooking.

Preparing egg noodles

Some egg noodles simply need to stand in boiling water to soften, but many require some boiling. Rinse to remove starch and use at once or toss in a little oil.

Preparing rice noodles

All dried rice noodles are just as starchy as the egg variety, so treat in the same way after boiling – rinse under cold running water. Stir once during cooking to separate the strands.

Deep-frying noodles

Both egg and rice noodles deep-fry well. Soften egg noodles first, then lower a handful into the hot oil and deep-fry for about 1 minute until crisp and golden.

Preparing rice for cooking

Both basmati and Thai fragrant rice need to be rinsed before cooking in order to remove excess starch and any pieces of grit. Simply place in a sieve and wash under running water. Drain thoroughly before cooking according to type.

Cooking basmati rice

Bring a saucepan of water to the boil. Add the rice to the pan, return to the boil and stir once. Lower the heat and cook, uncovered, fairly vigorously for about 12 minutes. As soon as it is cooked, drain and rinse with boiling water to remove excess starch.

Cooking Thai fragrant rice

Put the rice in a heavy-based saucepan with cold water. Cover and bring quickly to the boil, then remove the lid and stir over medium heat until the water has evaporated. Replace lid firmly and set over a low heat for 20 minutes allowing the rice to steam.

Making an omelette

Heat a little oil in a small frying pan, then pour in the beaten eggs. Cook over a low heat, stirring occasionally, until the omelette is just set. Remove with a spatula.

Slicing rolled omelette

Turn the omelette out onto a sheet of nonstick baking parchment and leave to cool. When the omelette is cold, roll up like a Swiss roll, and cut into thin slices to use as garnish.

Making ghee butter

Heat unsalted butter in a pan until melted and all bubbling stops. Remove from the heat and stand until the sediment has sunk to the bottom, then gently pour off the fat through muslin.

Using wonton wrappers

Place a heaped teaspoon of filling in the centre of each wonton wrapper and draw up the edges of the wrapper, pressing them together at the top to seal in the filling.

Wrapping prawn rolls

Place a prawn, with the tail shell still attached, at the end of a strip of prepared filo pastry. Then roll up the prawn in the pastry to enclose all but the tail.

Making poppadom baskets

Deep-fry a small poppadom and immediately place over a slim jar or can covered with foil. Quickly press a wider teacup over the poppadom to shape it into a basket. Drain when set.

STARTERS AND SNACKS

This chapter offers a selection of delicious lightweight dishes, ideal to serve as mouthwatering openers to meals, or as tasty everyday snacks. There's an interesting variety of soups, ranging from a tangy chicken soup with a hot and sour flavour, or a curried coconut soup packed with luxurious shellfish, to a delicate clear broth, laced with vegetables. A choice of tantalising meat snacks, including small spicy kebabs, chilli-flavoured pork wontons and bite-sized koftas, make tasty morsels to whet the appetite, while seafood appetisers – from delicately spiced prawns wrapped in light-as-air pastry to sesame-coated crab cakes, dipped in a sweet ginger sauce – will prove irresistible. Crisp vegetable fritters, a refreshing noodle dish with tofu and popular onion bhajis are just a few more delicacies to try.

Illustration: Beef Satay (recipe page 39)

Pork and Noodle Soup

PREPARATION TIME: 25 MINUTES

COOKING TIME: 35 MINUTES

FREEZING: NOT SUITABLE

300 CALS PER SERVING

SERVES 6

50 g (2 oz) peanuts or cashew nuts

4 garlic cloves

60 ml (4 tbsp) chopped fresh coriander

225 g (8 oz) minced pork

salt and pepper

3 lemon grass stalks

6 kaffir lime leaves or a little grated lime rind

1.7 litres (3 pints) chicken stock

15 ml (1 tbsp) light soy sauce

15 ml (1 tbsp) Thai fish sauce

juice of 2 limes

5 ml (1 tsp) Thai red curry paste

10 ml (2 tsp) caster sugar

125 g (4 oz) broccoli

125 g (4 oz) button mushrooms

125 g (4 oz) rice noodles or egg noodles

60 ml (4 tbsp) oil

COOK'S NOTE

Knead the meatballs well, with your hands, as it will help to bind them together and stops them breaking up during cooking.

1 Roughly chop the nuts. Peel and crush the garlic, then mix with the nuts, 30 ml (2 tbsp) chopped coriander, the minced pork and seasoning. Roll into 18 walnut-sized balls.

2 Finely chop the lemon grass and lime leaves, if using. Place in a large saucepan with the chicken stock, soy sauce, fish sauce, lime juice and lime rind, if using, red curry paste and sugar. Bring to the boil and simmer for 20 minutes.

3 Separate the broccoli into florets and slice the mushrooms. Cook the noodles according to packet instructions, then drain.

4 Meanwhile, heat 45 ml (3 tbsp) oil in a deep, heavy-based frying pan or saucepan and fry the meatballs in batches for 4-5 minutes or until a light golden colour and cooked through. Set aside.

5 Heat the remaining oil and stir-fry the mushrooms and broccoli for 1-2 minutes. Add the noodles and meatballs; strain the broth over. Garnish with the remaining coriander.

Thai Chicken Soup

PREPARATION TIME: 10 MINUTES
COOKING TIME: 20 MINUTES
FREEZING: NOT SUITABLE

265 CALS PER SERVING
SERVES 4

1 green chilli
2.5 cm (1 inch) piece fresh root ginger
2 garlic cloves
350 g (12 oz) skinless chicken flesh (breast, leg or thigh)
125 g (4 oz) creamed coconut
225 g (8 oz) mangetout

15 ml (1 tbsp) oil
750 ml (1½ pints) chicken stock
45 ml (3 tbsp) fresh lime juice (about 2 limes)
about 90 ml (6 tbsp) chopped fresh coriander
salt and pepper
a few chopped spring onions, to garnish

1 Halve, deseed and finely chop the chilli. Peel and finely chop the ginger. Peel and crush the garlic. Slice the chicken into chunks.

2 Roughly chop the creamed coconut, then dissolve in 300 ml (½ pint) boiling water. Slice the mangetout.

3 Heat the oil in a nonstick saucepan, add the chilli, ginger, chicken and crushed garlic and cook for 1-2 minutes.

4 Add the stock, coconut milk, lime juice and half the coriander. Bring to the boil, then cover the pan and simmer for 15 minutes. Add the mangetout and cook for a further 5 minutes or until the chicken is tender.

5 Add the remaining coriander and season to taste. Garnish with chopped spring onions to serve.

Hot and Sour Chicken Soup

PREPARATION TIME: 15 MINUTES
COOKING TIME: 25 MINUTES
FREEZING: NOT SUITABLE

50 CALS PER SERVING
SERVES 4

COOK'S NOTE
Look out for packs of Thai mixed herbs alongside the fresh herbs in larger supermarkets. Each pack usually contains a piece of lemon grass, some kaffir lime leaves, a couple of hot chillies and a few pieces of kuchai (garlic chives). If packs are unavailable, buy spices individually – try Oriental food stores.

1 packet fresh Thai mixed herbs
2 garlic cloves
2.5 cm (1 inch) piece fresh root ginger
handful of fresh coriander sprigs
1.1 litres (2 pints) good chicken stock
1 chicken breast fillet, skinned

125 g (4 oz) mushrooms, preferably shiitake or baby button mushrooms
juice of 2 limes
about 30 ml (2 tbsp) light soy sauce
spring onion curls, to garnish

1 To prepare the herbs, crush the lemon grass using a rolling pin. Slice 1 or 2 chillies (retaining the seeds) – the soup should be fairly hot. Peel the garlic and thinly slice. Thinly slice the unpeeled ginger. Put all the Thai herbs in a large saucepan with the garlic, ginger, half the coriander and the stock. Cover and bring to the boil.

2 Meanwhile, cut the chicken into strips and halve or slice any larger mushrooms. When the stock has come to the boil, reduce to a simmer and add the chicken and mushrooms. Cover and simmer gently for 20 minutes until the chicken is cooked.

3 Add the lime juice and soy sauce to the soup, then taste. The flavour should be fairly hot and faintly sour. If it needs more salt, add a little extra soy sauce. Add more chilli if necessary. Remove and discard the coriander sprigs.

4 Ladle the soup into warmed individual bowls and top each with a pile of onion curls and fresh coriander sprigs.

VARIATION
Replace the chicken with 225 g (8 oz) peeled raw prawns. Simmer the soup with the mushrooms for 20 minutes before adding the prawns. Add the prawns and simmer gently for 4-5 minutes or until the prawns are cooked through (they will look pink and opaque).

Indonesian Soup

PREPARATION TIME: 5 MINUTES

COOKING TIME: ABOUT 15 MINUTES

FREEZING: NOT SUITABLE

180 CALS PER SERVING

SERVES 6

2 garlic cloves
5 cm (2 inch) piece fresh root ginger
1 green chilli
15 ml (1 tbsp) sunflower oil
75 g (3 oz) creamed coconut
30 ml (2 tbsp) crunchy peanut butter
5 ml (1 tsp) ground coriander

75 g (3 oz) medium egg noodles
175 g (6 oz) cooked peeled prawns
75 g (3 oz) firm tofu
juice of 2 limes
5 ml (1 tsp) chopped fresh lemon grass
salt and pepper
spring onion strips, to garnish

1 Peel and crush the garlic. Peel and finely grate the ginger. Deseed and chop the chilli.

2 Heat the oil in a large saucepan, add the garlic, ginger and chilli and cook gently until softened.

3 Mix the coconut and peanut butter with 900 ml (1½ pints) boiling water and stir until dissolved.

4 Stir the ground coriander into the garlic mixture and cook for 1 minute. Add the coconut and peanut mixture to the pan and bring to the boil.

5 Add the noodles and the prawns to the soup and simmer gently for about 5 minutes until the noodles are just cooked. Meanwhile cut the tofu into 2.5 cm (1 inch) cubes.

6 Stir the lime juice into the soup. Add the tofu with the lemon grass. Season with salt and pepper. Simmer for a further 2-3 minutes. Serve immediately, garnished with spring onion.

Thai Shellfish Soup

PREPARATION TIME: 30 MINUTES

COOKING TIME: 1 HOUR

FREEZING: NOT SUITABLE

350 CALS PER SERVING

SERVES 4

Illustrated opposite

8 large raw prawns in shells
20 fresh mussels
4-8 small squid, cleaned
4 large cooked crab claws
900 ml (1½ pints) fish or vegetable stock
15 ml (1 tbsp) groundnut or sunflower oil

15-30 ml (1-2 tbsp) Thai red curry paste
300 ml (½ pint) coconut milk
30 ml (2 tbsp) light soy sauce
salt and pepper
coriander leaves, to garnish

1 Prepare the shellfish. Peel the prawns and place the heads and shells in a large saucepan. Scrub the mussels thoroughly in plenty of cold water and remove the beards. Discard any mussels which do not close when tapped firmly. Slice the squid into rings and halve the tentacles, if large. Separate the crab claws at the joints and crack the shells slightly with a mallet or nut crackers. Set all the shellfish aside.

2 Add the stock to the prawn shells, bring to the boil, cover the pan and simmer gently for 30 minutes. Strain and reserve the stock.

3 Meanwhile, place the mussels in a large saucepan with a little water. Cover with a tight-fitting lid and cook over a high heat for 3 minutes until the shells are steamed open. Drain the mussels and discard any that remain closed. Refresh the mussels immediately under cold running water and set aside.

4 Heat the oil in a clean pan, add the curry paste and fry, stirring, over a gentle heat for 2 minutes. Stir in the reserved prawn stock, coconut milk and soy sauce. Bring to the boil, cover and simmer gently for 20 minutes.

5 Add the prawns and crab claws to the soup. Simmer for 5 minutes, then add the squid and mussels. Heat through for a further 3-4 minutes and check the seasoning. Serve at once, garnished with the coriander leaves.

COOK'S NOTE
Cracking the crab claws prior to cooking makes getting into the flesh easier. Don't forget the finger bowls!

Hot and Sour Prawn Soup

PREPARATION TIME: 5 MINUTES

COOKING TIME: 20 MINUTES

FREEZING: NOT SUITABLE

140 CALS PER SERVING

SERVES 4

125 g (4 oz) onion
1 small green chilli
2.5 cm (1 inch) piece fresh root ginger
15 ml (1 tbsp) oil
50 g (2 oz) small oyster mushrooms
1.1 litres (2 pints) chicken stock

1 lemon grass stalk
15 ml (1 tbsp) white wine vinegar
350 g (12 oz) large cooked peeled prawns
1 bunch watercress
salt and pepper

1 Peel and chop the onion. Deseed and finely chop the chilli. Peel and chop the ginger.
2 Heat the oil in a large saucepan and fry the onion, chilli and ginger for 4-5 minutes. Add the mushrooms and continue to fry for 1-2 minutes.
3 Stir in the chicken stock, lemon grass and white wine vinegar. Bring to the boil, cover and simmer for 10-12 minutes.
4 Roughly chop the prawns and chop the watercress. Add to the pan and simmer for a further 2 minutes. Remove the lemon grass, adjust the seasoning and serve.

VARIATION
Try adding 60 ml (4 tbsp) chopped coriander to replace the watercress.

Spinach and Coconut Soup

PREPARATION TIME: 10 MINUTES

COOKING TIME: 25 MINUTES

FREEZING: NOT SUITABLE

150 CALS PER SERVING

SERVES 4

1 bunch spring onions
2 red chillies
1 garlic clove
2.5 cm (1 inch) piece fresh root ginger
1 lemon grass stalk
15 ml (1 tbsp) oil

450 g (1 lb) fresh spinach
300 ml (½ pint) coconut milk
600 ml (1 pint) vegetable or chicken stock
salt and pepper
crushed peppercorns, flat-leaf parsley, finely chopped spring onions, red chilli and coconut milk, to garnish

1 Thinly slice the spring onions. Deseed and finely chop the chillies. Peel and finely chop the garlic and ginger. Split open the lemon grass.
2 Heat the oil in a large saucepan and add the spring onions, chilli, garlic, ginger and lemon grass. Cook over a low heat for 5-7 minutes.
3 Wash the spinach in several changes of water and roughly chop. Add the spinach to the saucepan and continue cooking until it begins to wilt.
4 Add the coconut milk, stock and seasoning. Bring to the boil, then reduce the heat and simmer for 10-15 minutes. Leave to cool slightly.
5 Remove the lemon grass and discard. Place the mixture in a blender or food processor and purée until smooth. Re-heat, adjust the seasoning and serve garnished with peppercorns, parsley, onions, chilli and a swirl of coconut milk.

Vegetable, Noodle and Tofu Broth

PREPARATION TIME: 20 MINUTES

COOKING TIME: 1¼ HOURS, INCLUDING STOCK

FREEZING: SUITABLE – STOCK ONLY

135 CALS PER SERVING

SERVES 4

STOCK
1 onion
2 carrots
2 garlic cloves
15 g (½ oz) fresh root ginger
2 lemon grass stalks
2 celery sticks
4 kaffir lime leaves
4 coriander roots, scrubbed
5 ml (1 tsp) white peppercorns
5 ml (1 tsp) salt

BROTH
25 g (1 oz) dried black or shiitake mushrooms
1 large carrot
50 g (2 oz) cauliflower florets
50 g (2 oz) baby sweetcorn
125 g (4 oz) firm tofu
30 ml (2 tbsp) dark soy sauce
15 ml (1 tbsp) lemon or lime juice
50 g (2 oz) egg thread noodles
mint leaves and chilli oil, to serve

COOK'S NOTE
If you haven't time to prepare the stock, make up the required amount of liquid using a vegetable stock cube and add 15 ml (1 tbsp) each of lime and lemon juice and a pinch of sugar. Alternatively, use a good quality chicken stock instead.

1 Start by making the stock. Place 1.1 litres (2 pints) water in a large saucepan. Peel and roughly chop the onion, carrots, garlic and ginger. Chop the lemon grass and celery and add to the pan with the remaining ingredients. Bring to the boil, cover and simmer over a gentle heat for 1 hour.

2 Put the dried mushrooms in a bowl, pour over 100 ml (4 fl oz) boiling water and leave to soak for 30 minutes. Strain and reserve the liquid; chop the mushrooms.

3 Prepare the remaining vegetables. Cut the carrot into matchsticks; divide the cauliflower into small florets; halve the sweetcorn lengthways. Cube the tofu.

4 Strain the stock into a clean pan and stir in the soy sauce, lemon or lime juice and reserved mushroom liquid. Return to the boil and stir in the prepared vegetables, tofu and soaked mushrooms. Simmer for 5 minutes.

5 Plunge in the noodles and simmer for a further 5-6 minutes until the noodles and vegetables are tender. Ladle the soup into large warmed soup bowls. Serve at once, scattered with mint leaves and drizzled with a little chilli oil.

Spiced Dal Soup

PREPARATION TIME:
10 MINUTES, PLUS SOAKING

COOKING TIME: 1½ HOURS

FREEZING: NOT SUITABLE

200-130 CALS PER SERVING

SERVES 4-6

125 g (4 oz) yellow split peas
225 g (8 oz) tomatoes
5 ml (1 tsp) cumin seeds
10 ml (2 tsp) coriander seeds
3 dried red chillies
15 ml (1 tbsp) desiccated unsweetened coconut

30 ml (2 tbsp) ghee or oil
2.5 ml (½ tsp) ground turmeric
5 ml (1 tsp) treacle
5 ml (1 tsp) salt
coriander sprigs and lemon slices, to garnish

COOK'S NOTE
Poppadoms make an excellent accompaniment to this soup. To cook poppadoms, either fry for a few seconds in oil or brush with oil and grill for a few seconds on each side.

1 Put the split peas into a sieve and wash thoroughly under cold running water. Drain well, then transfer to a bowl, cover with cold water and soak for 8 hours. Drain, place in a large saucepan, cover with 600 ml (1 pint) water and boil rapidly for 10 minutes. Cover and simmer for at least 1 hour, or until tender.

2 Immerse the tomatoes in a bowl of boiling water for 30 seconds, then drain and remove the skins. Roughly chop the flesh. Set aside.

3 Finely grind the cumin, coriander, chillies and coconut in an electric spice grinder or with a pestle and mortar. Heat the ghee or oil in a heavy-based frying pan, add the spice mixture and fry, stirring, for 30 seconds. Set aside.

4 Purée the split peas and transfer to a large saucepan. Stir in the tomatoes, fried spices, turmeric, treacle, salt and a further 300 ml (½ pint) water.

5 Bring to the boil, then lower the heat, cover and simmer for about 20 minutes. Taste and adjust seasoning. Serve, garnished with coriander sprigs and lemon slices.

Mushroom and Omelette Soup

PREPARATION TIME:
25 MINUTES, PLUS SOAKING

COOKING TIME: 30 MINUTES

FREEZING: NOT SUITABLE

165 CALS PER SERVING

SERVES 4

Illustrated opposite

1.1 litres (2 pints) vegetable stock (see page 35)
15 g (½ oz) each dried black and dried shiitake mushrooms, or 25 g (1 oz) dried shiitake
1 bunch spring onions
1-2 garlic cloves
2 small green chillies
grated rind and juice of 1 lime
15 ml (1 tbsp) sunflower oil

10 ml (2 tsp) sesame oil
125 g (4 oz) oyster mushrooms
25 g (1 oz) canned bamboo shoots, drained
15 ml (1 tbsp) light soy sauce

OMELETTE
15 ml (1 tbsp) sunflower oil
2 eggs
salt and pepper

1 Strain the vegetable stock into a saucepan.

2 Place the dried mushrooms in a bowl, pour over 300 ml (½ pint) boiling water and leave to soak for 30 minutes. Strain and reserve the liquid; finely slice the shiitake and chop the black mushrooms.

3 Trim and slice the spring onions and set aside. Peel and roughly chop the garlic. Deseed and chop the chillies. Pound the garlic and chillies with the lime rind, using a pestle and mortar or a spice grinder, until well crushed.

4 Heat both the oils in a wok or frying pan and fry the garlic and chilli paste with the spring onions for 5 minutes until softened. Stir into the stock with the lime juice, soaked mushrooms and reserved liquid. Cover and simmer for 20 minutes.

5 Meanwhile, make the omelette. Heat the oil in a small frying pan. Beat the eggs with salt and pepper, then pour into the hot oil. Cook over a low heat, stirring occasionally, until the omelette is just set. Remove from the pan with a spatula and cut into thick strips or squares.

6 Add the oyster mushrooms, bamboo shoots and soy sauce to the soup and simmer for 4-5 minutes until all the mushrooms are tender. Stir in the omelette pieces and serve at once.

VARIATION
Instead of making an omelette, simply beat 2 eggs together and whisk into the just simmering soup at the end of cooking. Immediately remove from the heat.

Koftas

PREPARATION TIME: 20 MINUTES
COOKING TIME: 10 MINUTES
FREEZING: SUITABLE

40 CALS PER KOFTA
MAKES 24

COOK'S NOTE
If your frying pan is small you may need to cook the koftas in 2-3 batches.

1 small onion
1 garlic clove
2.5 cm (1 inch) piece fresh root ginger
5 ml (1 tsp) ground cumin
5 ml (1 tsp) ground coriander
45 ml (3 tbsp) ghee or oil
450 g (1 lb) minced beef
45 ml (3 tbsp) chopped fresh coriander
salt and pepper

1 egg (size 3), beaten
raita (see page 199), to serve
ONION RELISH
1 red onion
45 ml (3 tbsp) chopped fresh coriander
1 lime
1 large red chilli (optional)
1 garlic clove

1 First make the onion relish. Peel and quarter the onion, then slice thinly. Put into a bowl with the chopped coriander. Grate the lime rind into the bowl. Finely slice the chilli, if using, discarding the seeds if a milder flavour is preferred. Peel and chop the garlic. Add the chilli and garlic to the onion relish with a squeeze of lime juice. Toss to mix, then set aside.

2 To make the koftas, peel and quarter the onion; peel the garlic; peel and halve the ginger. Put these ingredients in a blender or food processor and work until finely chopped. Add the spices and process until evenly mixed.

3 Heat 15 ml (1 tbsp) of the ghee or oil in a frying pan and add the onion paste. Cook over a medium heat for 2-3 minutes, stirring all the time. Remove from the heat and allow to cool.

4 Put the minced beef in a bowl and break it up with a fork. Add the chopped coriander and season with salt and pepper. Add the cooled onion paste and mix thoroughly. Add just sufficient beaten egg to bind; don't add too much or the mixture will be too sticky to shape.

5 Using lightly floured hands, shape the spiced beef mixture into approximately 24 small balls.

6 Heat the remaining ghee or oil in the frying pan and add the koftas. Cook for about 5 minutes or until browned on all sides and cooked right through, shaking the pan as they cook to ensure they brown evenly. Drain the koftas on kitchen paper. Serve hot with the onion relish scattered over the koftas. Accompany with raita.

Beef Satay

PREPARATION TIME:
30 MINUTES, PLUS FREEZING
AND MARINATING

COOKING TIME: 4-5 MINUTES

FREEZING: NOT SUITABLE

110 CALS PER SERVING

SERVES 4

350 g (12 oz) fillet steak
2 garlic cloves
2.5 cm (1 inch) piece fresh root ginger
30 ml (2 tbsp) dark soy sauce
30 ml (2 tbsp) sweet sherry
15 ml (1 tbsp) rice or wine vinegar
10 ml (2 tsp) sesame oil
2.5 ml (½ tsp) chilli powder

PEANUT SAUCE
1 garlic clove
60 ml (4 tbsp) chopped peanuts
1.25 ml (¼ tsp) dried crushed chilli flakes
15 ml (1 tbsp) dark soy sauce
15 ml (1 tbsp) lime juice
5 ml (1 tsp) clear honey
100 g (3½ oz) creamed coconut

COOK'S NOTE
To make rice cubes for a garnish, cook 50 g (2 oz) Thai Fragrant rice until very soft. Refresh under cold water, drain, then press into a small oiled dish. Chill until required. Unmould and cut into cubes.

1 Place the beef in the freezer for 30 minutes until firm, to make it easier to slice.
2 Using a sharp knife, slice the beef across the grain into thin strips. Place in a shallow non-metallic dish. Peel and crush the garlic; peel and grate the ginger. Place the garlic and ginger in a bowl with the soy sauce, sherry, vinegar, sesame oil and chilli powder. Pour over the beef, stir well, cover and leave to marinate in a cool place for 2-4 hours.
3 Remove the beef from the marinade and thread onto bamboo skewers in a zig-zag fashion. Place the beef skewers on the grill rack and grill as close to the heat as possible for 4-5 minutes until tender, turning halfway through cooking.
4 Meanwhile make the peanut sauce. Peel and crush the garlic and put in a small saucepan with the peanuts, chilli flakes, soy sauce, lime juice and honey. Heat gently, then add the creamed coconut and cook, stirring, until smooth. Remove from the heat. Serve with the beef.

Seekh Kebabs

PREPARATION TIME: 20 MINUTES

COOKING TIME: 10 MINUTES

FREEZING: NOT SUITABLE

95-70 CALS PER KEBAB

MAKES 12-16

1 small onion
2 garlic cloves
2.5 cm (1 inch) piece fresh root ginger
1 hot red chilli
10 ml (2 tsp) coriander seeds
5 ml (1 tsp) ground fenugreek
5 ml (1 tsp) garam masala
5 ml (1 tsp) ground turmeric
15 ml (1 tbsp) ghee or oil, plus extra for brushing

450 g (1 lb) minced lamb
45 ml (3 tbsp) chopped fresh coriander
45 ml (3 tbsp) chopped fresh mint
salt and pepper
1 egg (size 3), beaten
mint sprigs and shredded coriander or chilli, to garnish
lemon wedges, to serve

COOK'S NOTES
If your grill pan is small, you may need to cook the kebabs in two batches.

To prevent scorching during grilling, pre-soak the bamboo skewers in water for about 10 minutes.

1 Peel and quarter the onion. Peel the garlic and ginger. Chop the chilli, discarding the seeds if a milder flavour is preferred. Put these ingredients into a blender or food processor and process until finely chopped.
2 Crush the coriander seeds with a pestle and mortar and add to the onion paste with the remaining spices. Process until evenly blended.
3 Heat 15 ml (1 tbsp) ghee or oil in a frying pan and add the onion paste. Cook over a medium heat for 2-3 minutes, stirring all the time. Remove from the heat and allow to cool.
4 Put the minced lamb in a bowl, stir in the chopped coriander and mint and season with salt and pepper. Add the cooled onion paste and mix thoroughly. Add just enough of the beaten egg to bind; don't add too much or you will make the mixture too wet to shape.
5 Divide the mixture into 12-16 portions. Using floured hands, shape each portion into a flattened sausage around one end of a bamboo skewer. Press the mixture firmly so that it sticks together. Repeat to make about 12-16 kebabs.
6 Brush the kebabs with melted ghee or oil. Cook under a very hot grill for about 10 minutes or until browned on the outside and cooked right through, turning the kebabs as they cook to ensure that they brown evenly. Serve garnished with mint and shredded coriander or chilli. Accompany with lemon wedges.

Momos

PREPARATION TIME:
50 MINUTES, PLUS CHILLING

COOKING TIME: 40 MINUTES

FREEZING: NOT SUITABLE

50 CALS PER MOMO

SERVES 6

1 small onion
15 g (½ oz) piece fresh root ginger
1 garlic clove
175 g (6 oz) lean minced lamb
15 ml (1 tbsp) garam masala
large pinch of chilli powder

salt and pepper
small handful fresh coriander leaves
125 g (4 oz) plain white flour
oil, for brushing
fresh tomato chutney (see page 199), to serve

1 Peel and roughly chop the onion and ginger. Peel the garlic. Place all three in a food processor with the lamb, garam masala, chilli powder, coriander and salt and blend to mix.
2 With floured hands, roll the mixture into 24 small balls. Cover and chill for 30 minutes.
3 Season the flour with salt and pepper, then mix to a soft dough with about 60-75 ml (4-5 tbsp) water. Knead until smooth. Divide into 24 pieces.
4 Roll out each piece of dough on a very well-floured surface to a thin round about 9 cm (3½ inches) across. Flour the dough well as you roll it, and keep turning it over to prevent sticking.
5 Place a ball of minced lamb in the centre of each round. Dampen the edges of the dough, then pinch them together over the lamb mixture to form money bag shapes. Place the momos on a baking sheet lined with nonstick paper. Cover and chill for at least 30 minutes.
6 Select a wire rack which will rest over a roasting tin. Cover the rack with foil and lightly oil the surface. Arrange the momos on top, brushing with oil. Half fill the roasting tin with boiling water, top with the wire rack and loosely cover with a second piece of foil to enclose the momos.
7 Steam bake at 180°C (350°F) Mark 4 for about 40 minutes. Serve hot, with chutney.

Lamb Samosas

PREPARATION TIME: 45 MINUTES

COOKING TIME: 20 MINUTES

FREEZING: SUITABLE

155 CALS PER SAMOSA

MAKES 24

Illustrated opposite

COOK'S NOTE
For convenience, the samosas can be made in advance and later reheated in the oven at 180°C (350°F) Mark 4 for about 15 minutes.

1 potato
1 onion
1 garlic clove
2.5 cm (1 inch) piece fresh root ginger
30 ml (2 tbsp) oil
5 ml (1 tsp) chilli powder
10 ml (2 tsp) ground coriander
10 ml (2 tsp) ground cumin
large pinch of grated nutmeg
large pinch of ground cloves
225 g (8 oz) lean minced lamb

handful of spinach leaves
30 ml (2 tbsp) each chopped fresh coriander and mint
salt and pepper
oil for deep-frying
lemon and lime wedges, to garnish

PASTRY
450 g (1 lb) plain white flour
5 ml (1 tsp) salt
5 ml (1 tsp) cumin seeds
60 ml (4 tbsp) oil, melted ghee or butter

1 Peel and finely chop the potato, onion, garlic and ginger. Heat the oil in a frying pan. Add the potato, onion and garlic and cook for about 5 minutes until the potato is softened.
2 Add the spices and cook, stirring, for 2 minutes. Add the minced lamb and cook for about 5 minutes until browned, stirring all the time. Add 30 ml (2 tbsp) water, lower the heat, cover and simmer for about 20 minutes or until the potato is tender and the mixture is fairly dry.
3 Trim and chop the spinach leaves. Add to the pan and cook for about 1 minute, until just wilted. Add the chopped herbs and plenty of seasoning. Leave to cool.
4 To make the pastry, mix together the flour, salt and cumin seeds in a bowl. Mix in the oil or melted fat and about 200 ml (7 fl oz) warm water to make a soft dough. Turn onto a lightly floured surface and knead for about 5 minutes.
5 Divide the dough into 12 even pieces; keep covered with a damp cloth to prevent them drying out. Roll out one piece to a circle, 15 cm (6 inches) in diameter. Cut in half.
6 Put a heaped teaspoonful of filling on each semi-circle. Dampen the edges, then fold over the filling and press together to seal. Repeat with the remaining pastry and filling.
7 Heat the oil in a deep-fat fryer. Test the temperature by dropping in a small piece of pastry – it should sizzle immediately on contact with the oil and rise to the surface.
8 Deep-fry the samosas in batches for about 3-5 minutes or until pale golden brown. Garnish.

Chillied Pork Dim Sum

PREPARATION TIME: 45 MINUTES

COOKING TIME: 15 MINUTES

FREEZING: NOT SUITABLE

145 CALS PER SERVING

SERVES 8

1 garlic clove
½ onion
2 whole dried red chillies
15 ml (1 tbsp) oil
125 g (4 oz) lean minced pork
15 ml (1 tbsp) finely chopped bamboo shoots
10 ml (2 tsp) dark soy sauce
15 ml (1 tbsp) oyster sauce
10 ml (2 tsp) tomato purée
5 ml (1 tsp) sesame oil
125 g (4 oz) self-raising flour

several good pinches of salt
20 g (¾ oz) lard
15 ml (1 tbsp) caster sugar
10 ml (2 tsp) sesame seeds

DIPPING SAUCE
15 ml (1 tbsp) soy sauce
15 ml (1 tbsp) lemon juice
5 ml (1 tsp) toasted sesame seeds
5 ml (1 tsp) caster sugar
1 crushed garlic clove
a little grated root ginger

COOK'S NOTE
Bamboo steamers (which stack on top of each other) are ideal for cooking this type of dim sum, as they can all be cooked at the same time. Move the stacks around to ensure even cooking – as those near the boiling water cook slightly more quickly.

1 Peel and crush the garlic. Peel and finely chop the onion. Finely chop the chillies, discarding the seeds if a milder flavour is preferred.

2 Heat the oil in a frying pan, add the pork, garlic, onion, chillies and bamboo shoots and stir-fry for 5 minutes. Add the soy sauce, oyster sauce and tomato purée and cook for 5 minutes, stirring occasionally. Stir in the sesame oil and leave to cool.

3 Sift the flour and salt into a bowl and rub in the lard finely. Stir in the sugar and sesame seeds. Add about 60 ml (4 tbsp) water and mix to form a soft dough. Divide into 24 portions. Form each into a ball and roll out on a lightly floured surface to an 9 cm (3½ inch) round.

4 Put a teaspoonful of pork mixture into the centre of each round. Dampen the edges and gather together, sealing well. Form each into a little pouch by twisting the tops together, sealing the edges well.

5 Cook in a bamboo steamer (or conventional steamer) over simmering water for about 15 minutes until cooked through.

6 To make the dipping sauce, mix the ingredients with 45 ml (3 tbsp) water until well blended.

7 Serve the dim sum hot accompanied by the sauce.

Spiced Pork Wontons

PREPARATION TIME: 30 MINUTES

COOKING TIME: ABOUT 15 MINUTES

FREEZING: NOT SUITABLE

100 CALS PER WONTON

MAKES 20-24

2.5 cm (1 inch) piece fresh root ginger
2 garlic cloves
1 small onion
2 hot chillies
5 ml (1 tsp) Chinese five-spice powder
90 ml (6 tbsp) chopped fresh coriander

700 g (1½ lb) lean minced pork
salt and pepper
20-24 wonton wrappers
1 egg, beaten
oil for deep-frying

1 Peel the ginger and cut in half. Peel the garlic. Peel and quarter the onion. Remove the stems from the chillies and, if a milder flavour is preferred, discard the seeds. Put all of these ingredients in a blender or food processor and process until finely chopped.

2 Add the five-spice powder, coriander and pork. Process again until evenly mixed. Season generously with salt and pepper.

3 Using lightly floured hands, shape the mixture into walnut-sized balls.

4 Wrap each one in a wonton wrapper, sealing the edges with beaten egg. Alternatively, stack the wonton wrappers in a neat pile and cut into thin shreds, using a large sharp knife. Spread them in a single layer on a plate. Dip the pork balls into the beaten egg then drop onto the shredded wontons and roll around on the plate until coated on all sides. The wonton strips should stick out, rather than lie flat.

5 Heat the oil in a deep-fat fryer to 175°C (345°F) or until a cube of bread dropped into the oil browns in about 1 minute. Deep-fry the wontons, in batches, for about 4 minutes until golden brown on all sides and the pork is cooked right through. Drain on crumpled kitchen paper. Serve warm.

Glazed Chicken Wings

PREPARATION TIME:
10 MINUTES, PLUS MARINATING

COOKING TIME: ABOUT 1 HOUR

FREEZING: NOT SUITABLE

175 CALS PER SERVING

SERVES 4

12 small chicken wings

4 garlic cloves

5-10 ml (1-2 tsp) hot chilli sauce

45 ml (3 tbsp) sweet soy sauce

15 ml (1 tbsp) preserved stem ginger syrup or clear honey

15 ml (1 tbsp) lemon juice

5 ml (1 tsp) ground coriander

2.5 ml (½ tsp) ground cinnamon

spring onion shreds and lime and/or lemon wedges, to garnish

1 Wash and dry the chicken wings. Tuck the tip of each wing under the thickest part of the wing, forming a triangular shape. Transfer to a large shallow, non-metallic dish.

2 Peel and crush the garlic and place in a bowl. Add all the remaining ingredients, mix well, then pour over the chicken wings. Toss to coat the wings thoroughly. Cover and leave to marinate in a cool place for at least 4 hours, preferably overnight.

3 Transfer the chicken wings and marinade juices to a roasting tin just large enough to hold them in a single layer. Bake at the top of the oven at 220°C (425°F) Mark 7 for 50-60 minutes, basting and turning frequently until the wings are glazed and tender. The flesh should almost fall from the bone. Serve hot, garnished with spring onion shreds and lime and/or lemon wedges.

VARIATION

Use the sauce as a glaze for spare ribs rather than chicken wings. Place 700 g (1½ lb) pork ribs in a pan, cover with cold water and add 30 ml (2 tbsp) distilled malt vinegar. Bring to the boil and simmer for 20 minutes, then drain and cool. Toss with the marinade and continue as above.

Thai Chicken Wontons

PREPARATION TIME: 25 MINUTES

COOKING TIME: ABOUT 30 MINUTES

FREEZING: NOT SUITABLE

345 CALS PER SERVING

MAKES 30

COOK'S NOTE
Keep the wontons well apart in the hot oil so that they do not stick together.

3 large red chillies
3 kaffir lime leaves
6 spring onions
2 lemon grass stalks, each 15 cm (6 inches) long
3 garlic cloves
450 g (1 lb) skinless chicken breast fillets
small handful fresh coriander sprigs

45 ml (3 tbsp) coconut milk
salt and pepper
225 g (8 oz) filo pastry
1 egg, beaten
oil for deep-frying
ready-made sweet chilli dipping sauce, to serve

1 Finely chop the chillies, kaffir lime leaves, spring onions and lemon grass. Peel and crush the garlic. Roughly chop the chicken. Place these ingredients in a food processor with the coriander, coconut milk and seasoning and work for 2-3 minutes.

2 Cut the filo into thirty 15 cm (6 inch) squares. Keep the filo squares covered with a lightly dampened tea-towel as you work on each one. Brush one square with the beaten egg. Place 10 ml (2 tsp) of the chicken mixture in the centre of the square. Scrunch the edges together roughly to seal. Set aside while you complete the remaining wontons.

3 Heat the oil in a deep-fat fryer to 175°C (345°F) or until a cube of bread dropped into the oil browns in about 1 minute. Deep-fry the wontons in batches for 4-5 minutes or until they are pale golden brown and cooked through. Drain the wontons on kitchen paper. Pile up on a serving platter and serve with a sweet chilli dipping sauce.

Chicken, Cashew and Noodle Salad

PREPARATION TIME:
25 MINUTES, PLUS MARINATING

COOKING TIME: 4-5 MINUTES

FREEZING: NOT SUITABLE

470 CALS PER SERVING

SERVES 4

350 g (12 oz) skinless chicken breast fillets
30 ml (2 tbsp) sunflower oil
5 ml (1 tsp) sesame oil
5 ml (1 tsp) ground coriander
1.25 ml (¼ tsp) chilli powder
pinch of Chinese five-spice powder
125 g (4 oz) dried egg noodles (½ packet)
50 g (2 oz) mangetout
50 g (2 oz) French beans, halved
15 ml (1 tbsp) chopped fresh mint
15 ml (1 tbsp) chopped fresh coriander

25 g (1 oz) cashew nuts, toasted
coriander sprigs, to garnish

DRESSING
45 ml (3 tbsp) peanut or sunflower oil
10 ml (2 tsp) sesame oil
1 garlic clove, crushed
5 ml (1 tsp) grated fresh root ginger
2.5 ml (½ tsp) crushed dried red chilli flakes
15 ml (1 tbsp) dark soy sauce
15 ml (1 tbsp) lemon juice

1 Very thinly slice the chicken breast, across the grain, then place in a shallow non-metallic dish. Combine 15 ml (1 tbsp) of the sunflower oil with the sesame oil, coriander, chilli powder and Chinese five-spice powder. Add to the chicken and stir until evenly coated. Cover and leave to marinate for at least 30 minutes.

2 Cook the noodles according to the packet instructions.

3 Heat the remaining sunflower oil in a large nonstick frying pan. When hot, add the marinated chicken pieces and stir-fry for 2 minutes until golden and crispy. Drain on kitchen paper.

4 Add the vegetables and herbs to the pan and stir-fry for 1 minute until tender. Add to the chicken pieces and keep warm.

5 To make the dressing, heat both oils in a small pan, add the garlic, ginger and chilli flakes and fry gently until softened but not coloured. Whisk in the soy sauce, lemon juice and 30 ml (2 tbsp) water. Bring to the boil and remove from the heat.

6 Drain the cooked noodles and immediately toss with the hot soy dressing and chicken and vegetable mixture. Sprinkle over the toasted cashews. Serve warm or cool, garnished with coriander.

Duck Dim Sum

PREPARATION TIME: 1 HOUR

COOKING TIME: 16 MINUTES

FREEZING: NOT SUITABLE

185 CALS PER DIM SUM

MAKES 16

450 g (1 lb) plain white flour

sesame oil, for brushing

30 ml (2 tbsp) oil

cucumber slivers and spring onion curls, to garnish

DUCK FILLING

2 duck breasts with skin, each weighing about 150 g (5 oz)

4 spring onions

75 g (3 oz) cucumber

15 ml (1 tbsp) hoisin sauce

30 ml (2 tbsp) plum jam

15 ml (1 tbsp) dark soy sauce

salt and pepper

1 Sift the flour into a bowl, add 350 ml (12 fl oz) boiling water and stir well. Sprinkle with 15 ml (1 tbsp) cold water and mix well. Leave until cool enough to handle, then knead until smooth. Cover with a damp cloth and leave for 30 minutes.

2 To make the filling, prick the duck breast skin all over with a fork and place, skin-side down, in a frying pan. Cook over a medium heat for 10 minutes or until golden brown all over.

3 Either mince the duck breasts and skin, or work in a food processor until finely chopped, then transfer to a bowl. Trim and chop the spring onions. Finely chop the cucumber. Add the spring onions and cucumber to the duck with the hoisin sauce, plum jam, soy sauce and salt and pepper to taste. Stir well.

4 Halve the dough and shape each piece into a roll about 23 cm (9 inches) long. Cut each roll into eight pieces and shape into balls. Roll out each ball into a 9 cm (3½ inch) round and, using a 7.5 cm (3 inch) round biscuit cutter, cut each piece to a neat round.

5 Lightly brush each one with sesame oil and place a teaspoonful of filling on each round. Spread out the filling to cover half of each round, leaving a clear border. Fold the plain sides over and seal the edges firmly together.

6 Heat 15 ml (1 tbsp) oil in a frying pan, add half the pancakes and fry for 2 minutes, turning frequently. Remove from the pan and cook the remainder in the same way.

7 Place each pancake on a small piece of greased greaseproof paper and steam in a tiered bamboo or metal steamer for 12 minutes.

8 Serve hot, garnished with slivers of cucumber and spring onion curls.

Marinated Trout

PREPARATION TIME:

15 MINUTES, PLUS MARINATING

COOKING TIME: NONE

FREEZING: NOT SUITABLE

120 CALS PER SERVING

SERVES 4

2 trout fillets, each about 125 g (4 oz)

salt and pepper

1 packet fresh Thai herbs

2 limes

1 orange

45 ml (3 tbsp) coconut milk powder

30 ml (2 tbsp) clear honey

1 large bag mixed salad leaves

125 g (4 oz) cooked peeled prawns

crispy fried onions, to garnish

1 Season the trout fillets with salt and pepper. Chop the Thai herbs. Sandwich the seasoned fillets together with the chopped herbs and place in a shallow, non-metallic dish. Squeeze over the lime and orange juices. Cover and leave to marinate in the refrigerator overnight.

2 Thickly slice the trout flesh and divide among 4 serving plates. Make a dressing by blending the coconut milk powder and honey with 200 ml (7 fl oz) water and half the coriander, lemon grass and chilli from the Thai herbs in the marinade.

3 Add the prawns to the salad leaves and toss with a little of the dressing. Arrange on top of the trout and garnish with the crispy onions. Serve the remaining dressing separately.

VARIATION

For a speedier dish, omit the trout and increase the prawns to 350 g (12 oz).

Sesame Mangetout with Prawns

PREPARATION TIME: 10 MINUTES

COOKING TIME: ABOUT 4 MINUTES

FREEZING: NOT SUITABLE

140 CALS PER SERVING

SERVES 6

COOK'S NOTE
Indian naan bread is available from most large supermarkets.

450 g (1 lb) mangetout
salt and pepper
45 ml (3 tbsp) sesame seeds
1 garlic clove
10 ml (2 tsp) vegetable oil

5 ml (1 tsp) sesame oil
125 g (4 oz) large cooked peeled prawns
50 g (2 oz) salted roasted cashew nuts
30 ml (2 tbsp) light soy sauce
warm naan bread, to serve (optional)

1 Trim the mangetout, then cook in boiling, salted water for 1 minute. Drain, then run under cold water to prevent further cooking.

2 Place the sesame seeds on a baking sheet and toast under the grill for about 5 minutes or until golden brown.

3 Peel and crush the garlic. Heat the oils in a wok or large frying pan with the crushed garlic. Stir in the mangetout, prawns, cashew nuts and soy sauce. Stir-fry for about 3 minutes. Add the sesame seeds and cook for a further 30 seconds.

4 Adjust the seasoning, then serve on warmed plates, with warm naan bread, if wished.

VARIATION
To make this dish suitable for vegetarians, add an extra 50 g (2 oz) of salted cashew nuts in place of the cooked prawns.

Spiced Quick-fried Prawns

PREPARATION TIME: ABOUT 20 MINUTES, PLUS MARINATING

COOKING TIME: ABOUT 20 MINUTES

FREEZING: NOT SUITABLE

440 CALS PER SERVING

SERVES 4

Illustrated opposite

COOK'S NOTE
If raw prawns are unobtainable, use cooked ones instead. Simmer in the coconut milk for 1-2 minutes only.

450 g (1 lb) large raw prawns in shells
2.5 cm (1 inch) piece fresh root ginger
1 garlic clove
5 ml (1 tsp) ground turmeric
5-10 ml (1-2 tsp) hot chilli powder
10 ml (2 tsp) black mustard seeds
5 green cardamoms, crushed
50 g (2 oz) ghee or butter

90 ml (6 tbsp) coconut milk
salt and pepper

POTATO RIBBONS
1 large elongated potato
oil for deep-frying
coarse sea salt
paprika

1 Peel the prawns leaving the tail end attached. Using a small sharp knife, make a shallow slit along the outer curve from the tail to the head end and remove the dark vein. Rinse under cold running water, drain and pat dry with kitchen paper.

2 Peel and grate the ginger. Peel and crush the garlic. Place the ginger and garlic in a bowl with the turmeric, chilli powder, mustard seeds and cardamoms. Add the prawns, turn to coat with the spice mixture and leave to marinate for about 20 minutes.

3 To make the potato ribbons, peel the potato and cut along its length into 5 mm (¼ inch) slices. Using a swivel potato peeler and working along the thin side of one slice of potato, pare wafer-thin strips. (They should not look like crisps – if they do, you are holding the potato the wrong way round!)

4 Heat the oil in a deep-fat fryer to 190°C (375°F). Test the temperature by dropping in a piece of potato – it should sizzle immediately on contact with the oil and rise to the surface.

5 Deep-fry a few potato strips at a time for 2-3 minutes, until golden brown and crisp. Drain on crumpled kitchen paper and sprinkle with a little coarse salt and paprika. Keep hot, while cooking the remainder and the prawns.

6 To cook the prawns, heat the ghee or butter in a frying pan until foaming. Add the prawns and cook very quickly, stirring all the time, for 2 minutes. Add the coconut milk and simmer for about 4 minutes until the prawns are pink and opaque. Season with salt and pepper.

7 Serve the prawns at once, accompanied by the potato ribbons.

Prawn Rolls

PREPARATION TIME: 40 MINUTES

COOKING TIME: ABOUT 10 MINUTES

FREEZING: NOT SUITABLE

320 CALS PER SERVING

SERVES 4

2 spring onions
1 garlic clove
1.25 ml (¼ tsp) salt
5 ml (1 tsp) grated fresh root ginger
5 ml (1 tsp) Thai red curry paste
15 ml (1 tbsp) chopped fresh coriander
5 ml (1 tsp) tamarind juice
1.25 ml (¼ tsp) sugar
16 large raw tiger prawns in shells

4-8 sheets filo pastry
1 egg white, beaten
oil for deep-frying

CHILLI DIPPING SAUCE
2 small red chillies
50 g (2 oz) caster sugar
50 ml (2 fl oz) rice vinegar
2.5 ml (½ tsp) salt

1 Start by making the dipping sauce. Finely chop the chillies, discarding the seeds if preferred, then place in a small pan with the sugar, vinegar, salt and 30 ml (2 tbsp) water. Bring slowly to the boil, stirring until the sugar is dissolved, then remove from the heat and set aside to cool.

2 To make the prawn rolls, trim the spring onions and roughly chop. Peel and roughly chop the garlic. Grind to a smooth paste with the salt, ginger, red curry paste and coriander, using an electric spice grinder or a pestle and mortar. Stir in the tamarind juice and sugar.

3 Cut the heads off the prawns, then peel away the shells, leaving the tail ends attached. Make a slit down the back of each prawn and remove the dark intestinal vein. Rinse well and pat dry. Cut the filo pastry into 16 strips, each 7.5 cm (3 inches) wide and 15 cm (6 inches) long. Keep covered with a lightly dampened tea-towel.

4 Working with one strip of pastry at a time, brush lightly with a little egg white. Spread 5 ml (1 tsp) of the spice mixture at one end of the pastry strip, top with a prawn and roll the pastry up to enclose all but the tail. Repeat to make 16 rolls.

5 Heat a 10 cm (4 inch) depth of oil in a deep, heavy-based saucepan to 180°C (350°F) or until a cube of bread dropped into the oil browns in 30 seconds. Fry the prawn rolls in the hot oil in batches for 2-3 minutes until crisp and golden. Drain on kitchen paper and serve hot with the sweet and sour dipping sauce.

Grilled King Prawns with Chilli Soy Sauce

PREPARATION TIME:
20 MINUTES, PLUS MARINATING

COOKING TIME: 6-8 MINUTES

FREEZING: NOT SUITABLE

115 CALS PER SERVING

SERVES 4

12 large raw tiger prawns in shells

MARINADE
1 garlic clove
1 red chilli
15 ml (1 tbsp) sesame oil
30 ml (2 tbsp) dark soy sauce
grated rind and juice of 2 limes
15-30 ml (1-2 tbsp) soft brown sugar

CHILLI SOY SAUCE
5 ml (1 tsp) dried crushed chilli flakes
15 ml (1 tbsp) lime juice
30 ml (2 tbsp) dark soy sauce
15 ml (1 tbsp) Thai fish sauce
30 ml (2 tbsp) soft brown sugar

1 Wash and dry the prawns and place in a shallow non-metallic dish. To make the marinade, peel and finely chop the garlic; deseed and finely chop the chilli. Mix the garlic and chilli with the remaining marinade ingredients. Pour over the prawns and stir well to coat. Cover the dish and leave to marinate in a cool place for at least 4 hours, preferably overnight.

2 To make the chilli soy sauce, place all the ingredients in a small saucepan with 30 ml (2 tbsp) cold water and bring to the boil, stirring until the sugar is dissolved. Leave to cool.

3 Just before serving, transfer the prawns to the grill pan and grill as close to the heat as possible for 6-8 minutes, turning and basting frequently with the marinade juices, until the prawns are pink and lightly charred.

4 Transfer to a warmed serving platter and serve with the sauce for dipping.

VARIATION
Pre-soak 4 bamboo skewers in water for 30 minutes, drain and thread 3 marinated prawns onto each skewer. Grill as close to the heat as possible for 2-3 minutes on each side.

Tandoori Prawns

PREPARATION TIME: 30 MINUTES

COOKING TIME: 6 MINUTES

FREEZING: NOT SUITABLE

160 CALS PER SERVING

SERVES 6

2.5 cm (1 inch) piece fresh root ginger
3 garlic cloves
juice of 1 lemon
90 ml (6 tbsp) natural yogurt
15 ml (1 tbsp) cumin seeds
10 ml (2 tsp) paprika
salt and pepper
75 g (3 oz) butter
300 g (11 oz) cooked peeled prawns
poppadom baskets (see page 27)

CORIANDER RELISH
75 g (3 oz) fresh coriander sprigs
1 large red chilli
15 ml (1 tbsp) lemon juice
salt and pepper
2.5 ml (½ tsp) ground cumin
30 ml (2 tbsp) mango chutney

1 To make the coriander relish, roughly chop the coriander. Deseed and roughly chop the chilli. Place in a blender or food processor with the lemon juice and remaining ingredients.

2 Process for 1-2 minutes or until the mixture forms a smooth paste. Cover and chill.

3 To make the prawn mixture, peel and finely chop the ginger. Peel and crush the garlic. Combine in a bowl with 20 ml (4 tsp) lemon juice, the yogurt, cumin, paprika and salt and pepper to taste.

4 Melt the butter in a large frying pan. Add the yogurt mixture and cook, stirring, for 3-4 minutes or until the butter separates. Stir in the prawns to coat in the butter. Cook for 1-2 minutes or until they are hot.

5 Serve the prawns in poppadom baskets, accompanied by the coriander relish.

Sesame Prawn Toasts

PREPARATION TIME:
25 MINUTES, PLUS CHILLING

COOKING TIME: ABOUT 10
MINUTES

FREEZING: NOT SUITABLE

250 CALS PER SERVING

SERVES 6

700 g (1½ lb) raw tiger prawns in shells, or frozen scampi, thawed

1 cm (½ inch) piece fresh root ginger

7.5 ml (1½ tsp) cornflour

10 ml (2 tsp) dry sherry

1 egg white, beaten

5 ml (1 tsp) salt

pinch of sugar

6-8 slices white bread, left out for about 2 hours

6 canned water chestnuts, drained and finely chopped (optional)

75 g (3 oz) sesame seeds

oil for deep-frying

spring onion curls, to garnish (optional)

chilli dipping sauce (see page 48), to serve

1 If using prawns, remove the heads and legs, and peel off the shells. With a sharp knife, make a slit down the centre of the back of each one and remove the intestinal vein. Wash well. If using scampi rinse and pat dry with kitchen paper.

2 Put the prawns or scampi into a food processor. Peel and chop the ginger and add to the prawns or scampi. Work to a smooth paste.

3 Mix together the cornflour, sherry, egg white, salt and sugar in a jug. Add gradually to the prawn paste. Do not overwork or the mixture will become too light when cooked. Cover and chill in the refrigerator for 30 minutes.

4 Meanwhile, cut the crusts off the bread and trim into neat squares.

5 If using water chestnuts, add them to the prawn mixture and stir well. Spread a generous amount of paste on one side of each slice of bread, about 0.6-1 cm (¼-½ inch) thick, thinner at the edges. Dip the prawn side of the bread into the sesame seeds to coat.

6 Heat the oil in a deep-fat fryer to 180°C (350°F) or until a cube of bread dropped into the oil browns in 30 seconds. Slide two prawn toasts at a time into the hot oil. Deep-fry for 3 minutes, turning once, until golden brown; drain. Keep warm.

7 Cut each prawn toast diagonally into four small triangles. Garnish with spring onion curls, if wished. Serve with chilli sauce.

Battered Mussels with Caramelised Chilli Paste

PREPARATION TIME: 25 MINUTES

COOKING TIME: 25-30 MINUTES

FREEZING: NOT SUITABLE

465 CALS PER SERVING

SERVES 4

48 large fresh mussels in shells

50 g (2 oz) plain white flour

15 g (½ oz) rice flour or cornflour

2.5 ml (½ tsp) salt

15 g (½ oz) desiccated coconut

15 ml (1 tbsp) chopped fresh chives

½ egg (or 1 size 5), beaten

15 ml (1 tbsp) rice wine or dry sherry

oil for deep-frying

lemon wedges and chives, to garnish

PICKLED CABBAGE

125 g (4 oz) white cabbage

125 ml (4 fl oz) white wine vinegar

2 shallots

1 garlic clove

15 ml (1 tbsp) sesame oil

CHILLI PASTE

2 shallots

1 garlic clove

15 ml (1 tbsp) sunflower oil

15 ml (1 tbsp) hot chilli sauce

50 g (2 oz) dark muscovado sugar

30 ml (2 tbsp) lemon juice

5 ml (1 tsp) salt

30 ml (2 tbsp) light soy sauce

1 First prepare the pickled cabbage. Shred the cabbage. Bring the vinegar to the boil in a small saucepan, then add the cabbage and simmer for 1 minute. Remove from the heat. Peel and finely chop the shallots and garlic. Heat the oil in a pan, add the shallots and garlic and fry for 2-3 minutes until softened. Stir in the cabbage and vinegar and simmer gently for 5 minutes. Set aside to cool.

2 Make the chilli paste. Peel and finely chop the shallots and garlic and fry in the oil for 3 minutes until softened. Add the remaining ingredients, bring to the boil and simmer fast for 3-4

minutes until the sauce is reduced and syrupy. Remove from the heat and leave to cool.

3 Scrub the mussels thoroughly under cold running water and remove their beards. Discard damaged ones and any that remain open when sharply tapped. Steam the mussels in a tightly covered large saucepan with just the water clinging to the shells for 3-4 minutes until opened. Discard any that remain closed. Plunge the mussels into cold water to cool, then remove them from their shells.

4 To make the batter, sift the flours and salt into a bowl, stir in the coconut and chives, then gradually beat in the egg, wine and 100 ml (3½ fl oz) water to form a batter.

5 Heat a 10 cm (4 inch) depth of vegetable oil in a deep, heavy-based saucepan to a temperature of 180°C (350°F) as registered on a thermometer or until a cube of bread dropped into the oil browns in 30 seconds. Deep-fry the mussels in batches. Dip into the batter, then carefully tip into the oil and fry for 30 seconds to 1 minute until crisp and golden. Drain on kitchen paper and serve hot, garnished with lemon wedges and chives and accompanied by the pickled cabbage and chilli paste.

Bean Sprout and Fish Fritters

PREPARATION TIME: 10 MINUTES

COOKING TIME: 20 MINUTES

FREEZING: NOT SUITABLE

75 CALS PER FRITTER

MAKES ABOUT 30

225 g (8 oz) cod fillet, skinned
2 red chillies
4 spring onions
3 garlic cloves
2.5 cm (1 inch) piece fresh root ginger
225 g (8 oz) bean sprouts
125 g (4 oz) plain white flour

10 ml (2 tsp) baking powder
5 ml (1 tsp) ground coriander
5 ml (1 tsp) light soy sauce
2 eggs
oil for deep-frying
salt and pepper
chilli dipping sauce (see page 48), to serve

1 Chop the fish into small pieces. Deseed and chop the chillies. Trim and thinly slice the spring onions. Peel and crush the garlic. Peel and finely chop the ginger.

2 In a bowl, mix together all the ingredients except the oil and seasoning.

3 Heat the oil in a deep-fat fryer to 180°C (350°F) or until a cube of bread dropped into the oil browns in 30 seconds. Drop six separate teaspoonfuls of batter into the oil at a time and fry for about 3 minutes or until crisp and cooked through. (Cook no more than six fritters at one time.)

4 Drain the fritters on kitchen paper. Serve hot or cold with chilli dipping sauce.

Sweet Potato Cakes with Baked Garlic

PREPARATION TIME: 45 MINUTES

COOKING TIME: 50 MINUTES

FREEZING: SUITABLE –
POTATO CAKES ONLY (STAGE 4)

470 CALS PER SERVING

SERVES 4

2 heads of garlic, about 125 g (4 oz) total weight
15 ml (1 tbsp) dark soy sauce
15 ml (1 tbsp) lemon juice
pinch of salt
pinch of sugar

PRAWN PASTE
2 garlic cloves
2-3 small green chillies
1.25 ml (¼ tsp) sea salt
30 ml (2 tbsp) dried shrimp
15 ml (1 tbsp) Thai fish sauce
15 ml (1 tbsp) dark muscovado sugar
30 ml (2 tbsp) lemon juice

POTATO CAKES
450 g (1 lb) sweet potatoes
225 g (8 oz) potato
15 g (½ oz) fresh coriander roots
30 ml (2 tbsp) chopped fresh coriander leaves
50 g (2 oz) desiccated coconut, toasted
15 g (½ oz) plain white flour
5 ml (1 tsp) sesame oil
pepper
flour, for dusting
50 g (2 oz) sesame seeds
oil for shallow-frying

COOK'S NOTE
The tangy prawn paste, called *nam prik* in Thailand, is a staple condiment of that country and can be served as a sauce or stirred into other dishes. You can make it yourself, or buy it ready-made from Oriental food suppliers.

1 Cut a small slice from the top of each garlic head and sit on a double layer of foil. Combine the soy sauce, lemon juice, salt and sugar in a bowl, then pour over the garlic. Seal the foil and bake in the oven at 200°C (400°F) Mark 6 for 30 minutes. Set aside until required.

2 Meanwhile, make the prawn paste. Peel and roughly chop the garlic. Deseed and chop the chillies. Grind the garlic and chillies to a smooth paste with the salt and dried shrimp, using an electric spice grinder or a pestle and mortar. Transfer to a dish and stir in the remaining ingredients. Set aside.

3 For the potato cakes, peel and cube all the potatoes and place in a saucepan. Scrub and chop the coriander roots and add to the pan. Add plenty of cold water to cover, bring to the boil and cook for 12-15 minutes until tender. Drain, return to the heat for a few seconds to dry out the potato, then mash with a potato masher. Allow to cool slightly.

4 Stir in the chopped coriander, coconut, flour and sesame oil. Season with salt and pepper to taste. With lightly floured hands, form the mixture into 12 small patties.

5 Dip the potato cakes in the sesame seeds to coat. Heat a shallow layer of oil in a heavy-based, nonstick frying pan. Fry the potato cakes in batches for 2-3 minutes each side until golden and heated through. Drain on kitchen paper.

6 Serve the potato cakes hot with the caramelised garlic cloves and a spoonful of prawn paste.

Crispy Crab Cakes

PREPARATION TIME:
40 MINUTES, PLUS CHILLING

COOKING TIME: 25 MINUTES

FREEZING: CRAB CAKES
SUITABLE (STAGE 4); DIP
SUITABLE WITHOUT SPRING
ONIONS, LIME AND CHILLI
SLICES

118 CALS PER CRAB CAKE
9 CALS PER 15 ML (1 TBSP) DIP
SERVES 8

COOK'S NOTE
If you do not want to serve
the crab cakes immediately,
they can be cooled and
refrigerated, lightly covered,
for up to 4 hours. To serve,
reheat on a baking sheet,
uncovered, at 200°C
(400°F) Mark 6 for 15
minutes or until hot through.

700 g (1½ lb) old potatoes
salt and pepper
6 spring onions
3 garlic cloves
5 cm (2 inch) piece fresh root ginger
2 small red chillies
50 g (2 oz) anchovy fillets
finely grated rind of 1 lime
45 ml (3 tbsp) each chopped fresh parsley and coriander
450 g (1 lb) frozen white crab meat, thawed
30 ml (2 tbsp) black or white sesame seeds
125 g (4 oz) fresh white breadcrumbs

seasoned flour for coating
2 eggs, beaten
oil for deep-frying
banana leaves, to garnish (optional)

SWEET GINGER DIP
2 spring onions
2.5 cm (1 inch) piece fresh root ginger
30 ml (2 tbsp) dark soy sauce
90 ml (6 tbsp) rice vinegar or cider vinegar
10 ml (2 tsp) sugar
lime slice and sliced chilli, to garnish

1 To make the dip, finely chop the spring onions. Peel and grate the ginger. Whisk together with the soy sauce, rice or cider vinegar and sugar.

2 To make the crab cakes, peel and quarter the potatoes. Cook in boiling, salted water for 10-15 minutes or until tender. Drain and mash with a fork.

3 Roughly chop the spring onions. Peel and finely chop the garlic and ginger. Chop the chillies, discarding the seeds if a milder flavour is preferred. Chop the anchovies.

4 Mix the spring onions, garlic, ginger, chillies and anchovies with the lime rind, parsley, coriander and crab meat; season well. Gently stir in the mashed potato. Shape the crab mixture into 16 balls, each the size of a golf ball, and chill for 10-15 minutes.

5 Mix the sesame seeds with the breadcrumbs. Dip the crab cakes in seasoned flour, beaten egg and the breadcrumb mixture.

6 Heat the oil in a deep-fat fryer to 170°C (325°F) and deep-fry the crab cakes in batches for about 8 minutes or until they are golden brown and hot through. Drain on kitchen paper and serve on banana leaves, if wished. Float a slice of lime and some chilli slices in the dip and serve with the crab cakes.

Spring Rolls

PREPARATION TIME: 15 MINUTES
COOKING TIME: 30 MINUTES
FREEZING: NOT SUITABLE

325 CALS PER SERVING
SERVES 4

1 large red pepper
75 g (3 oz) mangetout
5 spring onions
275 g (10 oz) cooked peeled prawns
30 ml (2 tbsp) sesame oil
10 ml (2 tsp) Thai red curry paste

50 g (2 oz) bean sprouts
10 ml (2 tsp) Thai fish sauce
225 g (8 oz) filo pastry
5 ml (1 tsp) sesame seeds
chilli dipping sauce (see page 48), to serve

1 Deseed and thinly slice the red pepper. Thinly slice the mangetout and spring onions. Roughly chop the prawns.

2 Heat 15 ml (1 tbsp) of the oil in a large frying pan and fry the vegetables for about 2 minutes. Add the curry paste and fry, stirring, for 30 seconds. Add the bean sprouts and fish sauce and fry for about 30 seconds until all the excess liquid has evaporated; leave to cool.

3 Stir the prawns into the cooled vegetable mixture. Cut the filo pastry into eight strips measuring 35.5 x 15 cm (14 x 6 inches). Keep the filo strips covered with a lightly dampened tea-towel as you work on each one. Spoon a little of the mixture at the top end of one strip. Fold in 1 cm (½ inch) of pastry down each side, then roll up. Repeat with the remaining strips.

4 Place the rolls on a baking sheet, seam side down. Brush with the remaining oil and sprinkle with the sesame seeds.

5 Cook at 190°C (375°F) Mark 5 for 20 minutes or until brown and cooked through. Serve with chilli dipping sauce.

Onion Bhajis

PREPARATION TIME: 20 MINUTES
COOKING TIME: 15 MINUTES
FREEZING: SUITABLE

180 CALS PER BHAJI
MAKES 12

450 g (1 lb) onions
1 garlic clove
2.5 cm (1 inch) piece fresh root ginger
1-2 hot red chillies
5 ml (1 tsp) ground turmeric
5 ml (1 tsp) ground cardamom seeds
125 g (4 oz) gram or plain wholemeal flour, sifted

50 g (2 oz) white self-raising flour
45 ml (3 tbsp) chopped fresh mint
salt and pepper
15 ml (1 tbsp) lemon juice
oil for deep-frying
mint sprigs and lime wedges, to garnish

COOK'S NOTES
About 12 cardamom pods will yield 5 ml (1 tsp) crushed seeds.

Bhajis can be prepared in advance and reheated on a baking sheet at 200°C (400°F) Mark 6 for about 10 minutes before serving.

1 Peel and halve the onions. Cut each half into very thin crescent-shaped slices. Peel and finely chop the garlic and ginger. Finely chop the chillies, discarding the seeds if a milder flavour is preferred.
2 Put the onions, garlic, ginger and chillies in a bowl. Add the ground spices and toss well. Add the flours, mint and salt and pepper. Mix thoroughly.
3 Add the lemon juice and about 75 ml (5 tbsp) cold water or enough to make the mixture cling together; do not make it too wet.
4 Heat the oil in a deep-fat fryer. Test the temperature by dropping in a small piece of bread – it should sizzle immediately on contact with the oil and rise to the surface; remove with a slotted spoon.
5 Meanwhile divide the mixture into 12 even portions. Using dampened hands, shape each portion into a ball. Pat firmly to ensure that it will hold together during cooking, but don't worry if it doesn't form a neat round.
6 Deep-fry 3-4 bhajis at a time in the hot oil for 5 minutes or until golden brown on all sides. Carefully remove from the hot oil and drain on crumpled kitchen paper. Serve warm, garnished with mint sprigs and lime wedges.

Vegetable Tempura

PREPARATION TIME: 20 MINUTES
COOKING TIME: 15 MINUTES
FREEZING: NOT SUITABLE

610 CALS PER SERVING
SERVES 4

125 g (4 oz) plain white flour
30 ml (2 tbsp) cornflour
30 ml (2 tbsp) arrowroot
salt and pepper
125 g (4 oz) cauliflower florets
2 large carrots
16 button mushrooms
2 courgettes

2 red peppers
30 ml (2 tbsp) plain white flour
oil for deep-frying
coriander sprigs, to garnish

DIPPING SAUCE
25 g (1 oz) fresh root ginger
60 ml (4 tbsp) dry sherry
45 ml (3 tbsp) soy sauce

1 Sift 125 g (4 oz) flour, the cornflour and arrowroot into a large bowl with a pinch each of salt and pepper. Gradually whisk in 300 ml (½ pint) ice-cold water to form a thin batter. Chill.
2 To make the dipping sauce, peel and grate the ginger, then put in a bowl with the sherry, soy sauce and 200 ml (7 fl oz) boiling water. Stir well to mix, then set aside.
3 Divide the cauliflower into tiny sprigs, discarding any thick, woody stalks. Peel the carrots and cut into thin sticks. Trim the mushroom stalks if necessary. Slice the courgettes. Cut the red peppers in half, remove the cores and seeds and slice flesh into thin strips.
4 Toss the vegetables in the remaining flour. Heat the oil in a wok or deep-fat fryer. Test the temperature by dropping in a small piece of bread – it should sizzle immediately on contact with the oil and rise to the surface; remove with a slotted spoon.
5 To cook a batch of vegetables, dip in the batter then remove with a slotted spoon, taking up a lot of the batter with the vegetables. Add the coated vegetables to the hot oil and deep-fry for 3-5 minutes or until crisp and golden.
6 Remove the vegetables with a slotted spoon and drain on kitchen paper; keep hot while cooking the remaining batches. Serve immediately, garnished with coriander and accompanied by the dipping sauce.

Thai Noodles with Tofu

PREPARATION TIME: 25 MINUTES

COOKING TIME: 35 MINUTES

FREEZING: NOT SUITABLE

400 CALS PER SERVING

SERVES 4

125 g (4 oz) firm tofu
8 shallots
1 garlic clove
2.5 cm (1 inch) piece fresh root ginger
30 ml (2 tbsp) sweet soy sauce
5 ml (1 tsp) rice vinegar
225 g (8 oz) rice noodles
25 g (1 oz) raw peanuts
30 ml (2 tbsp) sunflower oil
15 g (½ oz) dried shrimp (optional)

1 egg, beaten
25 g (1 oz) bean sprouts
basil leaves, to garnish
SAUCE
1 dried red chilli
30 ml (2 tbsp) lemon juice
15 ml (1 tbsp) Thai fish sauce
15 ml (1 tbsp) caster sugar
30 ml (2 tbsp) smooth peanut butter

1 Drain the tofu and cut into 2.5 cm (1 inch) cubes. Peel and halve the shallots and place in a small roasting pan with the tofu.

2 Peel and crush the garlic and ginger and blend with the sweet soy sauce, vinegar and 30 ml (2 tbsp) water. Pour over the tofu and shallots and toss well. Roast near the top of the oven at 200°C (400°F) Mark 6 for 30 minutes until the tofu and shallots are golden.

3 Meanwhile, soak the noodles according to the packet instructions. Drain, refresh under cold running water and set aside. Toast and chop the peanuts.

4 Make the sauce. Deseed and finely chop the chilli and place in a small saucepan with the remaining ingredients. Stir over a gentle heat until the sugar is dissolved. Keep warm.

5 Heat the oil in a wok or frying pan and stir-fry the dried shrimp, if using, for 1 minute. Add the noodles and egg to the wok and stir over a medium heat for 3 minutes. Add the tofu and shallots, together with any pan juices. Stir well, then remove from the heat.

6 Stir in the bean sprouts and sauce and divide between warmed serving plates. Sprinkle with the toasted peanuts and serve at once, garnished with basil.

Vegetable Sushi

PREPARATION TIME: 1 HOUR

COOKING TIME: 20 MINUTES

FREEZING: NOT SUITABLE

260 CALS PER SERVING

SERVES 6

350 g (12 oz) Japanese glutinous rice
30 ml (2 tbsp) rice vinegar or white wine vinegar
20 ml (4 tsp) caster sugar
5 ml (1 tsp) salt
15 ml (1 tbsp) mirin or dry sherry
DRESSING
15 g (½ oz) pickled ginger
60 ml (4 tbsp) rice vinegar or white wine vinegar
15 ml (1 tbsp) soy sauce
15 ml (1 tbsp) caster sugar

TO FINISH
1 egg
salt and pepper
10 ml (2 tsp) oil
5 cm (2 inch) piece cucumber
1 carrot
2 spring onions
½ small red pepper
4 sheets of toasted sushi nori
pickled ginger, to serve

1 Wash the rice in several changes of cold water and drain well. Put in a saucepan with 450 ml (¾ pint) water and bring to the boil. Cover and cook over a very low heat for 10-12 minutes until the water is completely absorbed. Stand, covered, for 10 minutes, then turn into a bowl.

2 Mix 30 ml (2 tbsp) vinegar with 20 ml (4 tsp) sugar, the salt and mirin or sherry. Add to the rice and stir gently until evenly combined. Leave to cool.

3 To make the dressing, shred the pickled ginger as thinly as possible. Mix 5 ml (1 tsp) with the vinegar, soy sauce and sugar until the sugar dissolves. Transfer to a small serving dish.

4 Beat the egg with a little seasoning. Heat the oil in a frying pan, then add the egg and cook over a low heat to make a thin omelette. Remove from the pan, drain and cut into thin strips.

5 Take a rounded dessertspoonful of the rice and, using wetted hands, press into a neat oval shape. Make 11 more in the same way. Place the rice ovals on a serving platter and decorate with the omelette strips and remaining shredded ginger from the dressing.

6 Peel the cucumber and remove the seeds. Cut the flesh into matchstick sized lengths. Peel and cut the carrot into similar sized pieces. Trim and shred the spring onion lengthways, removing the bulb ends. Deseed the pepper, then shred as thinly as possible.

7 Put a sheet of nori on a clean, heavy napkin with the long side facing you. Spoon a quarter of the remaining rice down the length of the nori, spreading in a thin layer to the short ends and to within 2.5 cm (1 inch) of the long sides. Brush with a little of the dressing. Arrange half the spring onion and red pepper along the centre. Roll up the nori inside the napkin, pressing the rice to shape a firm, neatly packed cylinder with the vegetables running through the centre.

8 Make 3 more rolls in the same way, using the remaining spring onions and red pepper in one, and the cucumber and carrot in the others.

9 Cut the sushi rolls into 2.5 cm (1 inch) slices. Arrange with the omelette sushi on the serving platter. Serve with the remaining dressing for dipping and extra pickled ginger.

MEAT DISHES

Beef, lamb and pork are flavoured with subtle combinations of spices and vegetables to create a selection of succulent meat dishes, varying from hot curries to light stir-fries. Beef steeped in a rich coconut sauce, or marinated steak, seared Japanese-style, are simple yet impressive, while thin slices of steak tossed with Chinese mushrooms and oyster sauce, and filling beef and noodle chow mein make easy informal food. A leg of lamb coated in a delicious spicy crust, or lean lamb cooked with potato and highlighted with cumin, turmeric and coriander are prime examples of Indian cuisine, while lamb and bamboo shoots flavoured with red curry paste is Thai food at its best. Pork served with sweet and spicy pineapple or tenderised in a fiery tomato sauce make memorable meals, while sticky-glazed spare ribs and Chinese-style red chops are good, fast food.

Illustration: Lamb with Potato (recipe page 78)

Beef in Coconut Milk

PREPARATION TIME: 20 MINUTES
COOKING TIME: 1½ - 1¾ HOURS
FREEZING: SUITABLE (STAGE 2)

460 CALS PER SERVING
SERVES 6

2 large red chillies
1 small red pepper
2.5 cm (1 inch) piece fresh root ginger
8 garlic cloves
225 g (8 oz) shallots or onions
2 lemon grass stalks, each 15 cm (6 inches) long
8 kaffir lime leaves or the grated rind of 1 lime

5 ml (1 tsp) ground cinnamon
5 ml (1 tsp) ground cloves
1.6 litres (2¾ pints) coconut milk
3 bay leaves
900 g (2 lb) cubed stewing beef
salt and pepper
shredded kaffir lime leaves and toasted coconut flakes, to garnish

1 Deseed and finely chop the chillies and red pepper. Peel and roughly chop the ginger, garlic and shallots. Roughly chop the lemon grass and lime leaves. Place these ingredients in a blender or food processor with the cinnamon, cloves and 150 ml (¼ pint) water and blend until smooth.

2 Place this paste in a large nonstick saucepan with the coconut milk, bay leaves and beef. Season well with salt, then bring to the boil, stirring. Simmer, uncovered, stirring occasionally, for 1½-1¾ hours until the meat is tender and the milk absorbed to make a thick coating. Adjust the seasoning.

3 Serve, garnished with lime leaves and toasted coconut flakes.

Thai Spiced Beef Curry

PREPARATION TIME: 30 MINUTES
COOKING TIME: 35-40 MINUTES
FREEZING: NOT SUITABLE

505 CALS PER SERVING
SERVES 4

450 g (1 lb) sirloin steak
4 cloves
5 ml (1 tsp) coriander seeds
5 ml (1 tsp) cumin seeds
seeds from 3 cardamom pods
2 garlic cloves
2.5 cm (1 inch) piece fresh root ginger
1 small onion
30 ml (2 tbsp) sunflower oil
15 ml (1 tbsp) sesame oil

15 ml (1 tbsp) Indian curry paste
5 ml (1 tsp) ground turmeric
225 g (8 oz) potatoes
4 tomatoes
5 ml (1 tsp) sugar
15 ml (1 tbsp) light soy suace
300 ml (½ pint) coconut milk
150 ml (¼ pint) beef or chicken stock
4 red chillies
50 g (2 oz) cashew nuts

1 Trim the steak of any fat and cut into 3 cm (1¼ inch) cubes.

2 Place the cloves and coriander, cumin and cardamom seeds in a small heavy-based frying pan. Roast over a high heat for 1-2 minutes until the spices are golden and release their aroma. Cool slightly, then grind to a powder in a spice grinder or with a pestle and mortar.

3 Peel and roughly chop the garlic, ginger and onion, then work in a blender or food processor to form a smooth paste. Heat the two oils together in a deep frying pan. Add the onion paste with the curry paste and stir-fry for 5 minutes, then add the roasted ground spices and turmeric and fry for a further 5 minutes.

4 Add the beef to the pan and fry for a further 5 minutes until browned on all sides. Peel and quarter the potatoes; quarter the tomatoes. Add the potatoes and tomatoes to the pan with the remaining ingredients, except the cashews. Bring to the boil, lower the heat and simmer, covered, for 20-25 minutes until the beef is tender and the potatoes are cooked.

5 Stir in the cashew nuts and serve at once.

Green Beef Curry

PREPARATION TIME: 5 MINUTES
COOKING TIME: 10 MINUTES
FREEZING: NOT SUITABLE

350 CALS PER SERVING
SERVES 4

700 g (1½ lb) rump steak
15 ml (1 tbsp) oil
15 ml (1 tbsp) Thai green curry paste
2.5 ml (½ tsp) ground cinnamon
15 ml (1 tbsp) Thai fish sauce
150 ml (¼ pint) coconut milk

grated rind of ½ a lime
5 ml (1 tsp) soft brown sugar
Thai fragrant rice, to serve
shredded kaffir lime leaves or coriander leaves, to garnish

1 Trim the steak of any fat and cut into finger-length strips. Heat the oil in a wok or frying pan and fry the meat in batches over a high heat to give it a good brown colour, removing each batch with a slotted spoon. Add more oil if necessary.

2 Return all the meat to the pan, add the remaining ingredients and cook, stirring, for 3 minutes or until the sauce has reduced slightly and the meat is tender. Serve at once, garnished with shredded kaffir lime or coriander leaves and accompanied by fragrant rice.

Red Beef Curry

PREPARATION TIME: 15 MINUTES

COOKING TIME: ABOUT 2 HOURS

FREEZING: SUITABLE

400 CALS PER SERVING

SERVES 4

2 onions

4 garlic cloves

1-2 red chillies (optional)

3 ripe juicy tomatoes

900 g (2 lb) stewing or braising beef

5 ml (1 tsp) black peppercorns

30 ml (2 tbsp) ghee or oil

15 ml (1 tbsp) paprika

5 ml (1 tsp) ground ginger

300 ml (½ pint) thick yogurt

salt

COOK'S NOTE

As this curry cooks the liquid reduces, leaving a rich, thick sauce clinging to the meat. Use a casserole dish with a tight-fitting lid and resist the temptation to keep lifting it during cooking, otherwise you will end up without any sauce and burnt meat! To improve the seal, cover the casserole with a double thickness of foil before positioning lid.

1 Peel and finely chop the onions and garlic. Chop the chillies if using, discarding the seeds if a milder flavour is preferred.

2 Immerse the tomatoes in boiling water to cover, leave for about 1 minute, then remove and peel away the skins. Finely chop the tomato flesh.

3 Remove any excess fat from the meat, then cut into 4 cm (1½ inch) cubes. Crush the peppercorns, using a pestle and mortar.

4 Heat the ghee or oil in a large flameproof casserole. Quickly fry the meat in batches until thoroughly browned on all sides, then remove with a slotted spoon and set aside.

5 Add the onions and garlic to the casserole and cook, stirring, over a high heat for about 2 minutes. Lower the heat and cook until the onions are lightly browned.

6 Return all the meat to the casserole along with any accumulated juices, then add the crushed peppercorns, paprika, ginger and chillies, if using. Cook for 2 minutes, stirring all the time. Stir in the tomatoes and cook for a few minutes until they start to disintegrate.

7 Add the yogurt, a spoonful at a time, then season with salt to taste. Bring to the boil, stir, then lower the heat and cover the casserole with a tight-fitting lid. Bake in the oven at 170°C (325°F) Mark 3 for about 1½-2 hours, until tender. If the meat is not tender after 1½ hours but quite dry, add 150 ml (¼ pint) water and return to the oven for a further 30 minutes.

Szechuan Shredded Beef

PREPARATION TIME:
15 MINUTES, PLUS CHILLING

COOKING TIME: ABOUT 12
MINUTES

FREEZING: NOT SUITABLE

250 CALS PER SERVING

SERVES 4

350 g (12 oz) beef skirt or rump steak
75 ml (5 tbsp) hoisin sauce
60 ml (4 tbsp) dry sherry
2 red or green chillies
1 large onion
2 garlic cloves
2 red peppers

2.5 cm (1 inch) piece fresh root ginger
30 ml (2 tbsp) oil
225 g (8 oz) can bamboo shoots, drained and sliced
15 ml (1 tbsp) sesame oil
a red chilli flower, to garnish (optional)

1 Put the steak in the freezer for at least 20 minutes, to make it easier to slice thinly. Cut the steak into thin slices, then stack several slices one on top of another. Cut lengthways into thin strips. Put the steak in a bowl, add the hoisin sauce and sherry and stir. Leave to marinate while preparing the vegetables.
2 Deseed and finely chop the chillies. Peel and thinly slice the onion. Peel and crush the garlic. Deseed the peppers and cut into diamond shapes. Peel and shred the ginger.
3 Heat the oil in a wok or large frying pan until smoking hot. Add the chillies, onion and garlic and stir-fry over medium heat for 3-4 minutes until softened. Remove with a slotted spoon and set aside. Add the red peppers, increase the heat and stir-fry for a few seconds. Remove with a slotted spoon.
4 Add the steak and marinade to the pan in batches. Stir-fry each batch over high heat for about 2 minutes, removing each batch with a slotted spoon.
5 Return the vegetables to the pan. Add the ginger and bamboo shoots, then the meat, and stir-fry for a further minute to heat through.
6 Transfer the mixture to a warmed serving dish, sprinkle with the sesame oil and serve, garnished with a chilli flower, if using.

Beef Rendang

PREPARATION TIME: 15 MINUTES

COOKING TIME: ABOUT 2 HOURS

FREEZING: SUITABLE

955 CALS PER SERVING

SERVES 6

COOK'S NOTE
This dish tastes even better if made the day before and reheated.

1 large onion, preferably red
6 garlic cloves
5 cm (2 inch) piece fresh root ginger
5 cm (2 inch) piece fresh or dried galangal
1 red pepper
4 dried hot chillies
10 ml (2 tsp) ground coriander
10 ml (2 tsp) ground cinnamon

5 ml (1 tsp) ground cloves
5 ml (1 tsp) ground turmeric
1.1 kg (2½ lb) stewing or braising beef
45 ml (3 tbsp) oil
1.7 litres (3 pints) coconut milk
1 lemon grass stalk, bruised
salt
finely shredded kaffir lime leaves, to garnish

1 Peel and quarter the onion. Peel the garlic, ginger and galangal. Halve the pepper, remove the core and seeds and roughly chop the flesh. Put all of these ingredients in a food processor or blender with the chillies, ground spices and 15 ml (1 tbsp) water. Process until smooth.
2 Remove any excess fat from the meat and discard. Cut the meat into large cubes, each about 6 cm (2½ inches).
3 Heat the oil in a large, wide flameproof casserole dish or a saucepan. Add the spice paste and cook over a medium heat for 3-5 minutes, stirring all the time.
4 Add the meat and cook for 2-3 minutes, stirring to coat in the spice mixture.
5 Add the coconut milk and bring to the boil, stirring all the time. Add the lemon grass and about 5 ml (1 tsp) salt. Reduce the heat and simmer very gently, uncovered, for about 2 hours, stirring from time to time. The beef is ready when it is really tender and almost falling apart; the sauce should be well reduced and quite thick.
6 If the sauce is too thin, transfer the meat to a warmed serving dish, using a slotted spoon; keep warm. Bring the sauce to the boil and boil vigorously, stirring frequently, until sufficiently reduced. Pour over the meat. Check the seasoning before serving, garnished with shredded lime leaves.

Chinese Beef with Mushrooms and Oyster Sauce

PREPARATION TIME:
15 MINUTES, PLUS SOAKING
AND MARINATING

COOKING TIME: ABOUT 15
MINUTES

FREEZING: NOT SUITABLE

330 CALS PER SERVING
SERVES 2

25 g (1 oz) dried black or shiitake mushrooms
175-225 g (6-8 oz) rump steak
30 ml (2 tbsp) oyster sauce
30 ml (2 tbsp) dry sherry
salt and pepper
1 small onion

1 garlic clove
2.5 cm (1 inch) piece fresh root ginger
2 carrots
30 ml (2 tbsp) oil
10 ml (2 tsp) cornflour

1 Place the dried mushrooms in a bowl, cover with boiling water and leave to soak for about 30 minutes.

2 Meanwhile, cut the steak into thin strips and place in a bowl. Add the oyster sauce, sherry and salt and pepper to taste. Stir well to mix, then cover and leave to marinate in a cool place.

3 Peel and thinly slice the onion. Peel and crush the garlic. Peel the ginger and carrots and cut into thin strips.

4 Heat the oil in a wok or large frying pan. Add the onion and garlic and stir-fry gently for about 5 minutes until soft but not coloured.

5 Drain the mushrooms and reserve the soaking liquid. Squeeze the mushrooms dry; discard any hard stalks.

6 Add the mushrooms, ginger and carrots to the wok and stir-fry over medium heat for about 5 minutes until slightly softened. Add the meat and marinade and stir-fry for a few minutes more, until the beef is tender.

7 Mix the cornflour to a paste with 60 ml (4 tbsp) of the soaking water from the mushrooms. Pour into the wok and stir-fry until the sauce is thickened. Taste and adjust the seasoning, if necessary. Serve at once.

Oriental Beef Stir-fry

PREPARATION TIME:
20 MINUTES, PLUS MARINATING

COOKING TIME: 10-15 MINUTES

FREEZING: NOT SUITABLE

200-135 CALS PER SERVING
SERVES 4-6

COOK'S NOTE
Stir-fried food is cooked in minutes in very little oil, so the natural flavours and textures are retained. Swirling the hot oil over the surface of the pan just before adding the food produces an even heat.

350 g (12 oz) fillet steak
2 bunches of spring onions
2 orange peppers
1 red chilli
225 g (8 oz) broccoli
175 g (6 oz) spinach or pak choi
15 ml (1 tbsp) chilli or stir-fry oil

MARINADE
30 ml (2 tbsp) sherry vinegar
30 ml (2 tbsp) black bean sauce
30 ml (2 tbsp) yellow bean sauce
2.5 cm (1 inch) piece fresh root ginger
15 ml (1 tbsp) dark soy sauce

1 First, prepare the marinade. Mix the sherry vinegar with the black and yellow bean sauces. Peel and crush the ginger and add to the mixture with the soy sauce.

2 Slice the fillet steak into thin finger-length strips. Stir into the marinade. Cover and leave to marinate in a cool place for at least 30 minutes or up to 12 hours in the refrigerator.

3 Trim the spring onions and cut into diagonal strips about 5 cm (2 inches) long. Deseed the peppers and slice into thin strips. Deseed the chilli and cut into fine strips. Cut the broccoli into small even florets. Shred the spinach.

4 Drain the meat from the marinade, using a slotted spoon. Reserve the marinade. Heat the oil in a large nonstick frying pan or wok, add the meat and cook for 3-4 minutes, stirring. Stir in the vegetables and cook for 3-4 minutes. Stir in the marinade and heat through for 3-4 minutes. Serve immediately.

Thai Rare Beef with Coconut Rice

PREPARATION TIME:
10-15 MINUTES

COOKING TIME: 15-20 MINUTES

FREEZING: NOT SUITABLE

830 CALS PER SERVING

SERVES 6

7.5 cm (3 inch) piece fresh root ginger
1 large red chilli
60 ml (4 tbsp) oil
90 ml (6 tbsp) white wine vinegar
90 ml (6 tbsp) caster sugar
700 g (1½ lb) beef fillet
salt and pepper
350 g (12 oz) basmati rice
50 g (2 oz) desiccated coconut, toasted

40 g (1½ oz) butter
75 g (3 oz) raisins
30 ml (2 tbsp) chopped fresh chives or spring onion tops
small handful fresh coriander leaves
75 g (3 oz) ready-made fried onion flakes or 1 sliced onion, fried until crisp
125 g (4 oz) salted, roasted cashew nuts
sprigs of fresh coriander, to garnish

1 Peel and finely chop the ginger; finely chop the chilli. Whisk together the oil, vinegar, sugar, ginger and chilli.

2 Season the beef with pepper and roast at 230°C (450°F) Mark 8 for 15-20 minutes for rare (20-25 minutes for medium), depending on the thickness of the fillet. Remove from the oven and set aside.

3 Meanwhile, cook the rice in boiling, salted water for about 15 minutes, then drain well. Stir in the next seven ingredients and season well.

4 Slice the beef thinly. Arrange the rice on plates with the beef. Spoon over the dressing, garnish with coriander and serve immediately.

Beef Teriyaki

PREPARATION TIME:
10 MINUTES, PLUS MARINATING

COOKING TIME: ABOUT 5
MINUTES

FREEZING: NOT SUITABLE

210 CALS PER SERVING

SERVES 6

COOK'S NOTE
Cooking the steaks for 1½
minutes on each side will
produce a rare result. For
medium-cooked steaks,
increase the cooking time
to 3 minutes on each side.

6 slices fillet steak, about 2 cm (¾ inch) thick
4 garlic cloves
6.5 cm (2½ inch) piece fresh root ginger
2.5 ml (½ tsp) caster sugar
30 ml (2 tbsp) oil

10 ml (2 tsp) cornflour
45 ml (3 tbsp) soy sauce
90 ml (6 tbsp) mirin or dry sherry
5 ml (1 tsp) rice vinegar

1 Trim the beef of any fat. Peel and crush the garlic. Peel and grate the ginger. Mix the garlic, ginger and sugar to a paste and spread over both sides of the beef. Cover and leave to marinate for 30 minutes.

2 Remove the excess paste from the beef and put the paste in a small saucepan. Heat the oil in a large frying pan or large griddle. Add the beef and fry quickly for 1½ minutes until browned. Turn the beef and fry for a further 1½ minutes.

3 Meanwhile, blend the cornflour with 30 ml (2 tbsp) water and add to the paste in the saucepan. Stir in the soy sauce, mirin or sherry, rice vinegar and an extra 60 ml (4 tbsp) water. Bring to the boil and cook, stirring, until thickened and glossy.

4 Transfer the beef to warmed serving plates and spoon the sauce over. Serve immediately.

Mee Goreng

PREPARATION TIME: 30 MINUTES

COOKING TIME: ABOUT 10 MINUTES

FREEZING: NOT SUITABLE

475-315 CALS PER SERVING

SERVES 4-6

125 g (4 oz) rump steak
2 garlic cloves
30 ml (2 tbsp) soy sauce
450 g (1 lb) squid
175 g (6 oz) large raw prawns
225 g (8 oz) egg noodles
salt
1-2 hot red chillies
2.5 cm (1 inch) piece fresh root ginger
2-3 spring onions

15 ml (1 tbsp) vegetable oil
15 ml (1 tbsp) sesame oil or peanut oil
30 ml (2 tbsp) hoisin sauce
15 ml (1 tbsp) lemon juice
30 ml (2 tbsp) Thai fish sauce
125 g (4 oz) bean sprouts
1 egg, beaten
shredded lettuce and lemon wedges, to garnish

COOK'S NOTE
For a less elaborate version of this Malaysian dish, simply omit the squid and replace the raw prawns with cooked peeled prawns, increasing the weight to 225 g (8 oz).

1 Cut the steak into wafer-thin slices across the grain and place in a shallow dish. Peel the garlic and add half to the dish. Add half of the soy sauce. Leave to stand.

2 Rinse the squid then, holding the body in one hand, firmly pull the tentacles with the other hand to remove the soft contents of the body. Cut the tentacles just in front of the eyes and discard the body contents. Cut the tentacles into small pieces.

3 Squeeze out the plastic-like quill from the body and discard. Rinse the body under cold running water, making sure that it is clean inside. Rub off the fine dark skin, then cut the body into rings or small rectangular pieces.

4 Peel the prawns, leaving the tail end attached. Using a small sharp knife, make a shallow slit along the outer curve from the tail to the head end and remove the dark intestinal vein. Rinse under cold running water, drain and pat dry with kitchen paper.

5 Soak the noodles according to the packet instructions.

6 Chop the chillies, discarding the seeds if a milder flavour is preferred. Peel and finely chop the ginger. Trim and slice the spring onions. Heat the oils in a wok or large frying pan, add the remaining garlic, chillies, ginger and spring onions and cook for 2 minutes, stirring all the time.

7 Add the beef and cook for 2 minutes. Add the squid and prawns and cook for 2 minutes. Add the hoisin sauce, lemon juice, fish sauce and remaining soy sauce; cook for 2 minutes.

8 Drain the noodles and add to the pan with the bean sprouts. Heat through for a couple of minutes, then add the beaten egg. Cook briefly until the egg is on the point of setting. Serve at once, garnished with shredded lettuce and a lemon wedge.

Beef Chow Mein

PREPARATION TIME:
15 MINUTES, PLUS MARINATING

COOKING TIME: 15 MINUTES

FREEZING: NOT SUITABLE

455 CALS PER SERVING

SERVES 4

225 g (8 oz) rump steak
10 ml (2 tsp) dark soy sauce
20 ml (4 tsp) sherry
5 ml (1 tsp) cornflour
5 ml (1 tsp) sugar
15 ml (1 tbsp) sesame oil
1 bunch of spring onions

1 large green chilli
125 g (4 oz) Chinese leaves, or cabbage
3 garlic cloves
175 g (6 oz) egg noodles
45 ml (3 tbsp) oil
50 g (2 oz) bean sprouts
salt and pepper

COOK'S NOTE
Many of the egg noodles are dried and packed in layers. As a general rule, allow one layer of noodles per person for a main dish.

1 Cut the steak into thin, finger-length strips. Whisk the next four ingredients with 5 ml (1 tsp) sesame oil and pour over the meat. Cover and marinate for at least 1 hour or overnight.

2 Slice the spring onions, chilli and Chinese leaves. Peel and crush the garlic.

3 Cook the noodles according to the packet instructions. Rinse in cold water and drain.

4 Drain the meat from the marinade; reserve the marinade. Heat the oil in a wok or large, nonstick frying pan and fry the meat over a brisk heat until well browned and tender. Remove with a slotted spoon and set aside.

5 Fry together the onions, garlic, chilli, Chinese leaves and bean sprouts for 2-3 minutes. Return the beef to the pan with the noodles and reserved marinade liquid. Bring to the boil, stirring all the time, and bubble for 2-3 minutes. Sprinkle over the remaining sesame oil. Season and serve immediately.

Stir-fried Beef with Noodles and Chilli

PREPARATION TIME: 20 MINUTES

COOKING TIME: 15 MINUTES

FREEZING: NOT SUITABLE

325 CALS PER SERVING

SERVES 4

Illustrated opposite

125 g (4 oz) egg thread noodles

1 small onion

2 garlic cloves

2.5 cm (1 inch) piece fresh root ginger

1 red pepper

125 g (4 oz) French beans

45 ml (3 tbsp) sunflower oil

15 ml (1 tbsp) dark soy sauce

4 kaffir lime leaves, shredded

225 g (8 oz) lean minced beef

30 ml (2 tbsp) Indian medium curry paste

5 ml (1 tsp) ground turmeric

2.5 ml (½ tsp) paprika

1.25 ml (¼ tsp) chilli powder

fried basil leaves or fresh coriander leaves, to garnish

SAUCE

30 ml (2 tbsp) tamarind juice

15 ml (1 tbsp) Thai fish sauce

10 ml (2 tsp) sugar

75 ml (3 fl oz) beef stock

1 Soak the noodles according to the packet instructions; drain well and pat dry.

2 Meanwhile prepare the sauce. Place the tamarind juice in a bowl and whisk in the remaining ingredients until smooth. Set aside.

3 Peel and finely chop the onion and garlic; peel and grate the ginger. Deseed and slice the red pepper; halve the French beans.

4 Heat 15 ml (1 tbsp) of the oil in a wok or large frying pan, add the noodles and soy sauce and stir-fry for 30 seconds. Remove from the pan and set aside.

5 Add the remaining oil to the pan. Add the onion, garlic, ginger and lime leaves and fry, stirring, for 5 minutes. Add the beef, curry paste and spices and stir-fry for 3 minutes.

6 Add the red pepper and beans and stir-fry for 3 minutes. Blend in the sauce and simmer for a further 3 minutes. Carefully stir in the noodles and heat through for 2 minutes. Transfer to a warmed serving dish. Garnish with the basil leaves or fresh coriander and serve at once.

VARIATION

Use thin strips of fillet or rump steak instead of mince.

Meatball Curry

PREPARATION TIME:
15 MINUTES, PLUS CHILLING

COOKING TIME: ABOUT 55 MINUTES

FREEZING: NOT SUITABLE

615 CALS PER SERVING

SERVES 4

2.5 cm (1 inch) piece fresh root ginger

2 garlic cloves

450 g (1 lb) finely minced beef

10 ml (2 tsp) garam masala

10 ml (2 tsp) ground turmeric

5 ml (1 tsp) ground cumin

5 ml (1 tsp) chilli powder

salt

1 egg, beaten

1 onion

50 ml (2 fl oz) ghee or oil

2.5 cm (1 inch) stick cinnamon

6 green cardamoms, crushed

4 whole cloves

10 ml (2 tsp) paprika

600 ml (1 pint) thin coconut milk

oil for deep-frying

1 Peel and finely chop the ginger. Peel and crush the garlic.

2 Put the minced meat in a bowl with half of the ginger, garlic, garam masala, turmeric, cumin and chilli powder. Add 5 ml (1 tsp) salt and mix well with your hands. Bind with the egg. With wetted hands, form the mixture into 24 balls. Chill for 30 minutes.

3 Meanwhile, peel and chop the onion. Heat the ghee in a heavy-based saucepan or flameproof casserole, add the onion with the remaining ginger and garlic and fry gently for about 5 minutes until softened.

4 Add the cinnamon, cardamoms, cloves and paprika with the remaining garam masala, turmeric, cumin and chilli powder. Fry, stirring, for 2 minutes. Pour in 600 ml (1 pint) water and the coconut milk. Add salt to taste and bring to the boil. Simmer until the sauce has reduced by about one-third.

5 Heat the oil in a deep-fat fryer to 190°C (375°F) and deep-fry the meatballs until golden. Drain the meatballs on kitchen paper, then add to the coconut sauce. Cover and simmer gently for 30 minutes. Serve at once.

Hot and Sour Beef Salad

PREPARATION TIME:
45 MINUTES, PLUS MARINATING

COOKING TIME: ABOUT 10 MINUTES

FREEZING: NOT SUITABLE

400-270 CALS PER SERVING

SERVES 4-6

45 ml (3 tbsp) sesame seeds

salt and pepper

2-3 hot chillies

1-2 garlic cloves

2 large thick rump steaks, each about 300 g (10 oz)

juice of 3 limes

30 ml (2 tbsp) soy sauce

45 ml (3 tbsp) vegetable oil

8 spring onions

1 orange pepper

1 red pepper

1 cucumber

4-6 red shallots, or 1 red onion

1 lemon grass stalk, sliced (optional)

1 cos lettuce, head of Chinese leaves, or other salad leaves

chilli oil, to taste

handful fresh mint leaves

handful fresh coriander leaves

COOK'S NOTE
Chilli oil adds a distinctive flavour to this salad. To make your own chilli oil, pack fresh chillies into a clean glass jar or bottle. Pour on olive oil to cover and leave to infuse for at least 2 weeks before using. It improves with age and keeps almost indefinitely.

1 Toast the sesame seeds in a dry small heavy-based frying pan over a low heat until golden brown, shaking the pan constantly. Allow to cool, then crush with a pinch of salt, using a pestle and mortar.

2 Finely chop the chillies, removing the seeds if a milder flavour is preferred. Peel and slice the garlic. Put the steaks in a large shallow dish and sprinkle with the chillies, garlic and lime juice. Mix the soy sauce with 30 ml (2 tbsp) of the vegetable oil and drizzle over the meat. Leave to marinate in a cool place for at least 1 hour or preferably overnight.

3 Meanwhile, trim the spring onions and shred very finely. Drop into a bowl of cold water. Quarter, core and deseed the peppers. Cut each pepper quarter into very thin shreds. Add to the bowl of water. Chill in the refrigerator.

4 Halve the cucumber lengthways and scoop out the seeds. Cut into thin strips, about 5 cm (2 inches) long. Cover and chill. Peel and finely slice the shallots or red onion.

5 Remove the meat from the marinade, reserving the marinade; scrape off any garlic and chilli. Heat the remaining oil in a large frying pan over a very high heat. Add 1 steak and press down to brown evenly and quickly. Turn and repeat on the other side. Lower the heat slightly and cook for a further 2-4 minutes, depending on thickness and preference; ideally it should be rare-medium. Cook the second steak in the same way. Cut into wafer-thin slices and place in a bowl.

6 Add the marinade to the pan with the lemon grass, if using. Simmer for 1 minute, then pour over the meat. Leave to cool.

7 Combine the lettuce, cucumber and half the drained shredded vegetables in a shallow serving dish. Toss with a little chilli oil and half of the toasted sesame seeds.

8 Add the shallot or red onion, mint and coriander to the beef and pile onto the salad. Top with the remaining vegetables and sesame seeds.

Chinese Beef Salad

PREPARATION TIME:
15 MINUTES, PLUS MARINATING

COOKING TIME: 15 MINUTES

FREEZING: NOT SUITABLE

200 CALS PER SERVING
SERVES 6

700 g (1½ lb) rump steak
2 large garlic cloves
grated rind and juice of 1 orange
60 ml (4 tbsp) rice vinegar or cider vinegar
45 ml (3 tbsp) hoisin sauce
15 ml (1 tbsp) clear honey
175 g (6 oz) spinach

125 g (4 oz) watercress, about 1 bunch
1 small radicchio
275 g (10 oz) assorted mushrooms, such as brown cap, oyster, shiitake
10 ml (2 tsp) sesame oil
salt and pepper
30 ml (2 tbsp) chopped fresh chives, to garnish

1 Slice the rump steak into thin, finger-length strips. Peel and crush the garlic.

2 Mix the orange rind and juice with the garlic, vinegar, hoisin sauce and honey. Add the steak and stir until evenly coated in the marinade. Cover and refrigerate overnight.

3 Remove any tough stalks and roughly tear the spinach, watercress and radicchio. Put in a serving bowl. Cover and refrigerate until required.

4 Slice any large mushrooms. Drain the beef from the marinade, reserving the marinade. Heat the oil in a wok or large nonstick frying pan and stir-fry the mushrooms for about 4 minutes or until golden brown and tender. Remove from the pan and keep warm.

5 Stir-fry the beef in batches for about 4 minutes or until browned and tender. Return all the beef and mushrooms to the pan with the marinade and bring to the boil, stirring, for 1 minute.

6 Toss the beef and mushroom mixture into the salad leaves. Season well and serve immediately, garnished with chives.

Beef Salad with Roasted Vegetable Paste

PREPARATION TIME:
20 MINUTES, PLUS MARINATING

COOKING TIME: 30-35 MINUTES

FREEZING: NOT SUITABLE

230 CALS PER SERVING
SERVES 4

225 g (8 oz) fillet steak
15 ml (1 tbsp) Szechuan peppercorns
5 ml (1 tsp) ground black pepper
5 ml (1 tsp) ground coriander
1.25 ml (¼ tsp) Chinese five-spice powder
125 g (4 oz) salad leaves
15 ml (1 tbsp) sesame seeds
lime wedges, to serve

VEGETABLE PASTE
225 g (8 oz) shallots
4-8 garlic cloves
2.5 cm (1 inch) piece fresh root ginger
2-3 large chillies
1 lemon grass stalk
5 ml (1 tsp) cumin seeds
45 ml (3 tbsp) sunflower oil
15 ml (1 tbsp) tamarind juice
15 ml (1 tbsp) light soy sauce
10 ml (2 tsp) sugar

COOK'S NOTE
This recipe is based on a Thai dish called *larp* which is similar to beef tartare.

1 Wash and dry the beef. Roughly grind the Szechuan peppercorns, using a pestle and mortar or spice grinder, and mix with the black pepper, ground coriander and five-spice powder. Spread on a board. Press the steak down into the spice mixture, turning to coat well on both sides. Cover and set aside for 2 hours.

2 Meanwhile, prepare the vegetable paste. Peel and halve any large shallots; peel and roughly chop the garlic and ginger; roughly chop the chillies; finely chop the lemon grass. Place these ingredients in a small roasting pan with the cumin seeds. Pour over the oil and toss well until evenly combined. Roast in the oven at 200°C (400°F) Mark 6 for 30 minutes until browned and softened. Allow to cool slightly.

3 Transfer the roasted vegetables to a food processor and add the tamarind juice, soy sauce and the sugar. Purée to form a rough paste, adding a little water if too thick.

4 Brush a griddle or heavy-based frying pan with a little oil and heat. As soon as the oil starts to smoke, add the beef fillet and sear by pressing down hard with a fish slice. Fry for 1 minute, turn the steak and repeat with the second side. Remove from the pan and rest for 2 minutes.

5 Divide the salad leaves between individual serving plates. Thinly slice the beef fillet and arrange on the plates. Spoon on a little of the roasted vegetable paste and scatter over the sesame seeds. Serve at once, with lime wedges.

Fragrant Lamb with Noodles

PREPARATION TIME: 20 MINUTES

COOKING TIME: 2 HOURS 40 MINUTES

FREEZING: NOT SUITABLE

550-415 CALS PER SERVING

SERVES 6-8

1.8 kg (4 lb) leg of lamb
45 ml (3 tbsp) oil
2.5 cm (1 inch) piece fresh root ginger
4 garlic cloves
1 red chilli
100 ml (4 fl oz) dry sherry
30 ml (2 tbsp) soft light brown sugar

5 ml (1 tsp) sesame seeds
100 ml (4 fl oz) hoisin or teriyaki sauce
pared rind and juice of 1 orange
pared rind of 1 lemon
1 bunch spring onions
1 small head Chinese leaves
125 g (4 oz) egg noodles

1 Place the leg of lamb in a deep, oiled roasting tin just large enough to hold the joint. Cook at 200°C (400°F) Mark 6 for 15 minutes.

2 Peel and slice the ginger and garlic. Deseed and slice the chilli. Add to the roasting tin with the next six ingredients and 600 ml (1 pint) water. Return to the oven for a further 15 minutes.

3 Reduce the oven temperature to 170°C (325°F) Mark 3, cover the lamb with a tent of foil and return to the oven for a further 2 hours or until the lamb is very tender. Baste regularly during the cooking time.

4 Transfer the lamb to a warmed serving platter. Cover and keep warm in a low oven.

5 Roughly chop the spring onions and thickly slice the Chinese leaves. Place the roasting tin on the hob and add the noodles to the pan juices. Bring to the boil and bubble gently for about 5 minutes until the noodles are tender. Stir in the spring onions and Chinese leaves, return to the boil and bubble for 1-2 minutes only. Serve immediately with the carved lamb.

Raan

PREPARATION TIME:
15 MINUTES, PLUS CHILLING

COOKING TIME: 2 HOURS

FREEZING: NOT SUITABLE

600 CALS PER SERVING

SERVES 6

2 onions
6 garlic cloves
5 cm (2 inch) piece fresh root ginger
75 g (3 oz) whole blanched almonds
5 cm (2 inch) stick cinnamon
10 green cardamoms
4 whole cloves
30 ml (2 tbsp) cumin seeds
15 ml (1 tbsp) ground coriander

2.5 ml (½ tsp) grated nutmeg
10 ml (2 tsp) ground turmeric
10 ml (2 tsp) chilli powder
10 ml (2 tsp) salt
30 ml (2 tbsp) lemon or lime juice
600 ml (1 pint) natural yogurt
2.3 kg (5 lb) leg of lamb, fat removed
25 g (1 oz) blanched flaked almonds
50 g (2 oz) sultanas

1 Peel and roughly chop the onions, garlic and ginger. Place all the remaining ingredients, except the lamb, flaked almonds and sultanas, in a blender or food processor and work until smooth.

2 With a sharp knife, make deep slashes all over the meat through to the bone.

3 Rub one-third of the yogurt mixture well into the lamb and place in an ovenproof baking dish or casserole. Pour the remaining yogurt mixture over the top of the meat and around the sides. Cover and chill for 12 hours.

4 Allow the dish to come to room temperature, then cover tightly with the lid or foil. Bake in the oven at 180°C (350°F) Mark 4 for 1¼ hours; uncover and bake for a further 45 minutes, basting occasionally until tender.

5 Transfer the lamb to a warmed serving dish, pour the sauce around the meat and scatter the almonds and sultanas over the top. Serve hot.

Chinese Barbecued Lamb

PREPARATION TIME:
10 MINUTES, PLUS MARINATING

COOKING TIME: 30-35 MINUTES

FREEZING: NOT SUITABLE

270 CALS PER SERVING

SERVES 8

1.1 kg (2½ lb) boned and flattened (butterflied) lamb shoulder
4 garlic cloves

MARINADE
2.5 cm (1 inch) piece fresh root ginger

150 ml (¼ pint) soy sauce
150 ml (¼ pint) dry or medium sherry
30 ml (2 tbsp) clear honey
pinch of ground or 3 whole star anise
30 ml (2 tbsp) chopped fresh coriander

1 First make the marinade. Peel and finely grate the ginger, then combine with the soy sauce, sherry, honey, star anise and coriander.

2 Open out the lamb and make a few small cuts all over the meat. Peel the garlic, cut into slivers, then insert into the cuts in the lamb. Place in a non-metallic dish and pour the marinade over. Cover and leave to marinate for 8 hours or overnight, turning occasionally.

3 Remove the lamb from marinade, reserving the liquid. Cook over a medium heat on the barbecue, basting frequently with the marinade, for 30-35 minutes (for medium rare). Alternatively, roast in the oven at 230°C (450°F) Mark 8 for 30 minutes then 180°C (350°F) Mark 4 for 30-35 minutes or until tender. Baste frequently.

VARIATION
Use a 1.8 kg (4 lb) whole, cleaned salmon instead of the lamb. Marinate the fish as above, then place on a piece of foil. Spoon over a little marinade; wrap securely. Cook on the barbecue for 30-40 minutes, turning occasionally, until the fish is cooked through.

Ginger and Coriander Lamb

PREPARATION TIME: 5 MINUTES
COOKING TIME: 6-10 MINUTES
FREEZING: NOT SUITABLE

470 CALS PER SERVING
SERVES 4

5 cm (2 inch) piece fresh root ginger
2 garlic cloves
30 ml (2 tbsp) clear honey
30 ml (2 tbsp) orange juice
5 ml (1 tsp) Chinese five-spice powder
125 g (4 oz) softened butter

salt and pepper
4 lamb chops, each about 175 g (6 oz)
30 ml (2 tbsp) white wine vinegar
30 ml (2 tbsp) dry sherry
30 ml (2 tbsp) chopped fresh coriander

1 Peel the ginger and garlic and place in a food processor with the honey and orange juice. Process to chop finely. Add the Chinese five-spice powder and softened butter and process again until evenly mixed.

2 Season the chops. Heat half the spiced butter in a frying pan. Brown the chops for 3-5 minutes on each side, then set aside. Add the remaining spiced butter, vinegar and sherry to the pan. Bring to the boil then add the coriander. Serve immediately with the chops.

Spiced Coconut Lamb

PREPARATION TIME: 10 MINUTES

COOKING TIME: 25 MINUTES

FREEZING: NOT SUITABLE

590 CALS PER SERVING

SERVES 4

1 onion
1 red chilli
2 garlic cloves
30 ml (2 tbsp) oil
25 g (1 oz) blanched almonds
2.5 ml (½ tsp) ground turmeric
2.5 ml (½ tsp) ground ginger
8 lean lamb cutlets, about 450 g (1 lb)
total weight

juice of 1 lemon
1 lemon grass stalk
5 ml (1 tsp) dark muscovado sugar
225 ml (8 fl oz) coconut milk
salt and pepper
banana leaves, to serve (optional)
coriander sprigs, to garnish

1 Peel and roughly chop the onion; deseed the chilli; peel and chop the garlic. Place in a food processor or blender with the oil, nuts and spices and blend to a paste.

2 Fry the paste in a large frying pan or wok for 1-2 minutes, stirring constantly. Add the cutlets and cook over a medium heat, until well browned on both sides.

3 Add the lemon juice, lemon grass, muscovado sugar, coconut milk and 150 ml (¼ pint) water. Bring to the boil, cover and simmer gently for about 15 minutes or until the cutlets are tender. Uncover and bubble down the juices for 3-4 minutes, to give a coating consistency. Stir occasionally to prevent the sauce from sticking to the pan.

4 Remove the lemon grass and adjust the seasoning. Serve on banana leaves, if wished, and garnish with coriander sprigs.

Spicy Cinnamon Lamb

PREPARATION TIME: 10 MINUTES

COOKING TIME: 25 MINUTES

FREEZING: NOT SUITABLE

510 CALS PER SERVING

SERVES 4

225 g (8 oz) onion
2 garlic cloves
2.5 cm (1 inch) piece fresh root ginger
700 g (1½ lb) lean boneless lamb
15 ml (1 tbsp) oil
225 g (8 oz) canned chopped tomatoes

30 ml (2 tbsp) dark soy sauce
10 ml (2 tsp) dark muscovado sugar
1.25 ml (¼ tsp) grated nutmeg
5 ml (1 tsp) ground cinnamon
pepper
spring onion shreds, to garnish

1 Peel and finely chop the onion. Peel and crush the garlic. Peel and chop the ginger. Slice the lamb into bite-sized pieces.

2 Heat the oil in a large frying pan, add the onion, garlic and ginger and cook for 2-3 minutes or until softened. Add the meat to the pan and cook over a high heat for 4-5 minutes or until the meat is well browned.

3 Stir in the tomatoes, soy sauce, sugar, nutmeg, cinnamon and pepper to taste. Add 150 ml (¼ pint) water and bring to the boil. Cover and simmer gently for about 20 minutes or until the meat is tender. Serve immediately, garnished with spring onion shreds.

Red Spiced Lamb

PREPARATION TIME: 5 MINUTES

COOKING TIME: 2 HOURS 25 MINUTES

FREEZING: NOT SUITABLE

420 CALS PER SERVING

SERVES 6

2.5 cm (1 inch) piece fresh root ginger
225 g (8 oz) onions
8 garlic cloves
1.1 kg (2½ lb) lean boneless lamb
60 ml (4 tbsp) oil
10 cardamom pods
2 bay leaves
6 whole cloves
10 peppercorns

2.5 cm (1 inch) stick cinnamon
5 ml (1 tsp) coriander seeds
10 ml (2 tsp) cumin seeds
20 ml (4 tsp) paprika
5 ml (1 tsp) cayenne pepper
90 ml (6 tbsp) natural yogurt
600-750 ml (1-1¼ pints) lamb stock
5 ml (1 tsp) salt

COOK'S NOTE
The meat should be well browned so that the juices have a rich, dark colour.

1 Peel and roughly chop the ginger and onions. Peel and crush the garlic. Pour 60 ml (4 tbsp) water into a blender or food processor, add the ginger, garlic and onion, then process until smooth. Cut the lamb into 4 cm (1½ inch) cubes.

2 Heat the oil in a large flameproof casserole and brown the meat in small batches. Set aside. Add a little more oil if necessary and stir in the cardamom pods, bay leaves, cloves, peppercorns and cinnamon. Cook until the cloves begin to swell and the bay leaves to colour, then add the onion paste and cook for 4 minutes, or until most of the liquid has evaporated, stirring all the time.

3 Add the remaining spices, meat and juices, and cook, stirring, for 1 minute. Add the yogurt a spoonful at a time, cooking and stirring after each addition. Stir in just enough stock to cover the meat. Add the salt and bring to the boil.

4 Cover and cook at 180°C (350°F) Mark 4 for 1½-2 hours or until the meat is very tender. Spoon off any excess fat and serve. (Warn guests to watch out for the whole spices.)

Lamb and Bamboo Shoot Red Curry

PREPARATION TIME: 10 MINUTES

COOKING TIME: 45 MINUTES

FREEZING: NOT SUITABLE

325 CALS PER SERVING

SERVES 4

Illustrated opposite

1 large onion
2 garlic cloves
450 g (1 lb) lean boneless lamb
30 ml (2 tbsp) sunflower oil
30 ml (2 tbsp) Thai red curry paste
150 ml (¼ pint) lamb or beef stock
30 ml (2 tbsp) Thai fish sauce

10 ml (2 tsp) soft brown sugar
200 g (7 oz) can bamboo shoots, drained
1 red pepper
30 ml (2 tbsp) chopped fresh mint
15 ml (1 tbsp) chopped fresh basil
25 g (1 oz) raw peanuts, toasted
basil leaves, to garnish

1 Peel the onion and cut into wedges; peel and finely chop the garlic. Cut the lamb into 3 cm (1¼ inch) cubes. Heat the oil in a wok or large frying pan, add the onion and garlic and fry over a medium heat for 5 minutes.

2 Add the lamb together with the curry paste and stir-fry for 5 minutes. Add the stock, fish sauce and sugar. Bring to the boil, lower the heat, cover and simmer gently for 20 minutes.

3 Meanwhile, slice the bamboo shoots; deseed and slice the red pepper. Stir into the curry with the herbs and cook, uncovered, for a further 10 minutes. Stir in the peanuts and serve at once, garnished with the basil leaves.

Sesame Lamb

PREPARATION TIME: 15 MINUTES

COOKING TIME: 15 MINUTES

FREEZING: NOT SUITABLE

640 CALS PER SERVING

SERVES 4

450 g (1 lb) lean boneless lamb
1 onion
3 carrots
225 g (8 oz) broccoli
2.5 cm (1 inch) piece fresh root ginger
125 g (4 oz) fresh white breadcrumbs
50 g (2 oz) sesame seeds
salt and pepper

2 eggs, beaten
90 ml (6 tbsp) oil
425 ml (¾ pint) chicken stock
30 ml (2 tbsp) dry sherry
25 ml (1½ tbsp) cornflour
15 ml (1 tbsp) dark soy sauce
a few drops of sesame oil, to serve

1 Cut the lamb into medallion-shaped slices, about 5 mm (¼ inch) thick. Peel the onion and slice lengthways. Peel and slice the carrots and cut into shapes using small cutters. Cut the broccoli into small florets and cut the stalks diagonally into thin slices. Peel and shred the ginger.

2 Mix the breadcrumbs with the sesame seeds and season with salt and pepper. Dip the lamb slices in the beaten egg and coat in the breadcrumb mixture, pressing on firmly with the fingertips.

3 Heat 30 ml (2 tbsp) oil in a wok or large frying pan, add half the lamb slices and fry for about 2 minutes on each side until golden. Remove from the pan, drain and keep warm. Cook the remaining lamb in the same way, using another 30 ml (2 tbsp) oil.

4 Wipe the pan clean and heat the remaining oil. Add the onion, carrots, broccoli and ginger, and stir-fry for 2 minutes. Add the stock and sherry, cover and steam for 1 minute.

5 Blend the cornflour with the soy sauce and 15 ml (1 tbsp) water, stir into the pan and cook for 2 minutes, stirring. Add the lamb slices and heat through. Sprinkle with sesame oil and serve.

Lamb with Potato

PREPARATION TIME: 20 MINUTES

COOKING TIME: 2 HOURS

FREEZING: SUITABLE

680-450 CALS PER SERVING

SERVES 4-6

1 large onion
3 garlic cloves
2.5 cm (1 inch) piece fresh root ginger
1-2 hot red chillies
45 ml (3 tbsp) desiccated coconut
900 g (2 lb) lean boneless lamb
550 g (1¼ lb) waxy potatoes
45 ml (3 tbsp) ghee or oil
10 ml (2 tsp) paprika

5 ml (1 tsp) ground fenugreek
5 ml (1 tsp) ground turmeric
10 ml (2 tsp) ground coriander
5 ml (1 tsp) ground cumin
150 ml (¼ pint) natural yogurt
300 ml (½ pint) meat or vegetable stock
salt
yogurt or raita (see page 199) and shredded chillies, to serve

COOK'S NOTE
If you're not certain that the potatoes you are using are waxy, add them to the casserole after 30 minutes of the cooking time.

1 Peel and quarter the onion. Peel the garlic. Peel and roughly chop the ginger. Chop the chillies, discarding the seeds if a milder flavour is preferred. Put the onion, garlic, ginger, chillies and coconut in a blender or food processor with 30 ml (2 tbsp) water and process until smooth.

2 Trim the meat of any excess fat and cut into 4 cm (1½ inch) cubes. Peel the potatoes and cut into large chunks.

3 Heat the ghee or oil in a flameproof casserole, add the onion paste and cook until golden brown, stirring all the time. Add the spices and cook, stirring, over a high heat for 2 minutes.

4 Brown the meat and potatoes in the casserole over a high heat, in batches if necessary, turning constantly until thoroughly browned on all sides. Lower the heat and return all the meat and potatoes to the casserole. Add the yogurt, a spoonful at a time, stirring after each addition.

5 Add the stock and season liberally with salt. Bring to the boil, then reduce the heat, cover and cook in the oven at 180°C (350°F) Mark 4 for about 2 hours or until the meat is very tender.

6 When the meat and potatoes are tender, remove with a slotted spoon; set aside. Bring the sauce to the boil and boil steadily until the sauce is well reduced and very thick. Return the meat and potatoes to the casserole and stir to coat with the sauce. Serve topped with raita or yogurt, and shredded chillies.

Spiced Lamb and Soured Cream Pot

PREPARATION TIME:
30 MINUTES, PLUS SOAKING

COOKING TIME: 2 HOURS 40 MINUTES

FREEZING: NOT SUITABLE

930 CALS PER SERVING

SERVES 4

275 g (10 oz) basmati rice
700 g (1½ lb) lean boneless lamb
225 g (8 oz) onions
5 cm (2 inch) piece fresh root ginger
2 large garlic cloves
75 ml (5 tbsp) oil
5 ml (1 tsp) ground cumin
5 ml (1 tsp) ground mace
5 ml (1 tsp) ground cinnamon
5 ml (1 tsp) garam masala
5 ml (1 tsp) paprika

300 ml (½ pint) soured cream
25 g (1 oz) butter
600 ml (1 pint) stock
salt and pepper
100 ml (4 fl oz) hot milk
1 large pinch saffron strands
25 g (1 oz) chopped fresh coriander or mint
50 g (2 oz) toasted slivered almonds
50 g (2 oz) seedless raisins
poppadoms, to serve

1 Wash the rice in several changes of cold water, cover with cold water and soak for 30 minutes.

2 Cut the lamb into large pieces. Peel and thinly slice the onions; peel and finely chop the ginger. Peel and crush the garlic. Heat 45 ml (3 tbsp) oil in a flameproof casserole and brown the lamb in batches. Set aside.

3 Lower the heat, add the remaining oil to the casserole and fry the onions until golden brown. Remove half the onions with a slotted spoon and set aside. Add the ginger, garlic and all the ground spices to the casserole and cook for 2-3 minutes.

4 Return the lamb to the casserole with half the soured cream and bring to the boil. Cover tightly and simmer for 1½ hours or until the lamb is tender and the sauce well reduced. Stir in the remaining soured cream.

5 Meanwhile, drain the rice. Melt the butter in a saucepan and stir in the rice. Add the stock and 5 ml (1 tsp) salt, bring to the boil then partially cover and simmer gently for 10-12 minutes or until most of the liquid has been absorbed. Cover the pan and turn off the heat. Leave the rice to steam for a further 15 minutes. Mix together the hot milk, saffron and coriander.

6 Stir the rice into the lamb with the milk mixture. Top with the reserved onions, cover and cook in the oven at 170°C (325°F) Mark 3 for 30 minutes. Turn off the heat and leave to rest for 10 minutes. Scatter over the almonds and raisins and serve with poppadoms.

Lamb Pasanda

PREPARATION TIME: 20 MINUTES

COOKING TIME: 2 HOURS

FREEZING: SUITABLE

865 CALS PER SERVING

SERVES 4

50 g (2 oz) blanched almonds
50 g (2 oz) unsalted cashew nuts
30 ml (2 tbsp) sesame seeds
2.5 cm (1 inch) piece fresh root ginger
2 garlic cloves
2 onions
30 ml (2 tbsp) ghee or oil
10 ml (2 tsp) ground cumin
10 ml (2 tsp) ground coriander

2.5 ml (½ tsp) ground turmeric
2.5 ml (½ tsp) ground cardamom
2.5 ml (½ tsp) ground cloves
700 g (1½ lb) lean boneless lamb, cubed
150 ml (¼ pint) double cream
150 ml (¼ pint) coconut milk
30 ml (2 tbsp) lemon juice
salt

COOK'S NOTE
It is important to ensure that the meat, nuts and onions are thoroughly browned, or the sauce will have an insipid colour.

1 Put the nuts in a heavy-based frying pan and dry-fry over a gentle heat until just golden brown. Remove from the pan and cool. Toast the sesame seeds in the same way; cool.

2 Peel and roughly chop the ginger. Peel the garlic. Peel and thinly slice the onions.

3 Tip the nuts into a blender or food processor and process briefly until finely chopped. Add the sesame seeds, ginger, garlic and 15 ml (1 tbsp) water and work to a purée.

4 Heat the ghee or oil in a large saucepan, add the onions and cook over a fairly high heat until tinged with brown. Add the nut mixture and cook over a moderately high heat for 2 minutes.

5 Add the ground spices and cook, stirring, for 2 minutes. Add the meat and cook over a high heat, turning constantly, until browned and sealed on all sides.

6 Add the cream, coconut milk and 150 ml (¼ pint) water. Stir in the lemon juice and season with salt to taste. Bring slowly to the boil, then lower the heat and simmer very gently for about 1½ hours or until the lamb is tender.

Rogan Josh

PREPARATION TIME: 30 MINUTES

COOKING TIME: 1½ HOURS

FREEZING: NOT SUITABLE

574-380 CALS PER SERVING

SERVES 4-6

2 onions
1 large garlic clove
2.5 cm (1 inch) piece fresh root ginger
900 g (2 lb) lamb fillet
75 ml (3 fl oz) ghee or oil
4 green cardamoms, crushed
10 ml (2 tsp) ground turmeric

10 ml (2 tsp) ground coriander
10 ml (2 tsp) paprika
2.5 ml (½ tsp) chilli powder
1 red and 1 green pepper
6 ripe tomatoes, skinned
300 ml (½ pint) natural yogurt
salt

1 Peel and thinly slice the onions. Peel and crush the garlic. Peel and finely chop the ginger. Trim the lamb and cut into cubes.

2 Heat 50 ml (2 fl oz) ghee or oil in a heavy-based saucepan or flameproof casserole, add the onion, garlic and ginger and fry gently for about 5 minutes until soft and lightly coloured.

3 Add the spices and fry gently for 2 minutes, stirring constantly. Increase the heat to moderate, add the meat and brown on all sides.

4 Halve and deseed the peppers. Chop half of the red pepper and half of the green pepper finely. Slice the other two halves into thin strips. Chop the tomatoes.

5 Reserve about 60 ml (4 tbsp) of the yogurt. Add the remainder to the pan, a spoonful at a time. Cook each addition over high heat, stirring constantly, until the yogurt is absorbed. Sprinkle in salt to taste. Add the chopped peppers and two-thirds of the tomatoes to the meat, increase the heat and fry until the juices run, stirring and tossing the contents of the pan.

6 Put a double thickness of foil over the top of the pan and seal tightly with the lid. Simmer gently for about 1½ hours, stirring occasionally, until the meat is tender.

7 Before serving, heat the remaining ghee in a frying pan, add the red and green pepper strips and fry over gentle heat for a few minutes until softened. Add the remaining chopped tomatoes with a pinch of salt, increase the heat and toss vigorously to combine with the peppers. Place the meat curry in a warmed serving dish and spoon the pepper and tomato mixture on top. Drizzle the remaining yogurt over and serve.

Lamb Tikka

PREPARATION TIME:
20 MINUTES, PLUS MARINATING

COOKING TIME: ABOUT 30
MINUTES

FREEZING: NOT SUITABLE

810-540 CALS PER SERVING
SERVES 4-6

900 g (2 lb) lean boneless lamb
1 onion
2 garlic cloves
7.5 cm (3 inch) piece fresh root ginger
5 ml (1 tsp) ground cumin
5 ml (1 tsp) ground turmeric
5 ml (1 tsp) cayenne pepper (optional)
30 ml (2 tbsp) finely chopped fresh coriander
60 ml (4 tbsp) thick yogurt
5 ml (1 tsp) salt
melted ghee, butter or oil, for brushing
juice of ½ lemon

5 ml (1 tsp) garam masala
fresh coriander chutney (see page 197), to serve

SAUCE
2.5 ml (½ tsp) saffron strands
25 g (1 oz) blanched almonds
25 g (1 oz) shelled unsalted pistachio nuts
200 ml (7 fl oz) double cream
15 ml (1 tbsp) ghee or oil
seeds of 3 cardamoms
salt
150 ml (¼ pint) yogurt

COOK'S NOTES
The sauce is improved if allowed to infuse for a while, so if you're marinating the meat overnight make the sauce the day before too.

If you haven't time to marinate the meat overnight, use lamb fillet rather than leg to ensure a tender result.

1 Trim the meat of excess fat, then cut into large cubes and place in a large non-metallic bowl.
2 Peel and finely chop the onion, garlic and ginger. Add to the lamb.
3 Add the cumin, turmeric, cayenne if using, chopped coriander, yogurt and salt. Toss thoroughly to coat. Cover the bowl and leave to marinate at cool room temperature for about 1 hour, or preferably overnight in the refrigerator.
4 Meanwhile, make the sauce. Put the saffron in a bowl with 30 ml (2 tbsp) boiling water and leave to soak.
5 Put the almonds and pistachio nuts in a blender or food processor and work until finely chopped. Add half of the cream and process again until the mixture is smooth.
6 Heat the ghee or oil in a heavy-based pan. Add the nut mixture, together with the saffron, the remaining cream, cardamom seeds and salt to taste. Bring to the boil, stirring. Simmer gently for about 5 minutes, stirring all the time. Remove from the heat and stir in the yogurt. Leave the sauce to stand for at least 30 minutes, or preferably overnight.
7 Thread the lamb onto kebab skewers. Place on the grill rack and cook under a moderately high heat for 15-25 minutes, turning occasionally, until evenly browned and cooked through. Brush with melted ghee, butter or oil during cooking.
8 Transfer the lamb to a warmed serving platter and sprinkle with the lemon juice and garam masala. Gently reheat the sauce. Serve the lamb with the sauce and coriander chutney.

Oriental Pork Chops

PREPARATION TIME:
10 MINUTES, PLUS MARINATING

COOKING TIME: 10 MINUTES

FREEZING: NOT SUITABLE

280 CALS PER SERVING

SERVES 4

2.5 cm (1 inch) piece fresh root ginger
4 garlic cloves
30 ml (2 tbsp) soy sauce
30 ml (2 tbsp) clear honey
30 ml (2 tbsp) chopped fresh coriander

30 ml (2 tbsp) chopped fresh rosemary
4 pork chops, each about 175 g (6 oz)
lime halves, to accompany
shredded spring onion and chilli, to garnish (optional)

1 Peel and finely chop the ginger. Peel and crush the garlic. Mix the ginger with the garlic, soy sauce, honey and herbs. Make 3 slashes in each side of the chops. Place in a shallow dish and coat with the marinade. Cover and refrigerate chops for at least 30 minutes, preferably overnight.

2 Pan-fry or grill the chops for about 5 minutes on each side, basting with the marinade. Serve with the pan juices and lime halves. Garnish with shredded spring onion and chilli, if wished.

Glazed Spare Ribs

PREPARATION TIME: 15 MINUTES

COOKING TIME: 1½ HOURS

FREEZING: SUITABLE FOR UP TO
1 MONTH

320-280 CALS PER SERVING

SERVES 2-4

900 g (2 lb) pork spare ribs
30 ml (2 tbsp) malt vinegar
30 ml (2 tbsp) sesame oil
75 ml (3 fl oz) rice or wine vinegar
50 ml (2 fl oz) dark soy sauce
10 ml (2 tsp) grated fresh root ginger

1 garlic clove, crushed
grated rind of 1 lime
60 ml (4 tbsp) soft brown sugar
2.5 ml (½ tsp) Chinese five-spice powder
coriander sprigs and lime wedges, to garnish

1 Wash and dry the spare ribs and place in a saucepan. Cover with plenty of cold water and add the malt vinegar. Bring to the boil and simmer for 20 minutes, skimming the surface from time to time to remove the scum.

2 Meanwhile, place the oil, vinegar, soy sauce, ginger, garlic, lime rind, sugar and five-spice powder in a small saucepan with 75 ml (3 fl oz) water. Bring to the boil and simmer for 5 minutes until reduced and thickened slightly.

3 Drain the ribs and transfer to a roasting dish that will hold the ribs in a single layer. Pour over the soy mixture and toss the ribs to coat evenly.

4 Cover loosely with foil and roast at 220°C (425°F) Mark 7 for 30 minutes. Remove the foil and cook for a further 30 minutes, turning and basting the ribs every 5 minutes. Leave to cool slightly for about 10 minutes before serving.

5 Garnish with coriander and lime wedges, and provide finger bowls.

VARIATION
Barbecued chicken wings make a tasty alternative to the pork ribs. Omit the par-boiling stage. Roast as above, coated with the glaze, for the same time or until glazed and tender.

Chinese Red Pork

PREPARATION TIME: 5 MINUTES,
PLUS MARINATING

COOKING TIME: 15 MINUTES

FREEZING: NOT SUITABLE

310 CALS PER SERVING

SERVES 4

2 garlic cloves
15 ml (1 tbsp) Chinese five-spice powder
75 ml (5 tbsp) hoisin sauce
45 ml (3 tbsp) soft brown sugar

30 ml (2 tbsp) soy sauce
30 ml (2 tbsp) orange juice
4 pork chops, each 175 g (6 oz)

1 Peel and crush the garlic, then mix with the Chinese five-spice powder, hoisin sauce, sugar, soy sauce and orange juice. Score the pork with a sharp knife and coat with the marinade. Cover and marinate for 30 minutes.

2 Cook under the grill, turning and basting with the marinade, for 15 minutes or until brown and crusty. Warm through any remaining marinade and serve with the chops.

Pork Chops in Almond Milk

PREPARATION TIME: 20 MINUTES

COOKING TIME: 1 HOUR

FREEZING: NOT SUITABLE

700 CALS PER SERVING

SERVES 4

4 whole cloves
4 green cardamoms
5 ml (1 tsp) black peppercorns
2.5 cm (1 inch) stick cinnamon
2 onions
2.5 cm (1 inch) piece fresh root ginger
75 ml (5 tbsp) ghee or oil

4 trimmed medium pork loin chops
600 ml (1 pint) milk
5 ml (1 tsp) ground turmeric
5 ml (1 tsp) salt
50 g (2 oz) blanched almonds
150 ml (¼ pint) double cream

1 Dry-fry the cloves, cardamoms, peppercorns and cinnamon stick in a large heavy-based frying pan for a few minutes, then grind.

2 Peel and thinly slice the onions. Peel and finely chop the ginger. Heat 60 ml (4 tbsp) ghee or oil in a flameproof casserole. Add the onions, ginger and ground spices and fry gently, stirring, for 10 minutes until softened. Transfer with a slotted spoon to a jug.

3 Put the remaining ghee or oil into a large, heavy-based frying pan, then add the pork chops. Fry until browned on both sides.

4 Stir the milk into the onion mixture, then add the turmeric and salt. Pour over the chops and bring to the boil. Cover and simmer for about 45 minutes until the chops are tender and the sauce is quite dry. Spoon the sauce over the chops occasionally during cooking.

5 Meanwhile, pound the almonds with a pestle and mortar or in an electric grinder, then mix the ground almonds with the cream in a bowl. Cover and leave to infuse for 30 minutes.

6 Transfer the cooked chops with some of the onions to a warmed serving plate and keep hot. Strain the cooking liquid and boil to reduce, then pour in the almond cream. Simmer for a few minutes, then pour over the chops.

Sweet and Spicy Pineapple Pork

PREPARATION TIME: 5 MINUTES

COOKING TIME: 35 MINUTES

FREEZING: NOT SUITABLE

240 CALS PER SERVING

SERVES 6

COOK'S NOTE
The ovenproof dish needs to be just large enough to hold the pork fillets side by side and deep enough to take the juice.

425 g (15 oz) canned pineapple pieces in natural juice
2 garlic cloves
700 g (1½ lb) pork tenderloin

15 ml (1 tbsp) oil
15 ml (1 tbsp) Indian mild curry paste
30 ml (2 tbsp) lemon juice
30 ml (2 tbsp) mango chutney

1 Drain the pineapple pieces, reserving the juice. Roughly chop the pineapple. Peel and crush the garlic.

2 Heat a nonstick frying pan and dry-fry the pork tenderloin at a high heat for 4 minutes or until golden brown. Set aside in a small ovenproof dish (see Cook's Note).

3 Lower the heat and add the oil, crushed garlic cloves and curry paste, then fry for 30 seconds. Stir in the pineapple and juice, lemon juice and chutney. Bring to the boil, then pour immediately over the pork.

4 Cook at 200°C (400°F) Mark 6 for about 25 minutes, basting occasionally. Serve, thickly sliced, with the pineapple and mango sauce.

Garlic and Honey Pork with Vegetable Noodles

PREPARATION TIME: 20 MINUTES

COOKING TIME: 25 MINUTES

FREEZING: NOT SUITABLE

490 CALS PER SERVING

SERVES 4

Illustrated opposite

2 pork tenderloins, each about 250 g (9 oz)
5 cm (2 inch) piece fresh root ginger
3 garlic cloves
30 ml (2 tbsp) clear honey
45 ml (3 tbsp) soy sauce
45 ml (3 tbsp) dry sherry
15 ml (1 tbsp) oil
10 ml (2 tsp) sesame seeds

VEGETABLE NOODLES
1 large yellow pepper
4 spring onions
2 lemon grass stalks
225 g (8 oz) bean sprouts
grated rind and juice of ½ lemon
15 ml (1 tbsp) sesame oil
125 g (4 oz) rice noodles
30 ml (2 tbsp) oil

1 Trim any fat and membrane from the pork tenderloins and prick them all over with a fork. Arrange side by side but not touching in a roasting tin.

2 Peel and grate the ginger. Peel and crush the garlic. Mix the ginger, garlic, honey, soy sauce, sherry and oil together in a bowl, then pour over the pork tenderloins, turning to coat all over.

3 Roast in the oven at 220°C (425°F) Mark 7 for 25 minutes, turning the pork, basting and sprinkling with the sesame seeds after 15 minutes.

4 Meanwhile, prepare the vegetable noodles. Halve the pepper lengthways. Remove the core and seeds, then shred finely. Trim the spring onions and slice diagonally. Remove the coarse outer leaves from the lemon grass, then shred the stalks very thinly. Rinse and drain the bean sprouts in a large colander. Mix the lemon rind and juice with the sesame oil.

5 When the meat is ready, leave to stand in the switched-off oven. Put the rice noodles in a heatproof bowl, pour on boiling water to cover and stir to separate the noodles.

6 Heat the oil in a wok or frying pan, add the yellow pepper, spring onions and lemon grass and stir-fry for 1 minute. Drain the noodles through the bean sprouts in the colander, shake well and add to the stir-fry.

7 Transfer the pork tenderloins to a carving board. Pour the liquid from the roasting tin over the noodle mixture. Add the lemon and sesame oil mixture and stir-fry briefly. Carve the meat into slices, about 5 mm (¼ inch) thick, and serve with the vegetable noodles.

Pork and Tomato Curry

PREPARATION TIME: 25 MINUTES

COOKING TIME: 1 HOUR

FREEZING: NOT SUITABLE

380 CALS PER SERVING

SERVES 4

4 large ripe tomatoes
2 garlic cloves
2.5 cm (1 inch) piece fresh root ginger
2 onions
75 ml (3 fl oz) natural yogurt
45 ml (3 tbsp) sunflower oil
700 g (1½ lb) lean pork, cubed

10 ml (2 tsp) ground cardamom
2.5 ml (½ tsp) ground cloves
10 ml (2 tsp) ground turmeric
2.5 ml (½ tsp) cayenne pepper
salt
15 ml (1 tbsp) cumin seeds
10 ml (2 tsp) chopped fresh coriander

1 Immerse the tomatoes in a bowl of boiling water for 15-30 seconds, then remove, cool slightly and peel away the skins. Peel and chop the garlic and ginger. Peel and roughly chop the onions.

2 Place the tomatoes, garlic and ginger in a food processor with the yogurt and process until the ingredients are reduced to a smooth paste. Set aside.

3 Heat the oil in a large flameproof casserole dish over a high heat, add the chopped onion and cook over a medium to high heat until softened and beginning to brown. Add the cubed pork and cook over a high heat until browned on all sides. Add the cardamom, cloves, turmeric, cayenne pepper and salt to taste and fry for 1 minute. Stir in the tomato and yogurt paste and cook, stirring occasionally, for 5 minutes.

4 Pour in 300 ml (½ pint) water, stir well and bring back to the boil. Cover tightly with a lid and cook in the oven at 170°C (325°F) Mark 3 for about 1 hour, until the pork is tender.

5 When the pork is nearly ready, dry-fry the cumin seeds in a heavy-based frying pan until browned – do not let them burn. Serve the pork with the cumin seeds and coriander sprinkled on top.

Spiced Chilli Pork

PREPARATION TIME:
10 MINUTES, PLUS MARINATING

COOKING TIME: ABOUT 25 MINUTES

FREEZING: NOT SUITABLE

425 CALS PER SERVING

SERVES 6

900 g (2 lb) pork fillet
50 g (2 oz) piece fresh root ginger
2 small green chillies
225 g (8 oz) onion
1 large garlic clove
30 ml (2 tbsp) garam masala
2.5 ml (½ tsp) ground turmeric
about 105 ml (7 tbsp) oil

salt and pepper
400 g (14 oz) canned chopped tomatoes
50 g (2 oz) creamed coconut
15 ml (1 tbsp) lemon juice
60 ml (4 tbsp) chopped fresh coriander
lemon wedges and chopped fresh coriander, to garnish

1 Slice the pork into pieces 5 mm (¼ inch) thick, discarding any skin or fat. Peel and finely chop the ginger. Halve, deseed and finely chop the chillies. Peel and slice the onion. Peel and crush the garlic.

2 Place the pork, ginger, chillies, onion, garlic and spices in a bowl. Stir in 60 ml (4 tbsp) oil with plenty of salt and pepper, mixing well. Cover and refrigerate for several hours, or overnight.

3 Heat 45 ml (3 tbsp) oil in a large frying pan or shallow flameproof casserole. Add about a quarter of the pork, onion and spice mixture and fry until the meat is well browned, stirring occasionally. Remove from the casserole. Brown the rest of the meat mixture in batches, adding a little more oil, if necessary.

4 Return all the pork, onion and spice mixture to the pan. Mix in the tomatoes with the grated creamed coconut and 60 ml (4 tbsp) water. Bring to the boil. Cover and simmer for 10-15 minutes or until the meat is tender.

5 Skim well, then add the lemon juice and coriander. Adjust the seasoning and serve garnished with lemon wedges and more chopped fresh coriander.

Pork Vindaloo

PREPARATION TIME: 20 MINUTES

COOKING TIME: ABOUT 2 HOURS

FREEZING: SUITABLE

475-315 CALS PER SERVING

SERVES 4-6

900 g (2 lb) lean shoulder of pork
225 g (8 oz) onions (preferably red)
60 ml (4 tbsp) ghee or oil
6 garlic cloves
2.5 cm (1 inch) piece fresh root ginger
4-6 dried hot red chillies
10 ml (2 tsp) cumin seeds
10 ml (2 tsp) coriander seeds
10 ml (2 tsp) fenugreek seeds

10 ml (2 tsp) black peppercorns
5 ml (1 tsp) ground turmeric
10 ml (2 tsp) sugar
5 ml (1 tsp) salt
60 ml (4 tbsp) wine vinegar
8 green cardamoms
1 cinnamon stick
6 ripe juicy tomatoes
30 ml (2 tbsp) tomato purée

1 Trim the pork of excess fat and cut into 4 cm (1½ inch) cubes. Set aside.

2 To make the vindaloo paste, peel and chop the onions. Heat 30 ml (2 tbsp) of the ghee or oil in a frying pan. Add the onions and cook over a fairly high heat until golden brown, stirring all the time. Remove from the pan with a slotted spoon and drain on kitchen paper.

3 Peel the garlic and ginger and put into a blender or food processor with the onions and spices, except the cardamoms, cinnamon and 1 or 2 of the chillies. Add the sugar, salt and vinegar, then process until smooth. Mix with the cardamoms and cinnamon.

4 Heat the remaining 30 ml (2 tbsp) ghee or oil in a large heavy-based saucepan or flameproof casserole. Quickly fry the pork in batches, turning constantly, until sealed and browned on all sides. Add the vindaloo paste and stir to ensure that the pork is evenly coated. Cook over a fairly high heat for about 5 minutes, stirring occasionally.

5 Roughly chop the tomatoes and add to the pan with the tomato purée, remaining chillies and 600 ml (1 pint) water. Bring to the boil, stirring, then lower the heat. Cover and simmer gently for about 1½ hours or until the pork is very tender. Check from time to time to make sure that the sauce hasn't evaporated completely; if it looks too dry add a little more water. Once the pork is cooked, adjust the seasoning and serve.

VARIATIONS

Replace the pork with lean boneless lamb or use braising or stewing beef instead of pork.

Stir-fried Pork

PREPARATION TIME:
15 MINUTES, PLUS MARINATING

COOKING TIME: 20 MINUTES

FREEZING: NOT SUITABLE

130 CALS PER SERVING

SERVES 4

350 g (12 oz) pork fillet or pork strips for stir-fry
2 garlic cloves
10 ml (2 tsp) light soy sauce
10 ml (2 tsp) dry sherry
10 ml (2 tsp) demerara sugar
2.5 ml (½ tsp) Chinese five-spice powder
125 g (4 oz) red pepper
125 g (4 oz) baby sweetcorn

125 g (4 oz) Chinese leaves
50 g (2 oz) bean sprouts
4 spring onions
125 g (4 oz) basmati rice
15 ml (1 tbsp) oil
60 ml (4 tbsp) chopped fresh coriander
salt and pepper
coriander sprigs, to garnish

1 Cut the pork into 2.5 cm (1 inch) strips, if necessary. Peel and crush the garlic. Mix together the pork, crushed garlic, soy sauce, sherry, sugar and five-spice powder. Cover and leave to marinate in the refrigerator for at least 30 minutes or overnight.

2 Deseed the pepper and cut into strips; halve the baby corn lengthways; roughly chop the Chinese leaves; rinse the bean sprouts. Roughly chop the spring onions.

3 Cook the rice according to the packet instructions. Drain and rinse with cold water.

4 Heat the oil until smoking in a large, heavy-based frying pan or wok. Remove the pork from marinade and stir-fry in batches for 1-2 minutes or until pale golden.

5 Add the red pepper, baby corn and Chinese leaves to the pan and stir-fry for 1-2 minutes. Return the pork with the rice and marinade and stir-fry for about 4 minutes. Stir in the bean sprouts, spring onions and coriander and seasoning. Garnish with sprigs of coriander and serve.

Twice-cooked Pork with Black Bean Sauce

PREPARATION TIME: 10 MINUTES

COOKING TIME: 38 MINUTES

FREEZING: NOT SUITABLE

570 CALS PER SERVING

SERVES 4

700 g (1½ lb) belly pork rashers
1 garlic clove
1 cm (½ inch) piece fresh root ginger
1 onion
4 spring onions
½ red pepper

½ yellow pepper
½ orange pepper
30 ml (2 tbsp) oil
15 ml (1 tbsp) light soy sauce
15 ml (1 tbsp) dry sherry
150 g (5 oz) black bean sauce

1 Cook the belly pork rashers in boiling water for 30 minutes. Drain well and allow to cool. Remove the rinds and any bones and cut the rashers into 2.5 cm (1 inch) pieces.

2 Peel and crush the garlic. Peel and finely chop the ginger. Peel the onion, quarter it lengthways, then cut in half crossways and separate into layers. Trim the spring onions and cut into 2.5 cm (1 inch) pieces. Deseed the peppers and cut into 1 cm (½ inch) squares.

3 Heat the oil in a wok or large frying pan, add the belly pork and stir-fry for 3-4 minutes or until crisp and light golden.

4 Add the garlic, ginger, onions and peppers to the pan and stir-fry for 2 minutes.

5 Add the remaining ingredients and stir-fry for 1-2 minutes or until heated through. Serve immediately.

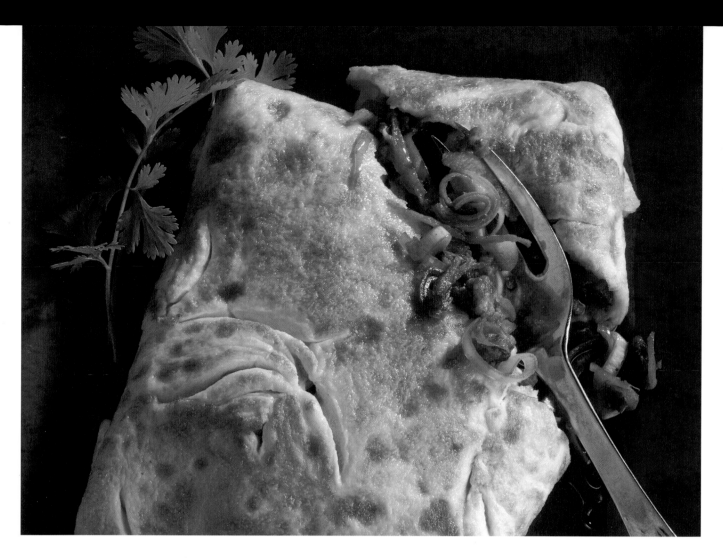

Stuffed Thai Omelette

PREPARATION TIME: 10 MINUTES

COOKING TIME: 7-8 MINUTES

FREEZING: NOT SUITABLE

460 CALS PER SERVING

SERVES 2

1 carrot
1 small leek
1 large garlic clove
2.5 cm (1 inch) piece fresh root ginger
1 tomato
3 eggs
salt and pepper

45 ml (3 tbsp) oil
125 g (4 oz) minced pork
5 ml (1 tsp) soft brown sugar
15 ml (1 tbsp) Thai fish sauce
10 ml (2 tsp) soy sauce
5-15 ml (1-3 tsp) rice vinegar or cider vinegar

1 Peel and grate the carrot. Trim and finely shred the leek. Peel and crush the garlic. Peel and grate the ginger. Skin the tomato and chop it finely.

2 In a bowl, beat the eggs together lightly, using a fork. Season with salt and pepper.

3 Heat half of the oil in a wok or frying pan. Add the pork with the garlic and ginger and fry, stirring constantly, until the pork is evenly coloured and cooked through.

4 Add the carrot and leek and stir-fry for 1 minute, then add the tomato, sugar, fish sauce, soy sauce and vinegar. Season generously with pepper and stir-fry for 2-3 minutes. Transfer to a warmed dish and keep warm.

5 Wipe out the wok or frying pan, place over a medium heat and add the remaining oil; swirl to distribute evenly. Pour in the beaten eggs, tilting the wok or pan to spread evenly.

6 When the omelette is just set but still moist, tip the filling into the middle and fold the four sides over the top to encase, like a parcel. Invert a warmed plate over the wok or pan, then invert both wok and plate to turn out the filled omelette. Serve immediately.

COOK'S NOTE

If preferred, you can make 2 individual omelettes, cooking half the beaten eggs at a time, and divide the filling between them.

VARIATIONS

Substitute minced beef for the pork. For a vegetarian option, omit the meat altogether and replace with another vegetable, such as bean sprouts.

POULTRY DISHES

A plentiful and cheap source of protein, chicken features strongly in Indian and Asian cuisine. Flavoured with distinctive ingredients, such as chilli, cardamom, soy sauce, garlic and lime, simple poultry pieces are transformed into delicious, authentic-tasting dishes with ease. From India, whole chicken marinated in a spiced yogurt sauce, or chicken pieces cooked with aubergines and lentils until meltingly tender make nourishing meals; for easy-to-prepare food with lots of aromatic flavour, tandoori-grilled chicken or poultry baked with whole spices are ideal. Chicken cooked in a coconut, ginger and lemon grass sauce, or lightly fried with a peanut curry paste are just two imaginative ideas with an Oriental flavour, while duck served with a mango sweet and sour sauce on crispy noodles is a dish combining interesting flavours from the Far East.

Illustration: Grilled Spiced Chicken with Tomato Chutney (recipe page 97)

Roast Chicken in Coconut Sauce

PREPARATION TIME: 5 MINUTES

COOKING TIME: 1 HOUR 20 MINUTES

FREEZING: NOT SUITABLE

310 CALS PER SERVING
SERVES 6

1 garlic clove
30 ml (2 tbsp) oil
5 ml (1 tsp) ground coriander
5 ml (1 tsp) ground cumin
5 ml (1 tsp) ground turmeric
5 ml (1 tsp) mild chilli powder
5 ml (1 tsp) salt

1 lemon grass stalk
225 g (8 oz) onions
600 ml (1 pint) coconut milk
1.4 kg (3 lb) oven-ready chicken
slices of lemon grass and lemon, and sprigs of coriander, to garnish

1 Peel and crush the garlic. Mix together the oil, garlic, spices and salt. Roughly chop the lemon grass, peel and grate the onions and add to the spices. Add a little of the coconut milk to produce a thick paste.

2 Brush the paste over the chicken inside and out and place in a roasting tin. Pour over the remaining coconut milk and place in the oven at 190°C (375°F) Mark 5 for about 1 hour 20 minutes or until the chicken is golden brown and tender. To test whether the chicken is cooked, pierce the thickest part of the chicken leg with a skewer. If the juices run clear it is cooked; if still pink, it needs longer. Baste occasionally with the coconut milk during cooking.

3 Remove the chicken. Skim the fat from the juices in the roasting tin, reheat if necessary and serve with the chicken. Garnish with the slices of lemon grass and lemon, and sprigs of coriander.

Cardamom Chicken with Peppers

PREPARATION TIME:
20 MINUTES, PLUS MARINATING

COOKING TIME: ABOUT 1 HOUR 20 MINUTES

FREEZING: NOT SUITABLE

380 CALS PER SERVING
SERVES 4

Illustrated opposite

5 ml (1 tsp) ground turmeric
salt
1.4 kg (3 lb) oven-ready chicken
3 garlic cloves
1 red chilli
2.5 cm (1 inch) piece fresh root ginger
5 ml (1 tsp) fennel seeds
4 black peppercorns
seeds from 8 green cardamoms

150 ml (¼ pint) yogurt
3 onions
45 ml (3 tbsp) ghee or oil
1 cinnamon stick
4 cloves
3 whole green cardamoms
2.5 ml (½ tsp) saffron strands
2 large red, yellow or orange peppers
coriander sprigs, to garnish

1 Mix the turmeric with 5 ml (1 tsp) salt and rub all over the chicken.

2 Peel and halve the garlic. Chop the chilli, discarding the seeds if a milder flavour is preferred. Peel the ginger and roughly chop. Put these ingredients in a blender or food processor with the fennel seeds, peppercorns and cardamom seeds. Process until finely chopped, then add the yogurt and salt to taste and process again until evenly blended.

3 Coat the chicken with the spiced yogurt mixture and leave to marinate at cool room temperature for 1 hour, or in the refrigerator overnight.

4 Peel and finely chop the onions. Heat the ghee or oil in a flameproof casserole. Add the cinnamon, cloves and cardamoms and fry for 2 minutes. Add the onions and cook for 10 minutes, stirring frequently, until soft and golden brown. Add the saffron and 300 ml (½ pint) boiling water. Bring to the boil, lower the heat and simmer for 2 minutes.

5 Add the chicken with any yogurt mixture. Cover with a lid and cook in the oven at 200°C (400°F) Mark 6 for 40 minutes.

6 Meanwhile, halve, core and deseed the peppers, then cut the flesh into thin strips.

7 Add the peppers to the casserole. If most of the water has evaporated, add a little extra boiling water so that the peppers do not burn. Cook, uncovered, for a further 40 minutes or until the chicken is cooked through and browned.

8 To serve, spoon the pepper and onion mixture onto a warmed platter. Put the chicken on top and moisten with a little of the cooking liquid. Garnish with coriander and serve immediately.

Almond Roast Chicken

PREPARATION TIME: 15 MINUTES

COOKING TIME: 1¼ HOURS

FREEZING: NOT SUITABLE

600-400 CALS PER SERVING

SERVES 4-6

175 g (6 oz) onions
2 garlic cloves
2.5 cm (1 inch) piece fresh root ginger
2 large oranges
45 ml (3 tbsp) oil
10 ml (2 tsp) cumin seeds
pinch of saffron
400 g (14 oz) canned chopped tomatoes

300 ml (½ pint) white wine
1 cinnamon stick or pinch of ground cinnamon
125 g (4 oz) whole, blanched almonds, toasted
45 ml (3 tbsp) clear honey
1.4 kg (3 lb) oven-ready chicken
salt and pepper

1 Peel and slice the onions. Peel and crush the garlic. Peel and finely chop the ginger. Cut each whole orange into eight segments.

2 Heat 30 ml (2 tbsp) oil in a saucepan. Add the onions, ginger, garlic, cumin seeds and saffron. Cook, stirring, over a medium heat for about 7 minutes. Add the chopped tomatoes, white wine, cinnamon, almonds and honey, bring to the boil and simmer for 3-4 minutes.

3 Place two orange segments inside the chicken cavity, season and brush with the remaining oil. Place the chicken in a roasting tin lying on one breast.

4 Cook at 200°C (400°F) Mark 6 for 1¼ hours. After 20 minutes cooking time, turn the chicken onto the other breast. Spoon over the sauce and the remaining orange segments. After a further 20 minutes turn the chicken onto its back for the remainder of the cooking time. To test whether the chicken is cooked, push a fine skewer into the thickest part of the thigh. If the juices run clear, the chicken is cooked; if still pink, it needs longer cooking. Cover with foil if the chicken shows signs of over-browning.

5 Season the pan juices and serve with the chicken.

Chicken Vindaloo

PREPARATION TIME: 20 MINUTES

COOKING TIME: ABOUT 1 HOUR

FREEZING: SUITABLE

330 CALS PER SERVING

SERVES 4

900 g (2 lb) chicken pieces, such as thighs, drumsticks and breast fillets
2 onions
60 ml (4 tbsp) ghee or oil
6 garlic cloves
2.5 cm (1 inch) piece fresh root ginger
10 ml (2 tsp) cumin seeds
10 ml (2 tsp) coriander seeds
10 ml (2 tsp) fenugreek seeds

10 ml (2 tsp) black peppercorns
5 ml (1 tsp) ground turmeric
10 ml (2 tsp) sugar
2.5 ml (½ tsp) salt
60 ml (4 tbsp) red or white wine vinegar
8 green cardamoms
1 cinnamon stick
4-6 dried hot red chillies
30 ml (2 tbsp) tomato purée

1 Remove any skin from the chicken and cut any large portions in half.

2 Peel and chop the onions. Heat 30 ml (2 tbsp) of the ghee or oil in a frying pan. Add the onions and cook over a fairly high heat until golden brown, stirring all the time. Remove from the pan with a slotted spoon and drain on kitchen paper.

3 Peel the garlic cloves and ginger. Put these in a blender or food processor with the onions, cumin, coriander, fenugreek, peppercorns, turmeric, sugar, salt and vinegar. Process until smooth, then mix with the cardamoms, cinnamon and chillies.

4 Heat the remaining 30 ml (2 tbsp) ghee or oil in a large saucepan or flameproof casserole. Cook the chicken, in batches, until sealed on all sides. Add the vindaloo paste and stir so that the chicken is coated on all sides. Cook over a fairly high heat for about 5 minutes, stirring occasionally.

5 Add the tomato purée and 300 ml (½ pint) water. Bring to the boil, then lower the heat, cover and simmer gently for about 45 minutes or until the chicken is very tender. Check from time to time to make sure that the sauce hasn't evaporated completely – if it looks too dry, simply add a little more water. If the chicken is cooked and the sauce is too thin, cook over a high heat for a few minutes to boil off some of the liquid. Adjust seasoning and serve.

Chicken Baked with Spices

PREPARATION TIME:
15 MINUTES, PLUS MARINATING

COOKING TIME: ABOUT 25 MINUTES

FREEZING: NOT SUITABLE

260 CALS PER SERVING

SERVES 6

2 garlic cloves
30 ml (2 tbsp) mild paprika
10 ml (2 tsp) ground coriander
5-10 ml (1-2 tsp) cayenne pepper
finely grated rind and juice of 1 large lemon
30 ml (2 tbsp) chopped fresh mint
30 ml (2 tbsp) chopped fresh coriander

45 ml (3 tbsp) grated fresh coconut (optional)
200 ml (7 fl oz) thick yogurt
salt and pepper
6 chicken supremes, or other portions
melted ghee, butter or oil, for brushing
lemon or lime wedges, to serve

1 Peel and crush the garlic and mash with the paprika, coriander, cayenne pepper and lemon rind and juice. Put the herbs, and coconut if using, in a bowl and stir in the yogurt. Beat in the garlic mixture. Add salt and pepper to taste.
2 Skin each chicken supreme and make 2 or 3 deep cuts in the thickest part of the flesh.
3 Drop the chicken portions into the yogurt mixture and turn the portions in the mixture so that they are thoroughly coated on all sides. Make sure that the marinade goes well into the slashes. Leave to marinate in a cool place for at least 30 minutes, or overnight if possible.
4 Arrange the chicken in a single layer in a roasting tin and brush with melted ghee, butter or oil. Roast in the oven at 200°C (400°F) Mark 6, basting from time to time, for about 25 minutes until the chicken is cooked right through. Serve garnished with lemon or lime wedges.

Chicken Dhansak

PREPARATION TIME: 20 MINUTES

COOKING TIME: 1 HOUR

FREEZING: SUITABLE

445 CALS PER SERVING

SERVES 6

6 chicken quarters
3 tomatoes
3 onions
6 garlic cloves
2.5 cm (1 inch) piece fresh root ginger
2-3 red chillies
15 ml (1 tbsp) coriander seeds
15 ml (1 tbsp) cumin seeds
5 black peppercorns
seeds from 4 cardamoms

10 ml (2 tsp) ground turmeric
10 ml (2 tsp) ground cinnamon
45 ml (3 tbsp) ghee or oil
175 g (6 oz) masoor dal (red split lentils)
175 g (6 oz) chana dal
5 ml (1 tsp) salt
3 small thin aubergines, or 1 medium one
15 ml (1 tbsp) dark brown sugar
30 ml (2 tbsp) lemon juice

1 Skin the chicken quarters and cut each one into 2 or 3 pieces. Immerse the tomatoes in boiling water for 30 seconds, then drain and peel away the skins. Finely chop the tomatoes.

2 Peel and quarter the onions. Peel and halve the garlic. Peel and roughly chop the ginger. Chop the chillies, discarding the seeds if a milder flavour is preferred.

3 Put the onions, garlic, ginger and chillies in a food processor or blender with about 30 ml (2 tbsp) water. Process until very finely chopped. Add the spices and process again.

4 Heat the ghee or oil in a large heavy-based casserole. Add the spice paste and cook over a medium heat, stirring frequently, for about 10 minutes or until the onion is softened and golden brown. Add the chicken, increase the heat and cook, turning, for a few of minutes to seal.

5 Add the dals with the tomatoes and cook for 2 minutes, stirring all the time. Add enough water to just cover the dal and chicken and bring to the boil. Lower the heat, add the salt, cover and simmer for 20 minutes.

6 Halve the small aubergines (or cut the medium one into large chunks). Add to the dhansak with the sugar and lemon juice. Re-cover and simmer for a further 20-30 minutes or until the chicken is tender and the lentils are mushy. Check from time to time to make sure that the dhansak is not sticking to the base of the pan – add a little extra water if it starts to look too dry.

7 Using a potato masher, mash the dals to break them down slightly. Check the seasoning and serve.

Chicken with Cashews

PREPARATION TIME: 15 MINUTES

COOKING TIME: ABOUT 50 MINUTES

FREEZING: SUITABLE

400-270 CALS PER SERVING

SERVES 4-6

about 1.4 kg (3 lb) chicken pieces
2 large onions
3 garlic cloves
2.5 cm (1 inch) piece fresh root ginger
50 g (2 oz) cashew nuts
45 ml (3 tbsp) oil
1 cinnamon stick
15 ml (1 tbsp) coriander seeds

10 ml (2 tsp) cumin seeds
4 cardamom pods
150 ml (¼ pint) thick natural yogurt
salt and pepper
45 ml (3 tbsp) chopped fresh coriander (optional)
30 ml (2 tbsp) chopped fresh mint (optional)
natural yogurt, and garam masala, to serve

1 Skin the chicken pieces. If there are any large ones, such as breasts, cut into 2 or 3 pieces.

2 Peel and chop the onions. Peel and crush the garlic. Peel the ginger and chop it finely.

3 Put the cashew nuts in a blender or food processor with 150 ml (¼ pint) water and work until smooth.

4 Heat the oil in a large flameproof casserole and add the onions, garlic, ginger and all the spices. Cook over a high heat for 2-3 minutes, stirring all the time. Add the cashew purée and cook for 1-2 minutes. Add the chicken and stir to coat in the spices.

5 Lower the heat, then add the yogurt a spoonful at a time, followed by another 150 ml (¼ pint) water. Season with salt and pepper. Lower the heat, cover and cook gently for about 45 minutes or until the chicken is cooked right through.

6 Add the coriander and mint if using, and check the seasoning. Serve each portion topped with a spoonful of yogurt and sprinkled with garam masala.

Sweet Spicy Chicken

PREPARATION TIME: 15 MINUTES

COOKING TIME: 45 MINUTES

FREEZING: NOT SUITABLE

300 CALS PER SERVING

SERVES 6

1 medium onion
1 large red chilli
4 cm (1½ inch) piece fresh root ginger
2 garlic cloves
550 g (1¼ lb) tomatoes
15 ml (1 tbsp) oil
1.1 kg (2½ lb) chicken pieces (breast, thighs or drumsticks), with skin

2.5 ml (½ tsp) ground turmeric
1 cinnamon stick
450 ml (¾ pint) chicken stock
90 ml (6 tbsp) coconut milk powder or 75 g (3 oz) creamed coconut
deep-fried onion rings and chilli pieces, to garnish

1 Peel and slice the onion; finely chop the chilli; peel and grate the ginger. Peel and crush the garlic. Plunge the tomatoes into boiling water for 30 seconds, then drain and peel away the skins; cut into quarters.

2 Heat the oil in a large flameproof casserole, about 3.1 litres (5½ pints) in size. Fry the chicken joints for about 5 minutes or until well browned. Remove and drain on kitchen paper.

3 Lower the heat, add the onion to the casserole and fry for about 10 minutes until soft and golden brown. Add the chilli, ginger, garlic, turmeric and cinnamon stick and fry for a further 2-3 minutes. Stir in the chicken stock and coconut. Bring up to a gentle simmer, stirring all the time, then bubble for about 5 minutes.

4 Add the tomatoes and return the chicken to the casserole and simmer, uncovered, for about 25 minutes. Serve at once, garnished with deep-fried onion rings and chilli pieces.

Grilled Spiced Chicken with Tomato Chutney

PREPARATION TIME:
40 MINUTES, PLUS MARINATING

COOKING TIME: 30-35 MINUTES

FREEZING: NOT SUITABLE

440 CALS PER SERVING

SERVES 4

4 large chicken breast quarters, each about 300 g (10 oz)
coriander sprigs, to garnish
lemon wedges, to serve
SPICE PASTE
2 large thin red chillies
2 garlic cloves
15 ml (1 tbsp) sunflower oil
10 ml (2 tsp) sesame oil
5 ml (1 tsp) cumin seeds
5 ml (1 tsp) fennel seeds
15 ml (1 tbsp) chopped fresh basil
5 ml (1 tsp) turmeric

15 ml (1 tbsp) dark brown sugar
30 ml (2 tbsp) rice or wine vinegar
30 ml (2 tbsp) tomato purée
2.5 ml (½ tsp) salt
TOMATO CHUTNEY
225 g (8 oz) shallots
1 garlic clove
30 ml (2 tbsp) sunflower oil
75 ml (3 fl oz) rice vinegar or wine vinegar
30 ml (2 tbsp) rice wine or dry sherry
50 g (2 oz) caster sugar
175 g (6 oz) firm cherry tomatoes
30 ml (2 tbsp) sweet soy sauce

1 Start by making the spice paste. Deseed and chop the chillies; peel and crush the garlic. Heat the two oils together in a small saucepan and stir the chillies into the pan with the garlic, cumin, fennel, basil and turmeric. Fry gently for 5 minutes. Add the remaining ingredients and stir until the sugar is dissolved. Remove from the heat and leave to cool.

2 Wash and dry the chicken and, using a sharp knife, cut a few deep slashes on both sides of each quarter. Spread the spice paste over the chicken and place in a shallow, non-metallic dish. Cover and leave to marinate in a cool place for at least 4 hours, preferably overnight.

3 Make the tomato chutney. Peel and halve any large shallots; peel and chop the garlic. Heat the oil in a saucepan, add the shallots and garlic, and fry gently for 15 minutes until golden. Carefully add the vinegar, rice wine or sherry, sugar and 50 ml (2 fl oz) water. Bring the mixture to the boil and boil steadily over a high heat for 10 minutes.

4 Halve the cherry tomatoes and add to the pan with the soy sauce. Simmer for a further 5-10 minutes until the tomatoes are softened and the liquid reduced. Leave to cool.

5 Spear each chicken quarter with two skewers. Transfer to the grill pan and cook under the grill for 15-20 minutes on each side, basting frequently until the chicken is cooked through. Serve garnished with coriander and accompanied by the tomato chutney and lemon wedges.

Chicken Cooked with Whole Spices

PREPARATION TIME: 30 MINUTES

COOKING TIME: 45 MINUTES

FREEZING: SUITABLE

445 CALS PER SERVING

SERVES 4

COOK'S NOTE

In Indian cooking it is usual to cook the chicken on the bone because it improves the flavour, but you could use chicken breasts fillets if preferred.

450 g (1 lb) onions
2-3 garlic cloves
45 ml (3 tbsp) blanched almonds
4 chicken quarters
45-60 ml (3-4 tbsp) ghee or oil
1 cinnamon stick
8 curry leaves

3 black cardamoms
4 cloves
4 black peppercorns
10 ml (2 tsp) cumin seeds
1-2 dried red chillies
3 large ripe tomatoes, skinned if preferred
salt

1 Peel the onions and cut into wedges. Peel and chop the garlic. Finely chop the almonds. Halve each chicken quarter, discarding the skin.

2 Heat 45 ml (3 tbsp) ghee or oil in a large flameproof casserole or heavy-based pan. Add the onions and garlic and cook over a medium heat, stirring frequently, for 10-15 minutes until the onions are softened and golden brown.

3 Add the whole spices and cook over a high heat for 2 minutes, stirring all the time. Add the almonds and cook for 1-2 minutes until they are lightly browned.

4 Remove the onions, almonds and spices from the pan, using a slotted spoon. Add a little extra ghee or oil to the pan if there is none remaining and heat until very hot. Add the chicken, a few pieces at a time, and cook over a high heat until browned on all sides.

5 Return all the browned chicken to the pan with the browned onions, almonds and spices.

6 Chop the tomatoes and add to the pan with 450 ml (¾ pint) water and salt to taste. Bring to the boil, then lower the heat. Cover and simmer for 45 minutes until the chicken is tender.

7 If the sauce is too thin once the chicken is cooked, transfer the chicken to a warmed serving dish and boil the sauce rapidly, uncovered, over a high heat for a few minutes until reduced. Pour the sauce over the chicken and serve immediately. (Remind guests that the whole spices are not intended to be eaten.)

Tandoori-style Chicken

PREPARATION TIME:
15 MINUTES, PLUS MARINATING

COOKING TIME: 25 MINUTES

FREEZING: NOT SUITABLE

265 CALS PER SERVING

SERVES 4

Illustrated opposite

2-3 garlic cloves
2.5 cm (1 inch) piece fresh root ginger
1-2 hot green chillies
600 ml (1 pint) thick yogurt
15 ml (1 tbsp) ground coriander
15 ml (1 tbsp) ground cumin
10 ml (2 tsp) Indian curry paste or tandoori paste
30 ml (2 tbsp) chopped fresh coriander

30 ml (2 tbsp) chopped fresh mint (optional)
salt
few drops each of red and yellow food colouring (optional)
8 chicken supremes, skinned
melted ghee, butter or oil, for basting
fresh lemon or lime juice, to taste
lime or lemon wedges, to garnish

COOK'S NOTE

If your grill pan is very small you may find it difficult to grill 8 chicken supremes, so either cook them in batches or bake in the oven at 200°C (400°F) Mark 6 for about 30 minutes.

1 Peel and crush the garlic. Peel and finely chop the ginger. Chop the chillies, discarding the seeds if a milder flavour is preferred.

2 Put the yogurt in a large non-metallic dish and add the garlic, ginger and chillies. Add the ground spices and curry or tandoori paste and mix thoroughly. Add the chopped coriander and mint if using. Season with salt and add a few drops of food colouring to enhance the colour if desired.

3 Make 3-4 deep cuts in each chicken portion, being careful not to cut right through. Add the chicken to the marinade and turn to thoroughly coat. Rub the mixture well into the cuts. Cover the bowl and leave the chicken to marinate in the refrigerator overnight.

4 Remove the chicken from the marinade and place on the grill (or barbecue) rack and cook fairly close to high heat for about 25 minutes, basting with melted ghee, butter or oil and turning frequently to ensure that it cooks evenly. To check that the chicken is cooked pierce the thickest part with a skewer; the juices should run clear – if they are at all pink cook for longer.

5 Serve sprinkled with lime or lemon juice and garnished with lime or lemon wedges.

Thai Grilled Chicken

PREPARATION TIME:
10 MINUTES, PLUS MARINATING

COOKING TIME: 12 MINUTES

FREEZING: NOT SUITABLE

270 CALS PER SERVING

SERVES 4

1 medium red chilli
2 garlic cloves
5 spring onions
10 ml (2 tsp) sugar
125 g (4 oz) creamed coconut

10 ml (2 tsp) Thai fish sauce
15 ml (1 tbsp) chopped fresh coriander
4 chicken breast fillets, each about 125 g (4 oz)

1 Halve the chilli and discard the seeds. Place in a food processor with 150 ml (¼ pint) warm water and all the ingredients except the chicken. Blend until almost smooth.

2 Cut four slashes in each chicken breast, then place in a non-metallic dish and spoon the marinade over. Turn to coat thoroughly, then cover and marinate for 1 hour.

3 Place the chicken on a foil-lined grill pan and coat with half the marinade. Grill for 6 minutes, then turn the chicken and spread the remaining marinade over the second side of the chicken. Cook for a further 6 minutes or until cooked.

VARIATION

Turkey breasts may be used instead of chicken. Turkey contains less fat than chicken, making it one of the lowest fat meats available – 125 g (4 oz) turkey-breast fillet contains about 1.1 g fat and 103 calories, while chicken-breast fillet contains 4.3 g fat and 121 calories.

Thai Chicken Omelette

PREPARATION TIME: 30 MINUTES

COOKING TIME: 20 MINUTES

FREEZING: NOT SUITABLE

350 CALS PER SERVING

SERVES 4

15 ml (1 tbsp) light soy sauce
30 ml (2 tbsp) peanut satay sauce (see Cook's Note)
5 ml (1 tsp) soft brown sugar
30 ml (2 tbsp) tomato ketchup
225 g (8 oz) skinless chicken breast fillets
125 g (4 oz) red pepper
125 g (4 oz) baby sweetcorn
50 g (2 oz) bean sprouts

4 spring onions
2.5 cm (1 inch) piece fresh root ginger
2 garlic cloves
6 eggs
30 ml (2 tbsp) Thai fish sauce (optional)
pepper
60 ml (4 tbsp) chopped fresh coriander
sunflower oil for frying

COOK'S NOTE
Ready-made satay sauce is delicious with chicken and is a handy ingredient for quick supper dishes. It is available from most supermarkets.

1 To make the marinade, combine the soy sauce with the satay sauce, sugar and tomato ketchup in a bowl. Cut the chicken into thin 2.5 cm (1 inch) long strips, add to the marinade and toss to coat well. Cover the bowl and leave to marinate in the refrigerator.

2 Deseed the red pepper and cut into strips. Halve the sweetcorn lengthways. Rinse the bean sprouts. Chop the spring onions; peel and finely chop the ginger; peel and crush the garlic.

3 In a small bowl, lightly beat the eggs with the fish sauce, if using, and pepper to taste. Add 30 ml (2 tbsp) chopped coriander and set aside.

4 Heat 30 ml (2 tbsp) oil in a large, nonstick frying pan. Cook the chicken in batches with the garlic and ginger for 1-2 minutes or until golden. Add the red pepper, baby sweetcorn, bean sprouts and spring onions and cook, stirring, for another 3 minutes or until just tender. Turn into a bowl and stir in the remaining coriander.

5 Wipe out the pan, add a little oil and half the beaten egg. Cook for 2-3 minutes or until the outside edge of the omelette is golden brown and the middle nearly set. Add half the chicken mixture and fold the omelette over. Keep warm while cooking the remaining egg and chicken filling in the same way; add more oil, if necessary.

6 Serve half an omelette per person.

Chicken and Coconut Curry

PREPARATION TIME: 15 MINUTES

COOKING TIME: 30 MINUTES

FREEZING: SUITABLE

775-520 CALS PER SERVING

SERVES 4-6

2 garlic cloves
1 onion
1 lemon grass stalk
2.5 cm (1 inch) piece fresh root ginger
2 small hot chillies
small handful of fresh coriander
5 ml (1 tsp) ground coriander
grated rind and juice of 1 lime

2 large tomatoes
6 skinless chicken breast fillets
30 ml (2 tbsp) oil
30 ml (2 tbsp) Thai fish sauce
900 ml (1½ pints) thick coconut milk
salt and pepper
toasted fresh coconut and coriander leaves, to garnish

1 Peel the garlic cloves. Peel and quarter the onion. Halve the lemon grass. Peel the ginger and cut in half. Put these ingredients in a food processor with the chillies, fresh coriander, ground coriander, lime rind and juice. Process until reduced to a chunky paste, adding a couple of spoonfuls of water if the mixture gets stuck under the blades.

2 Immerse the tomatoes in a bowl of boiling water for 15-30 seconds, then remove, cool slightly and peel away the skins. Roughly chop the tomato flesh. Cut each chicken breast into 3 pieces.

3 Heat the oil in a large heavy-based frying pan or flameproof casserole. Add the spice paste and cook over a fairly high heat for 3-4 minutes, stirring all the time. Add the chicken and cook for about 5 minutes, stirring to coat in the spice mixture.

4 Add the tomatoes, fish sauce and coconut milk. Bring to the boil, then cover and simmer very gently for about 25 minutes or until the chicken is cooked. Season to taste with salt and pepper. Serve garnished with toasted fresh coconut and coriander leaves.

Chilli-fried Chicken with Coconut Noodles

PREPARATION TIME:
15-20 MINUTES

COOKING TIME: 15 MINUTES

FREEZING: NOT SUITABLE

340 CALS PER SERVING

SERVES 6

30 ml (2 tbsp) plain white flour

5 ml (1 tsp) each mild chilli powder and ground ginger

2.5 ml (½ tsp) salt

5 ml (1 tsp) caster sugar

6 skinless chicken breast fillets, each about 150 g (5 oz)

250 g (9 oz) thread egg noodles

1 large bunch of spring onions

150 g (5 oz) salted roasted peanuts

45 ml (3 tbsp) peanut oil

7.5 ml (1½ tsp) Thai red curry paste or tandoori paste

90 ml (6 tbsp) coconut milk

1 Mix the flour, chilli powder, ground ginger, salt and sugar in a bowl. Cut each chicken fillet diagonally into three. Dip into the spiced flour and coat well.

2 Cook the noodles according to packet instructions. Slice the spring onions. Finely chop the peanuts or process them in a food processor. Drain the noodles.

3 Heat the oil in a frying pan and fry the chicken for 5 minutes or until cooked. Remove from the pan and keep warm. Fry the onions for 1 minute; remove from the pan and keep warm.

4 Add the curry paste to the pan with 75 g (3 oz) of the chopped peanuts and fry for 1 minute. Add the noodles and fry for 1 minute. Stir in the coconut milk and toss the noodles over a high heat for 30 seconds.

5 Serve the chicken and spring onions on the coconut noodles. Sprinkle with the remaining peanuts.

Thai Chicken and Noodle Soup

PREPARATION TIME: 20 MINUTES

COOKING TIME: ABOUT 20 MINUTES

FREEZING: NOT SUITABLE

690-460 CALS PER SERVING

SERVES 4-6

225 g (8 oz) firm tofu
oil for shallow or deep-frying
275 g (10 oz) cooked chicken, skinned
2.5 cm (1 inch) piece fresh root ginger
2.5 cm (1 inch) piece fresh or dried galangal (optional)
1-2 garlic cloves
2 lemon grass stalks
175 g (6 oz) cauliflower florets
1 large carrot
few green beans

3 spring onions
5 ml (1 tsp) chilli powder
2.5 ml (½ tsp) ground turmeric
600 ml (1 pint) coconut milk
600 ml (1 pint) chicken or vegetable stock, or water
125 g (4 oz) thin or medium egg noodles
125 g (4 oz) peeled prawns (optional)
75 g (3 oz) bean sprouts
30 ml (2 tbsp) soy sauce

COOK'S NOTE
Dried galangal requires soaking for 30 minutes before using.

1 Pat the tofu dry with kitchen paper, then cut into small cubes. Heat the oil in a wok or deep-fat fryer and fry the tofu, in batches, until golden brown on all sides. Drain on kitchen paper.
2 Cut the chicken into bite-sized pieces. Peel and finely chop the ginger. Peel and finely slice the galangal, if using. Peel and crush the garlic. Halve each lemon grass stalk and bruise with a rolling pin or the heel of your hand.
3 Break the cauliflower into tiny florets, thinly slicing any thick stems. Peel the carrot and cut into matchstick strips. Trim and halve the beans. Trim and finely slice the spring onions.
4 Heat 30 ml (2 tbsp) oil in a large saucepan. Add the ginger, galangal, garlic, lemon grass, chilli powder, turmeric and chicken and cook for 2 minutes, stirring all the time. Add the cauliflower and carrot.
5 Add the coconut milk and stock and bring to the boil, stirring. Reduce the heat and simmer for 10 minutes. Add the beans and simmer for 5 minutes.
6 Meanwhile, cook the noodles according to the packet instructions.
7 Drain the noodles and add to the soup with the prawns if using, tofu, spring onions, bean sprouts and soy sauce. Simmer gently for 5 minutes or until heated through. Serve immediately, in deep soup bowls.

Thai Green Curry

PREPARATION TIME: 10 MINUTES

COOKING TIME: 12 MINUTES

FREEZING: NOT SUITABLE

290 CALS PER SERVING

SERVES 6

1 green chilli
4 cm (½ inch) piece fresh root ginger
1 lemon grass stalk
350 g (12 oz) skinless chicken breast fillets
10 ml (2 tsp) oil
225 g (8 oz) brown-cap or oyster mushrooms
15 ml (1 tbsp) Thai green curry paste

300 ml (½ pint) coconut milk
150 ml (¼ pint) chicken stock
15 ml (1 tbsp) Thai fish sauce
5 ml (1 tsp) light soy sauce
350 g (12 oz) cooked peeled king prawns
30 ml (2 tbsp) chopped fresh coriander

1 Deseed and finely chop the chilli. Peel and finely grate the ginger. Cut the lemon grass into 3 large pieces. Cut the chicken into bite-sized pieces.
2 Heat the oil in a wok or large frying pan and stir-fry the chilli, ginger, lemon grass and mushrooms together for about 3 minutes or until the mushrooms begin to turn golden. Add the curry paste and fry for a further 1 minute.
3 Pour in the coconut milk, stock, fish sauce and soy sauce and bring up to the boil. Stir in the chicken and simmer for about 8 minutes or until the chicken is cooked. Add the prawns and cook for a further 1 minute.
4 Garnish with coriander and serve immediately.

Chicken Korma

PREPARATION TIME: 15 MINUTES

COOKING TIME: 40 MINUTES

FREEZING: NOT SUITABLE

390 CALS PER SERVING

SERVES 4

Illustrated opposite

COOK'S NOTE

For best results, use a good thick yogurt; rich Greek-style yogurt is ideal. Don't be tempted to use a low-fat yogurt, as this would curdle and make the sauce unappetising.

3 large onions
30-45 ml (2-3 tbsp) ghee or oil
2-3 garlic cloves
4 cloves
4 cardamom pods
1 cinnamon stick
10 ml (2 tsp) ground coriander
2.5 ml (½ tsp) ground turmeric

2.5 ml (½ tsp) ground ginger
2.5 ml (½ tsp) ground cumin
4 skinless chicken breast fillets
squeeze of lemon juice
600 ml (1 pint) thick yogurt
salt
coriander sprigs, to garnish (optional)

1 Peel and thinly slice half of the onions. Heat 30 ml (2 tbsp) ghee or oil in a frying pan, add the sliced onions and fry until browned and crisp. Remove with a slotted spoon and drain thoroughly on crumpled kitchen paper; set aside.

2 Finely chop the remaining onion. Peel and crush the garlic. Cook the onion and garlic in the ghee or oil remaining in the pan until softened, adding a little extra if necessary. Add the spices and cook, stirring constantly, for 2 minutes until the onions are lightly browned.

3 Cut each chicken breast fillet into 3 pieces. Add these to the pan with a squeeze of lemon juice and lower the heat. Add the yogurt, a tablespoon at a time, stirring thoroughly after each addition. Gradually stir in 150 ml (¼ pint) water.

4 Half-cover the pan with a lid and simmer gently for about 30 minutes until the chicken is tender and cooked right through. Season with salt to taste.

5 Serve sprinkled with the crisp browned onions, and garnished with coriander, if desired.

VARIATION

Replace the chicken with 700 g (1½ lb) shelled large raw prawns or 450 g (1 lb) cooked peeled prawns. Add to the sauce at stage 4. Cook for about 4 minutes if using raw prawns, until they turn pink. Cooked prawns only need to be heated through, for about 2 minutes.

Oriental Chicken Parcels

PREPARATION TIME:
20 MINUTES, PLUS MARINATING

COOKING TIME: 35 MINUTES

FREEZING: NOT SUITABLE

215 CALS PER SERVING

SERVES 4

3 oranges
juice of 1 lemon
30 ml (2 tbsp) dark soy sauce
30 ml (2 tbsp) yellow bean sauce
15 ml (1 tbsp) dry sherry
15 ml (1 tbsp) oil
salt and pepper

50 g (2 oz) stem ginger or 2.5 cm (1 inch) piece fresh root ginger
1 bunch of spring onions
125 g (4 oz) carrot
4 skinless chicken breast fillets, each 125 g (4 oz)

1 Finely grate the rind of one orange into a bowl, then squeeze the orange and add 60 ml (4 tbsp) orange juice to the bowl. Add the lemon juice, soy sauce, yellow bean sauce, sherry and oil. Season well with salt and pepper.

2 Thinly slice the stem ginger or peel and slice the fresh ginger. Cut the spring onions and carrot into 5 cm (2 inch) shreds.

3 Lightly slash the chicken breasts all over and stir into the marinade with the ginger, spring onions and carrot. Refrigerate overnight.

4 The next day, peel and segment the remaining oranges. Cut four 30.5 cm (12 inch) squares of foil and pull the edges to make open purses. Divide the chicken and marinade among the foil pieces and top with orange segments. Pinch the corners of the foil together and place in a roasting tin.

5 Cook in the oven at 180°C (350°F) Mark 4 for about 35 minutes or until the chicken is tender.

6 To serve, open the parcels into soup bowls as there is quite a lot of juice.

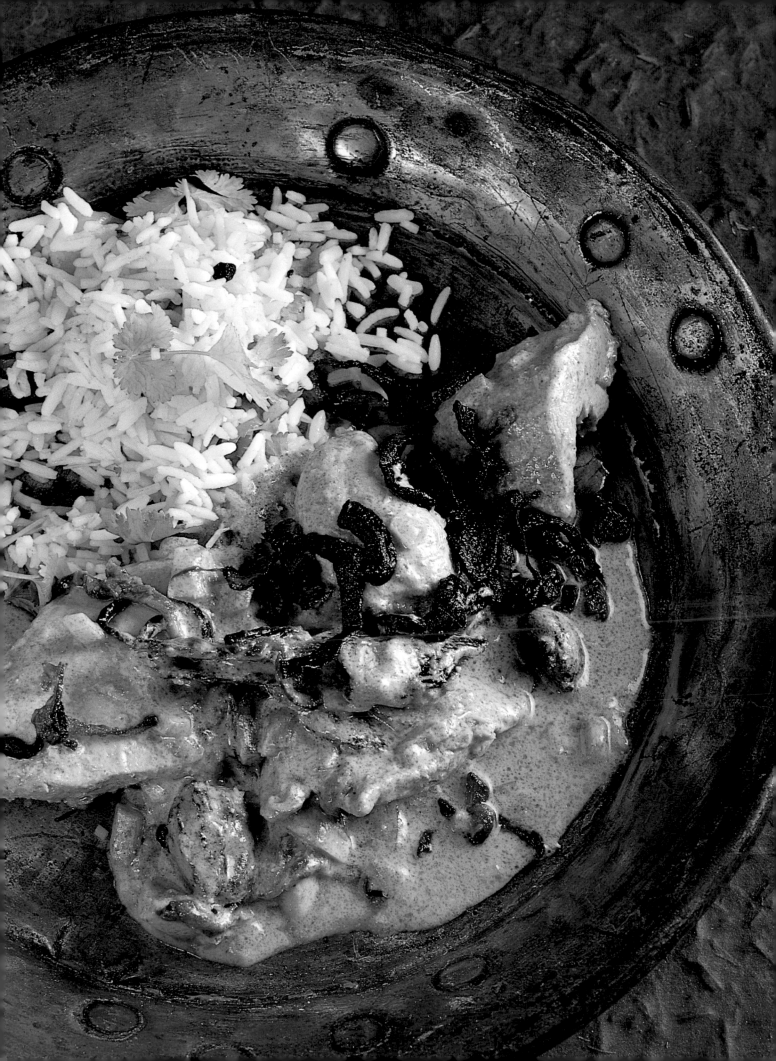

Chicken with Oyster Sauce

PREPARATION TIME: 10 MINUTES

COOKING TIME: 15 MINUTES

FREEZING: NOT SUITABLE

410 CALS PER SERVING

SERVES 4

450 g (1 lb) skinless chicken breast fillets
90 ml (6 tbsp) vegetable oil
45 ml (3 tbsp) oyster sauce
15 ml (1 tbsp) dark soy sauce
100 ml (4 fl oz) chicken stock
10 ml (2 tsp) lemon juice
6-8 large flat mushrooms, about 250 g (9 oz)
total weight

1 garlic clove
125 g (4 oz) mangetout
5 ml (1 tsp) cornflour
15 ml (1 tbsp) sesame oil
salt and pepper

1 Slice the chicken into bite-sized pieces. Heat 45 ml (3 tbsp) oil in a wok or frying pan. Add the chicken and cook over a high heat, stirring continuously for 2-3 minutes, until lightly browned. Remove with a slotted spoon; drain on kitchen paper.

2 In a bowl, mix the oyster sauce with the soy sauce, chicken stock and lemon juice. Add the chicken and stir until thoroughly combined.

3 Slice the mushrooms. Peel and finely slice the garlic. Heat the remaining vegetable oil over a high heat and stir-fry the garlic for about 30 seconds; add the mushrooms and cook for 1 minute. Add the chicken mixture, cover and simmer for 8 minutes.

4 Stir in the mangetout and cook for a further 2-3 minutes. Mix the cornflour with 15 ml (1 tbsp) water. Remove the wok or frying pan from the heat and stir in the cornflour mixture. Return to the heat, add the sesame oil and stir until the sauce has thickened. Adjust the seasoning and serve at once.

Chicken with Vegetables and Noodles

PREPARATION TIME: 10 MINUTES

COOKING TIME: ABOUT 10 MINUTES

FREEZING: NOT SUITABLE

730 CALS PER SERVING

SERVES 2

1 skinless chicken breast fillet
1 red pepper
4 spring onions
2 carrots
125 g (4 oz) shiitake or button mushrooms
2.5 cm (1 inch) piece fresh root ginger
1 garlic clove
225 g (8 oz) thin egg noodles

about 30 ml (2 tbsp) oil
few bean sprouts (optional)
45 ml (3 tbsp) hoisin sauce
30 ml (2 tbsp) light soy sauce
15 ml (1 tbsp) chilli sauce
shredded spring onion and sesame seeds, to garnish

1 Cut the chicken into very thin strips. Halve, core and deseed the pepper, then cut the flesh into thin strips. Cut the spring onions and carrots into similar-sized strips. Halve the mushrooms. Peel the ginger and garlic then chop finely.

2 Cook the noodles according to the packet instructions. Drain thoroughly and toss with a little of the oil to prevent them sticking together; set aside.

3 Heat the remaining oil in a wok or a large frying pan. Add the chicken, ginger and garlic and cook over a very high heat until the chicken is browned on the outside and cooked right through.

4 Add all the vegetables to the wok or pan and stir-fry over a high heat for a few minutes or until they are just cooked, but still crunchy.

5 Add the hoisin sauce, soy sauce and chilli sauce and stir to mix. Add the noodles and cook for a couple of minutes to heat through. Serve immediately, sprinkled with shredded spring onion and a few sesame seeds.

VARIATION
Replace the chicken with thinly sliced turkey escallops. Increase the heat of the dish by frying a chopped chilli with the onion and ginger.

Hiyashi Chuka

PREPARATION TIME: 20 MINUTES

COOKING TIME: ABOUT 35 MINUTES

FREEZING: NOT SUITABLE

480 CALS PER SERVING

SERVES 4

2 chicken breast fillets, with skin on
salt
10 ml (2 tsp) hoisin sauce
225 g (8 oz) thread egg noodles
1 small cucumber
1 carrot
4 seafood sticks

DRESSING
30 ml (2 tbsp) sesame oil
60 ml (4 tbsp) light soy sauce
75 ml (5 tbsp) sherry
30 ml (2 tbsp) rice vinegar or wine vinegar
5 ml (1 tsp) chilli oil or sauce

1 First make the dressing. In a bowl, whisk the sesame oil with the soy sauce, sherry, vinegar and chilli oil or sauce.

2 Place the chicken breasts in a small roasting tin. Generously salt the skin of the breasts, then drizzle and spread 5 ml (1 tsp) hoisin sauce over each one.

3 Pour half the dressing around the chicken breasts and roast at 200°C (400°F) Mark 6 for 30-35 minutes until cooked through. Remove from the tin and allow to cool. Reserve the pan juices and stir into the remaining dressing.

4 Cook the noodles according to the packet instructions. Drain and allow to cool.

5 Cut the cucumber in half, remove the seeds and cut into fine sticks. Peel the carrot and cut into fine sticks; cut the seafood sticks and cooled chicken into thins strips.

6 Spoon the noodles into a bowl and arrange the cucumber, carrot, seafood sticks and chicken on top. Pour over the dressing and serve at room temperature.

Hot Red Jungle Curry

PREPARATION TIME: 10 MINUTES

COOKING TIME: 15 MINUTES

FREEZING: NOT SUITABLE

200 CALS PER SERVING

SERVES 4

350 g (12 oz) skinless chicken breast fillets
2.5 cm (1 inch) piece fresh root ginger
125 g (4 oz) aubergine
125 g (4 oz) baby sweetcorn
75 g (3 oz) green beans
75 g (3 oz) button or brown-cap mushrooms
15 ml (1 tbsp) oil
30 ml (2 tbsp) Thai red curry paste

2-3 kaffir lime leaves (optional)
450 ml (¾ pint) chicken stock
30 ml (2 tbsp) Thai fish sauce
grated rind of ½ a lime
5 ml (1 tsp) tomato purée
15 ml (1 tbsp) soft brown sugar
pared lime rind, to garnish

1 Cut the chicken into finger-length strips; peel the ginger and finely slice. Cut the aubergine into bite-sized pieces and halve the corn lengthways. Top the beans and halve the mushrooms, if necessary.

2 Heat the oil in a wok or large frying pan. Add the chicken and cook, stirring, for 5 minutes or until the chicken turns golden brown.

3 Add the red curry paste and cook for a further minute. Add the vegetables and lime leaves, if using, and stir until coated in the red curry paste. Add all the remaining ingredients, except the garnish, and bring to the boil. Simmer gently for 10-12 minutes or until the chicken and vegetables are just tender. Serve immediately, garnished with pared lime rind.

VARIATION

If you like them, add a drained 227 g (8 oz) can of bamboo shoots with other vegetables in stage 3.

Spiced Tikka Kebabs

PREPARATION TIME: 10 MINUTES,
PLUS MARINATING

COOKING TIME: 7-10 MINUTES

FREEZING: NOT SUITABLE

130 CALS PER SERVING

SERVES 4

350 g (12 oz) skinless chicken breast fillets
3 spring onions
30 ml (2 tbsp) tikka paste
150 ml (¼ pint) natural low-fat yogurt

juice of 1 lime
salt and pepper
lime slices and celery leaves, to garnish

1 Cut the chicken into bite-sized pieces. Thread the chicken pieces loosely onto skewers and place in a non-metallic dish.

2 Trim and chop the spring onions. Mix together the tikka paste, yogurt and lime juice, then stir in the chopped spring onions and season to taste. Spoon the mixture over the kebabs, cover and leave to marinate for 3-4 hours in the refrigerator.

3 Grill the kebabs for 7-10 minutes, turning and basting with the marinade, until the chicken is cooked through. Serve garnished with lime slices and celery leaves.

Oriental Chicken Skewers

PREPARATION TIME:
10 MINUTES, PLUS MARINATING

COOKING TIME: 15 MINUTES

FREEZING: NOT SUITABLE

175 CALS PER SERVING

SERVES 4

COOK'S NOTE
Soaking the wooden satay
sticks in water overnight
helps to prevent them from
burning.

450 g (1 lb) skinless chicken breast fillets or
boned thighs
2.5 cm (1 inch) piece fresh root ginger
2 large garlic cloves
30 ml (2 tbsp) dark soy sauce

30 ml (2 tbsp) dry sherry
25 ml (5 tsp) caster sugar
noodles and stir-fried vegetables, to serve

1 Slice the chicken into thick, finger-length strips (about 12 in total). Peel and grate the ginger.
Peel and crush the garlic.

2 Combine the ginger, crushed garlic, soy sauce, sherry and sugar in a non-metallic bowl. Add
the chicken and stir well to coat in the marinade. Cover and refrigerate overnight. Soak 12
wooden satay sticks in water overnight.

3 Thread a strip of chicken onto each stick and place in a foil-lined grill pan with any remaining
marinade. Cover the exposed part of the sticks with foil.

4 Cook under a hot grill for about 15 minutes, turning occasionally. Serve 3 skewers per
person with noodles and stir-fried vegetables.

Oriental Chicken and Crispy Noodle Salad

PREPARATION TIME:
20 MINUTES, PLUS MARINATING

COOKING TIME: 15 MINUTES

FREEZING: NOT SUITABLE

510 CALS PER SERVING

SERVES 4

4 small skinless chicken breast fillets, each about 125 g (4 oz)
300 ml (½ pint) chicken stock
4 star anise
8 large spring onions
225 g (8 oz) mangetout
225 g (8 oz) broccoli florets
1 sheet thin egg noodles
oil for deep-frying
toasted sesame seeds, to garnish

DRESSING
60 ml (4 tbsp) hoisin sauce
60 ml (4 tbsp) rice vinegar
30 ml (2 tbsp) dark soy sauce
30 ml (2 tbsp) peanut oil
10 ml (2 tsp) sesame oil
20 ml (4 tsp) clear honey
salt and pepper

COOK'S NOTE
For this dish, the chicken can be cooked and marinated well ahead of time for convenience.

1 Wash and dry the chicken breasts. Place the chicken stock in a frying pan with the star anise and bring to the boil. Add the chicken breasts and simmer for 10 minutes.
2 Meanwhile, blend all the ingredients for the dressing together, seasoning with salt and pepper to taste.
3 Remove the cooked chicken from the poaching liquid and add 30 ml (2 tbsp) of the liquid to the dressing. Slice the chicken, toss with half of the dressing and leave to marinate for 30 minutes.
4 Meanwhile, prepare the vegetables. Trim and cut the spring onions into 5 cm (2 inch) lengths. Top and tail the mangetout. Blanch the vegetables separately in lightly salted, boiling water: allow 2 minutes for the broccoli; 1 minute for the mangetout; 1 minute for the spring onions. Drain, refresh under cold water and dry on kitchen paper. Toss with the remaining dressing and set aside for 30 minutes.
5 Soak the noodles in hot water according to the instructions on the packet; drain well and dry thoroughly.
6 Just before serving, heat a 10 cm (4 inch) depth of vegetable oil in a deep saucepan to 190°C (375°F), or until a cube of bread dropped into the oil browns in 30 seconds. Immerse a pile of noodles in the hot oil, fry for 1 minute until golden, then drain on kitchen paper. Repeat with the remaining noodles.
7 Toss the chicken and vegetables together and divide between individual serving plates. Top with the crispy noodles and serve at once, sprinkled with toasted sesame seeds.

Warm Chinese Chicken Salad

PREPARATION TIME:
20 MINUTES, PLUS MARINATING
COOKING TIME: 20 MINUTES
FREEZING: NOT SUITABLE

300 CALS PER SERVING
SERVES 4

2.5 cm (1 inch) piece fresh root ginger
1 large garlic clove
200 ml (7 fl oz) orange juice
60 ml (4 tbsp) lemon juice
60 ml (4 tbsp) light soy sauce
60 ml (4 tbsp) dry sherry
15 ml (1 tbsp) white wine vinegar
5 ml (1 tsp) clear honey
4 skinless chicken breast fillets, about 450 g (1 lb) total weight

175 g (6 oz) baby sweetcorn
salt and pepper
125 g (4 oz) bean sprouts
1 small head Chinese leaves
1 head radicchio lettuce
1 bunch spring onions
15 ml (1 tbsp) sunflower oil
15 ml (1 tbsp) toasted sesame seeds, to garnish

1 Peel and chop the ginger. Peel and crush the garlic. Mix together with the next six ingredients and place in a large, shallow, non-metallic dish.

2 Make three shallow cuts in the flesh of each chicken breast and place in the marinade. Cover and refrigerate for at least 3-4 hours, the longer the better.

3 Meanwhile prepare the salad vegetables. Halve the baby sweetcorn lengthways and boil in salted water for about 5 minutes. Add the bean sprouts and cook for 30 seconds. Drain on kitchen paper, then cool. Shred the Chinese leaves and radicchio; trim and slice the spring onions.

4 Remove the chicken breasts from the marinade with a slotted spoon, reserving the marinade. Heat the oil in a large nonstick frying pan and cook the chicken breasts for 10-12 minutes, turning frequently, until browned and cooked through.

5 Add the reserved marinade and simmer to thicken slightly. Adjust the seasoning. Mix together the salad vegetables and place on a large serving plate. Serve the warm chicken breasts on top of the salad, spooning over the pan juices. Garnish with sesame seeds.

Turkey Curry

PREPARATION TIME: 15 MINUTES
COOKING TIME: 35 MINUTES
FREEZING: SUITABLE

325 CALS PER SERVING
SERVES 4

1 onion
2 garlic cloves
30 ml (2 tbsp) oil
5 ml (1 tsp) ground turmeric
5 ml (1 tsp) black mustard seeds
2.5 ml (½ tsp) chilli powder
2.5 ml (½ tsp) ground cardamom
7.5 ml (1½ tsp) ground cumin

7.5 ml (1½ tsp) ground coriander
400 g (14 oz) canned chopped tomatoes
salt
500 g (1¼ lb) cooked turkey
5 ml (1 tsp) garam masala
150 ml (5 fl oz) natural yogurt
chopped fresh coriander, to garnish

1 Peel and chop the onion; peel and finely chop the garlic. Heat the oil in a heavy-based saucepan, add the onion and garlic and fry until golden.

2 Add the turmeric, mustard seeds, chilli powder, cardamom, cumin and coriander; cook, stirring, for 1 minute.

3 Add the tomatoes and season with salt. Bring to the boil, cover and simmer for 20 minutes. Meanwhile, chop the turkey into large chunks, discarding any bones and skin.

4 Stir the garam masala and 60 ml (4 tbsp) of the yogurt into the tomato mixture. Add the turkey, stir well, cover and cook gently for 10 minutes. Stir in the remaining yogurt and sprinkle with coriander before serving.

Crispy Duck with Mangetout

PREPARATION TIME: 15 MINUTES
COOKING TIME: 35 MINUTES
FREEZING: NOT SUITABLE

325 CALS PER SERVING
SERVES 6

4 duck breast fillets, each 175 g (6 oz)
salt
25 ml (1½ tbsp) clear honey
1 bunch of spring onions
2 garlic cloves
1 large green pepper
225 g (8 oz) mangetout

45 ml (3 tbsp) oil
2-3 good pinches Chinese five-spice powder
45 ml (3 tbsp) caster sugar
45 ml (3 tbsp) dark soy sauce
45 ml (3 tbsp) wine vinegar
16 water chestnuts, sliced
40 g (1½ oz) toasted cashew nuts

1 Prick the duck breast skin all over with a skewer or fork and rub well with salt to help crisp the skin. Place, skin-side up, on a rack or trivet in a roasting tin.
2 Bake in the oven at 180°C (350°F) Mark 4 for 15 minutes. Brush the skin with the honey and cook for a further 15 minutes or until cooked through. Leave to cool, then cut into strips.
3 Cut the spring onions into 2.5 cm (1 inch) lengths. Peel and crush the garlic. Cut the green pepper into thin strips, discarding the core and seeds. Top and tail the mangetout.
4 Heat the oil in a wok or large frying pan. Add the spring onions, green pepper, mangetout, garlic and five-spice powder and stir-fry for 2 minutes. Add the sugar, soy sauce, vinegar and duck strips and toss in the sauce to heat through and glaze. Add the water chestnuts and heat through.
5 Serve at once, sprinkled with toasted cashew nuts.

Duck with Pineapple and Kumquats

PREPARATION TIME: 15 MINUTES
COOKING TIME: ABOUT 45 MINUTES
FREEZING: NOT SUITABLE

815 CALS PER SERVING
SERVES 4

4 duck breasts fillets, each about 175 g (6 oz)
salt
10 ml (2 tsp) clear honey
3 carrots
1 bunch spring onions
2.5 cm (1 inch) piece fresh root ginger
1 garlic clove
125 g (4 oz) mangetout

½ small fresh pineapple
45 ml (3 tbsp) dark soy sauce
45 ml (3 tbsp) malt vinegar
45 ml (3 tbsp) caster sugar
15 ml (1 tbsp) cornflour
175 ml (6 fl oz) fresh orange juice
4 fresh kumquats, sliced, to garnish

1 Prick the duck skin all over with a fork and sprinkle with salt. Place the breasts, skin-side up, on a rack in a roasting tin and cook, uncovered, at 180°C (350°F) Mark 4 for 30 minutes.
2 Remove the duck breasts from the oven and brush the skins with honey. Return to the oven for a further 10-15 minutes or until golden.
3 Meanwhile, peel the carrots and cut into thin strips. Trim the spring onions and slice diagonally. Peel the ginger and cut into very thin strips. Peel and crush the garlic. Top and tail the mangetout.
4 Remove the duck breasts from the oven, transfer to a plate and leave to rest for 5 minutes. Reserve the duck fat in the roasting tin.
5 To make the sauce, heat 45 ml (3 tbsp) duck fat in a wok or large frying pan, add the carrots, spring onions, ginger, garlic and mangetout and stir-fry for 2 minutes. Using a slotted spoon, remove the vegetables from the pan and reserve.
6 Peel the pineapple, core and cut lengthways into 4 slices. Cut each wedge of pineapple lengthways into two slices, add to the pan and fry gently for a few seconds on each side to heat through. Remove from the pan and keep warm.
7 Stir the soy sauce, vinegar and sugar into the pan. Blend the cornflour with the orange juice, add to the pan and cook for 2 minutes, stirring. Return the vegetables to the pan and heat.
8 Cut the duck breasts diagonally into fairly thin slices and arrange on hot serving plates with the pineapple. Spoon the sauce and vegetables around the duck and pineapple. Garnish with sliced kumquats and serve.

Crispy Noodles with Sweet-sour Duck

PREPARATION TIME:
15 MINUTES, PLUS MARINATING

COOKING TIME: ABOUT 20
MINUTES

FREEZING: NOT SUITABLE

380 CALS PER SERVING

SERVES 4

225 g (8 oz) duck breast fillet
45 ml (3 tbsp) dark soy sauce
15 ml (1 tbsp) dry sherry
5 ml (1 tsp) sesame oil
50 g (2 oz) rice vermicelli noodles
oil for deep-frying
125 g (4 oz) aubergine
1 red onion
1 garlic clove

125 g (4 oz) carrot
1 mango
15 ml (1 tbsp) sugar
10 ml (2 tsp) cornflour
45 ml (3 tbsp) distilled malt vinegar
15 ml (1 tbsp) tomato ketchup
60 ml (4 tbsp) vegetable oil
125 g (4 oz) sugar snap peas or mangetout

COOK'S NOTE
If you do not want to deep-fry the noodles, boil them as directed on the packet and toss in a little sesame oil and chopped spring onion to accompany the sweet-sour duck.

1 Thinly slice the duck breast. Mix together 15 ml (1 tbsp) soy sauce with the sherry and sesame oil, pour over the duck and leave to marinate for at least 30 minutes.

2 Deep-fry the raw noodles in hot oil for about 1-2 minutes until puffed and crispy. Drain well and keep warm, uncovered, in a low oven.

3 Slice the aubergine. Peel and slice the onion, garlic and carrot. Peel and stone the mango, then slice the flesh thinly.

4 Mix together the sugar, cornflour, vinegar, ketchup and remaining 30 ml (2 tbsp) soy sauce.

5 Heat half the vegetable oil in a wok or large, nonstick frying pan. Drain the duck from the marinade and reserve the marinade. Fry the duck slices over a high heat until golden and the fat is crisp. Set aside.

6 Add 15 ml (1 tbsp) more oil and fry the aubergine until golden. Add the remaining oil and fry the onion, garlic and carrot for 2-3 minutes, then add the sugar snap peas and fry for a further 1-2 minutes. Add the mango and return the duck with the soy sauce mixture and the reserved marinade. Bring to the boil, stirring gently all the time, and bubble for 2-3 minutes until lightly thickened. Serve immediately with the crispy noodles.

Crispy Duck, Mango and Sesame Salad

PREPARATION TIME: 30 MINUTES

COOKING TIME: 15 MINUTES

FREEZING: NOT SUITABLE

560 CALS PER SERVING

SERVES 4

2 small duck breast fillets, each about 125 g (4 oz)

30 ml (2 tbsp) clear honey

5 ml (1 tsp) Chinese five-spice powder

2.5 ml (½ tsp) sea salt

30 ml (2 tbsp) oil

1 onion

125 g (4 oz) sugar snap peas, trimmed

1 large mango

175 g (6 oz) assorted salad leaves, such as frisée (curly endive), watercress, chicory, baby spinach

30 ml (2 tbsp) sesame seeds, toasted

coriander sprigs, to garnish

DRESSING

60 ml (4 tbsp) peanut oil

30 ml (2 tbsp) sesame oil

15 ml (1 tbsp) rice vinegar

15 ml (1 tbsp) soy sauce

5 ml (1 tsp) grated fresh root ginger

30 ml (2 tbsp) chopped fresh coriander

pepper

1 Wash and dry the duck breasts. Blend the honey, five-spice powder and salt together and brush all over the duck.

2 Heat half of the oil in a heavy-based frying pan and fry the duck breasts for 1-2 minutes on each side until well browned. Transfer to a baking tray and roast in the oven at 200°C (400°F) Mark 6 for 6-8 minutes. Leave to rest for 5 minutes.

3 Meanwhile, peel and thinly slice the onion and fry in the remaining oil for 5 minutes until crisp and golden; set aside.

4 Blanch the sugar snap peas in lightly salted boiling water for 2 minutes. Drain, refresh under cold water and set aside.

5 Peel and stone the mango, then slice the flesh thinly. Wash and dry the salad leaves and place in a large bowl.

6 Shake all the dressing ingredients together in a screw-topped jar until evenly combined. Pour a little of the dressing over the salad leaves and divide between individual serving plates. Gently heat the remaining dressing.

7 Thinly slice the duck breasts and arrange on the salad leaves. Add the mango slices, sugar snap peas and crispy onions. Drizzle over the warm dressing and scatter over the sesame seeds. Serve immediately, garnished with coriander sprigs.

Duck Breasts with Pickled Plums

PREPARATION TIME:
15 MINUTES, PLUS MARINATING

COOKING TIME: 15 MINUTES

FREEZING: NOT SUITABLE

270 CALS PER SERVING

SERVES 6

6 duck breast fillets, each about 175 g (6 oz)

15 ml (1 tbsp) sunflower oil

150 ml (¼ pint) chicken stock

30 ml (2 tbsp) oyster sauce

MARINADE

2 garlic cloves

5 ml (1 tsp) hot chilli sauce

pinch of salt

10 ml (2 tsp) clear honey

10 ml (2 tsp) dark muscovado sugar

30 ml (2 tbsp) lime juice

15 ml (1 tbsp) dark soy sauce

PICKLED PLUMS

6 large under-ripe plums

50 g (2 oz) caster sugar

50 ml (2 fl oz) distilled malt vinegar

1.25 ml (¼ tsp) dried crushed chilli flakes

5 ml (1 tsp) salt

pinch of ground cinnamon

1 First make the marinade. Peel and crush the garlic and mix with the remaining marinade ingredients.

2 Skin the duck breasts, wash well and dry thoroughly. Cut a few deep slashes in each duck breast and place in a shallow, non-metallic dish. Spread evenly with the marinade, then cover and leave to marinate for at least 4 hours, turning the duck breasts several times.

3 Meanwhile, prepare the pickled plums. Wash and dry the plums, halve and remove the stones. Place the remaining ingredients in a saucepan with 50 ml (2 fl oz) water and heat gently, stirring until the sugar is dissolved. Add the plums, bring to the boil and simmer gently for 5 minutes or until the plums have just softened. Set aside to cool.

4 When ready to serve, remove the duck breasts from the marinade and pat dry, reserving the marinade juices. Heat the oil in a large nonstick frying pan and brown the duck quickly on both sides. Add the stock, marinade juices and oyster sauce and simmer gently, covered, for 5 minutes. Remove the duck breasts with a slotted spoon and keep warm.

5 Remove the plums from their liquid with a slotted spoon and carefully add to the duck sauce. Bring to the boil and simmer, uncovered, for a further 5 minutes. Slice the duck breasts and arrange on warmed serving plates with the plum halves. Spoon the sauce over the duck slices and serve at once.

FISH AND SHELLFISH DISHES

There are literally countless species of fish found in the waters around India and Asia, many of which are purely local to a tiny area. However, by combining the traditional flavourings and cooking methods of these areas with fish varieties commonly found in the West, you can create authentic-tasting dishes that capture all the character of Indian and Asian cooking. White fish fillets bathed in a pale yellow coconut and spice sauce or served with a tomato, coriander and chilli sauce bring a touch of India to the table, while salmon glazed with soy and ginger, or fish cakes flavoured with kaffir lime leaves are delicious ideas drawn from Oriental cuisines. Seafood is used to great effect in Far-Eastern cooking – prawns stir-fried with Chinese greens, a salad of mussels with crispy vegetables, or tender squid in a black bean sauce are just a few temptations.

Illustration: Green Curry of Fish and Seafood (recipe page 136)

Fish Fillets with Spicy Tomato Sauce

PREPARATION TIME:
30 MINUTES, PLUS MARINATING

COOKING TIME: 10-15 MINUTES

FREEZING: NOT SUITABLE

160 CALS PER SERVING

SERVES 6

1 large red chilli
175 g (6 oz) shallots or onions
175 g (6 oz) spring onions
450 g (1 lb) tomatoes
4 garlic cloves
60 ml (4 tbsp) white wine vinegar
5 ml (1 tsp) ground coriander
2.5 ml (½ tsp) chilli powder
5 ml (1 tsp) ground ginger

450 g (1 lb) fish fillets, such as cod, haddock or salmon
30 ml (2 tbsp) oil
2.5 ml (½ tsp) ground turmeric
30 ml (2 tbsp) soft brown sugar
5 ml (1 tsp) mustard
15 ml (1 tbsp) lemon juice
15 ml (1 tbsp) tomato purée

1 Deseed and slice the chilli. Peel and slice the shallots. Trim and slice spring onions. Deseed and roughly chop the tomatoes.
2 Peel and crush the garlic cloves. Combine half the garlic with half the vinegar, the coriander, chilli powder and half the ginger. Arrange the fish fillets in a shallow, non-metallic dish and pour over the marinade. Cover and marinate the fish for 1 hour, turning occasionally.
3 Meanwhile make the sauce. Heat the oil in a large frying pan, add the shallots, sliced chilli and remaining crushed garlic and cook, stirring, for 1 minute. Add the remaining ginger and the turmeric and cook for another 1 minute. Stir in the remaining vinegar, the sugar, mustard, lemon juice, tomato purée and 150 ml (¼ pint) water. Bring to the boil and simmer for 15 minutes. Stir in the spring onions and tomatoes.
4 Drain the fish from the marinade and place in a single layer on a large, shallow baking tray. Cook at 200°C (400°F) Mark 6 for 10-15 minutes or until just cooked. Serve with the hot spicy tomato sauce.

Fish Baked with Hot Spices

PREPARATION TIME:
15 MINUTES, PLUS MARINATING

COOKING TIME: 10-15 MINUTES

FREEZING: NOT SUITABLE

280 CALS PER SERVING

SERVES 4

4 large white fish fillets, such as cod, haddock, monkfish, sea bass, each 175 g (6 oz)

SPICE MIXTURE
3 garlic cloves
grated rind and juice of 1 lemon
grated rind of 1 lime
30 ml (2 tbsp) chopped fresh coriander
30 ml (2 tbsp) chopped fresh parsley
large pinch of powdered saffron

large pinch of ground turmeric
5 ml (1 tsp) ground cumin
2.5 ml (½ tsp) ground cinnamon
5-10 ml (1-2 tsp) hot chilli sauce
10 ml (2 tsp) brown sugar
15 ml (1 tbsp) paprika
60 ml (4 tbsp) olive oil
salt and pepper

COOK'S NOTE
Don't be tempted to leave the fish marinating for longer than an hour or the acid in the marinade will begin to 'cook' the fish.

1 Peel and crush the garlic, then combine with all the ingredients for the spice mixture in a glass bowl, adding plenty of salt and pepper. Whisk together with a fork.
2 Rub the spice mixture into the fish fillets, making sure that each piece is completely coated. Leave to marinate in a cool place for 30 minutes to 1 hour.
3 Wrap each fish fillet in a piece of foil and place on a baking sheet. Bake in the oven at 200°C (400°F) Mark 6 for about 10-15 minutes or until the fish flakes easily when tested with a fork. The cooking time will depend on the thickness of the fillets: if using chunky fillets like monkfish or cod they will take longer than thinner, more delicate fillets.
4 Unwrap and transfer each fillet to a warmed serving plate. Pour the liquid from each parcel over the fish. Serve at once.

Coconut Fish Curry

PREPARATION TIME: 15 MINUTES

COOKING TIME: 20 MINUTES

FREEZING: SUITABLE (STAGE 2)

415 CALS PER SERVING

SERVES 6

2.5 cm (1 inch) piece fresh root ginger
6 garlic cloves
225 g (8 oz) onions
1 large red chilli
60 ml (4 tbsp) oil
10 ml (2 tsp) ground cumin

2.5 ml (½ tsp) ground turmeric
400 ml (14 fl oz) coconut milk
2.5 ml (½ tsp) salt
450 g (1 lb) cod or haddock fillet
coriander sprigs, lime wedges and whole chillies, to garnish

COOK'S NOTE
If you are reconstituting powdered or creamed coconut, make it up to the consistency of single cream.

1 Peel and roughly chop the ginger and garlic. Pour 150 ml (¼ pint) water into a blender or food processor. With the machine running, add the ginger and garlic and process until smooth. Peel, halve and slice the onions; deseed and slice the chilli.

2 Heat the oil in a large frying pan. Add the onion and cook for 5-7 minutes or until beginning to colour. Add the cumin and turmeric and cook, stirring, for 30 seconds. Add the ginger paste and chilli, and cook, stirring, for 2 minutes or until all the liquid has evaporated. Pour in the coconut milk and add the salt. Bring to the boil and bubble until reduced by half.

3 Cut the fish into 5 cm (2 inch) pieces and place in the hot sauce. Bring back to the boil and baste the fish with the hot sauce. Simmer very gently for 4-6 minutes or until the fish is just cooked when tested with a fork.

4 Serve garnished with coriander sprigs and lime wedges.

Coconut Fish Pilau

PREPARATION TIME: 10 MINUTES

COOKING TIME: 30 MINUTES

FREEZING: NOT SUITABLE

375 CALS PER SERVING

SERVES 4

125 g (4 oz) onion
1 garlic clove
175 g (6 oz) skinless cod fillet
15 ml (1 tbsp) oil
15 ml (1 tbsp) Thai green curry paste or Indian curry paste
225 g (8 oz) Thai fragrant rice or basmati rice
600 ml (1 pint) fish stock

150 ml (¼ pint) coconut milk
125 g (4 oz) blanched sugar snap peas
125 g (4 oz) cooked peeled tiger prawns
25 g (1 oz) blanched toasted almonds
15 ml (1 tbsp) lemon juice
salt and pepper
chopped fresh coriander, to garnish

1 Peel and roughly chop the onion. Peel and crush the garlic. Cut the cod fillet into large, bite-sized pieces.

2 Heat the oil in a large, nonstick frying pan, add the onion and garlic and fry for 4-5 minutes or until golden. Stir in the curry paste and cook, stirring, for 1-2 minutes.

3 Add the rice, stock and coconut milk. Bring to the boil. Cover and simmer gently for about 15 minutes, stirring occasionally with a fork.

4 When the rice is tender and all the liquid has been absorbed, add the cod. Cook for a further 3-5 minutes or until the fish is cooked through.

5 Stir in the sugar snap peas, prawns, almonds and lemon juice. Season with salt and pepper. Heat through for about 1 minute then serve immediately, garnished with coriander.

Cod Fillets with Spicy Yogurt Crust

PREPARATION TIME:
10 MINUTES, PLUS MARINATING

COOKING TIME: 5-7 MINUTES

FREEZING: NOT SUITABLE

120 CALS PER SERVING

SERVES 4

1 garlic clove
2.5 cm (1 inch) piece fresh root ginger
45 ml (3 tbsp) chopped fresh coriander
2.5 ml (½ tsp) ground cumin
2.5 ml (½ tsp) ground coriander
1.25 ml (¼ tsp) cayenne pepper

5 ml (1 tsp) salt
150 ml (¼ pint) low-fat natural yogurt
4 cod fillets, each about 125 g (4 oz)
pepper
flat-leaf parsley and fresh lime, to garnish

1 Peel and crush the garlic; peel and grate the ginger. Mix the two with the fresh coriander. Add the ground cumin and coriander, cayenne pepper, salt and natural yogurt.

2 Place the fish in the yogurt mixture and coat well. Cover and refrigerate for 2-3 hours.

3 Transfer the fish to a foil-lined grill pan and cook under a hot grill for about 5-7 minutes or until cooked through. Season with pepper and garnish with flat-leaf parsley and fresh lime.

Spiced Fried Fish

PREPARATION TIME: 20 MINUTES
COOKING TIME: 10 MINUTES
FREEZING: NOT SUITABLE

285 CALS PER SERVING
SERVES 4

COOK'S NOTE
For this dish you will need firm fillets that won't break up during cooking. Firm-textured monkfish is the best choice but it is quite expensive. Although a little more delicate, cod and haddock fillet – cut from the thickest part of the fish – also work well.

700 g (1½ lb) firm white fish fillets
1-2 hot red chillies
1 bunch of fresh coriander
1 garlic clove
10 ml (2 tsp) plain white flour
large pinch of salt

5 ml (1 tsp) cumin seeds
10 ml (2 tsp) coriander seeds
finely grated rind of 1 lime
oil for shallow-frying
lime wedges, to garnish

1 Skin the fish fillets and cut into large chunks. Chop the chillies, discarding the seeds if a milder flavour is preferred. Trim the roots (if still attached) and most of the tough stems from the coriander, then finely chop the leaves. Peel the garlic and chop very finely.
2 Put the coriander, chillies and garlic in a large bowl and mix with the flour and salt.
3 Heat a small heavy-based frying pan. Add the cumin and coriander seeds and dry-fry for 2 minutes, stirring all the time so that they do not burn. Allow to cool, then finely crush the spices using a pestle and mortar. Add them to the flour mixture with the grated lime rind.
4 Add the prepared fish to the spiced flour mixture and toss carefully to ensure that each piece is coated on all sides.
5 Heat the oil in a frying pan. Cook the fish, a few pieces at a time, until browned and crisp on the outside and cooked right through. Drain on kitchen paper and keep warm while cooking the rest of the fish. Serve at once, garnished with lime wedges.

Spiced Fish Kebabs

PREPARATION TIME:
15 MINUTES, PLUS MARINATING

COOKING TIME: 15 MINUTES

FREEZING: NOT SUITABLE

290 CALS PER SERVING

SERVES 4

2 green chillies
2.5 ml (1 inch) piece fresh root ginger
1 garlic clove
60 ml (4 tbsp) natural yogurt
10 ml (2 tsp) cumin seeds
5 ml (1 tsp) black peppercorns
2.5 ml (½ tsp) ground turmeric

2.5 ml (½ tsp) salt
700 g (1½ lb) thick white fish fillets, such as monkfish, halibut, haddock or cod
12 large peeled prawns
1 large green pepper
50 ml (2 fl oz) melted butter
lime or lemon wedges, to serve

1 To make the marinade, deseed and roughly chop the chillies. Peel and chop the ginger and garlic. Put the yogurt in a blender or food processor with the chillies, ginger, garlic, cumin seeds, peppercorns, turmeric and salt. Work to a paste.

2 Cut the white fish into 16 large chunks, discarding the skin and any bones. Place in the marinade, together with the prawns. Cover and marinate in the refrigerator for 4 hours.

3 Meanwhile, cut the green pepper in half, remove the seeds and cut the flesh into 12 neat squares.

4 When ready to cook, thread the ingredients onto 4 oiled flat kebab skewers, allowing 4 pieces of white fish, 3 pieces of green pepper and 3 prawns on each skewer.

5 Cook the kebabs on the barbecue or under the grill, brushing frequently with the butter, for about 15 minutes or until the fish is cooked.

Cod Steaks with Fennel

PREPARATION TIME:
10 MINUTES, PLUS MARINATING

COOKING TIME: 20 MINUTES

FREEZING: NOT SUITABLE

175 CALS PER SERVING

SERVES 4

COOK'S NOTE
Ask your fishmonger to remove the scales from the skin. When grilled it will be crisp and delicious to eat.

15 ml (1 tbsp) hoisin sauce
60 ml (4 tbsp) light soy sauce
60 ml (4 tbsp) dry vermouth
60 ml (4 tbsp) orange juice
2.5 ml (½ tsp) Chinese five-spice powder
2.5 ml (½ tsp) ground cumin

1 garlic clove
4 thick cod fillets or steaks, each 150 g (5 oz) (see Cook's Note)
2 bulbs fennel, about 700 g (1½ lb)
15 ml (1 tbsp) oil
10 ml (2 tsp) sesame seeds

1 First make the marinade. Combine the hoisin and soy sauces with the vermouth, orange juice, five-spice powder and cumin. Peel and crush the garlic and add to the marinade.

2 Place the cod in a shallow non-metallic dish and pour the marinade over. Cover and leave in a cool place for 1 hour.

3 Thinly slice the fennel, reserving the tops. Remove the fish, reserving the marinade. Place the fish under a hot grill or on a lightly oiled hot griddle for 4 minutes, then turn over and cook for 3-4 minutes or until cooked.

4 Heat the oil in a frying pan and cook the fennel briskly for 5-7 minutes or until brown and beginning to soften. Add the marinade, bring to the boil and bubble until reduced and sticky. Place the fish on a bed of fennel, spoon round any pan juices and sprinkle over the sesame seeds. Garnish with fennel tops.

Thai Fish Cakes

PREPARATION TIME: 25 MINUTES

COOKING TIME: ABOUT 20 MINUTES

FREEZING: SUITABLE

100 CALS PER FISH CAKE

MAKES ABOUT 10

450 g (1 lb) white fish fillets, such as cod or haddock
4 kaffir lime leaves
30 ml (2 tbsp) chopped fresh coriander
15 ml (1 tbsp) Thai fish sauce
15 ml (1 tbsp) lime juice

30 ml (2 tbsp) Thai red curry paste
salt and pepper
flour, for coating
oil for shallow-frying
salad leaves, shredded spring onion, 1 sliced mild red chilli and lime halves, to serve

1 Remove any skin from the fish, then place the fish in a food processor or blender and work until smooth.

2 Finely chop the lime leaves and add to the fish with the coriander, fish sauce, lime juice and red curry paste. Season with salt and pepper. Process until well mixed.

3 Using lightly floured hands, divide the mixture into about 10 pieces and shape each one into a cake, about 6 cm (2½ inches) in diameter.

4 Heat a 1 cm (½ inch) depth of oil in a frying pan. Cook the fish cakes, a few at a time, for about 4 minutes each side. Drain on crumpled kitchen paper and keep hot while cooking the remainder.

5 Serve the fish cakes as soon as they are all cooked, on a bed of salad leaves scattered with shredded spring onion and chilli slices. Serve with lime halves.

Fish Masala

PREPARATION TIME: 15 MINUTES

COOKING TIME: 20 MINUTES

FREEZING: SUITABLE – SAUCE ONLY

360 CALS PER SERVING

SERVES 4

Illustrated opposite

COOK'S NOTE
If you are short of time, stage 5 can be omitted.

5 large juicy tomatoes
1 onion
2 garlic cloves
1-2 hot green chillies
2.5 cm (1 inch) piece fresh root ginger
60 ml (4 tbsp) chopped fresh coriander
juice of 2 limes
15 ml (1 tbsp) coriander seeds
5 ml (1 tsp) fenugreek seeds

5 ml (1 tsp) ground turmeric
30 ml (2 tbsp) oil
15 ml (1 tbsp) garam masala
salt
4 white fish steaks, such as cod, haddock, halibut
about 30 ml (2 tbsp) plain white flour, for coating
oil for shallow-frying

1 Immerse the tomatoes in boiling water for 30 seconds, then drain and peel away the skins. Finely chop the tomatoes. Peel and quarter the onion. Peel the garlic. Halve the chillies, discarding the seeds if a milder flavour is preferred. Peel and halve the ginger.

2 Put the onion, garlic, chillies, ginger, chopped coriander and lime juice in a blender or food processor and process to make a fairly thick paste.

3 Crush the coriander and fenugreek seeds using a pestle and mortar, then add to the spice paste with the turmeric and mix well.

4 Heat the oil in a large frying pan. Add the spice paste and cook, stirring constantly, for about 5 minutes. Stir in the chopped tomatoes, garam masala and salt to taste. Cook for about 5 minutes or until the tomatoes have broken down and their liquid has evaporated.

5 Coat the fish steaks with the flour. Heat the oil in another frying pan. Add the fish steaks and quickly brown on both sides.

6 Transfer the fish steaks to the frying pan containing the sauce, arranging them in a single layer. Spoon a little of the sauce over each fish steak and cover the pan with a lid or a baking sheet. Simmer gently for about 8-10 minutes, depending on the thickness of the fish, until the fish is cooked right through. Serve at once.

Citrus Spiced Haddock

PREPARATION TIME: 20 MINUTES

COOKING TIME: 30-35 MINUTES

FREEZING: NOT SUITABLE

205 CALS PER SERVING

SERVES 6

1 onion
1 cm (½ inch) piece fresh root ginger
3 firm tomatoes
30 ml (2 tbsp) sunflower oil
6 thick skinless haddock fillets, each 150 g (5 oz)
300 ml (½ pint) natural yogurt

grated rind and juice of ½ lemon
5 ml (1 tsp) cornflour
10 ml (2 tsp) ground cumin
30 ml (2 tbsp) ground coriander
1.25 ml (¼ tsp) cayenne pepper
salt
45 ml (3 tbsp) chopped fresh coriander

1 Peel and finely slice the onion. Peel and grate the ginger. Immerse the tomatoes in boiling water for 30 seconds, then drain and peel away the skins. Deseed the tomatoes and cut into even-sized strips.

2 Heat the oil in a small frying pan and fry the onion for 3-5 minutes until softened and beginning to brown. Add the tomatoes to the onion, mix well, then spread over the base of a shallow ovenproof dish.

3 Cut the haddock fillets in half diagonally and arrange in a single layer on top of the onions and tomatoes.

4 In a bowl, mix together the yogurt, lemon rind and juice, cornflour, cumin, ground coriander, cayenne pepper and salt to taste. Stir the ginger into the yogurt mixture with half of the fresh coriander.

5 Pour the yogurt mixture over the fish and cover tightly. Bake in the oven at 190°C (375°F) Mark 5 for 30-35 minutes until the fish is just cooked. Scatter the remaining fresh coriander on top and serve at once.

Sole in a Lemon Grass and Coconut Sauce

PREPARATION TIME:
15 MINUTES, PLUS CHILLING

COOKING TIME: 10 MINUTES

FREEZING: NOT SUITABLE

220 CALS PER SERVING

SERVES 4

Illustrated opposite

6 sole or plaice fillets, about 700 g (1½ lb) total weight

15 cm (6 inch) lemon grass stalk

2.5 cm (1 inch) piece fresh root ginger

grated rind and juice of 1 lime

300 ml (½ pint) coconut milk

10 ml (2 tsp) Thai fish sauce

shredded lemon grass, to garnish

1 Skin the sole fillets and halve each one lengthways. Roll the fillets up and place in the refrigerator for about 30 minutes.

2 Slice the lemon grass in half and finely chop. Peel and finely slice the root ginger.

3 Place the lemon grass, ginger, 15 ml (1 tbsp) lime juice, the coconut milk and fish sauce in a frying pan. Bring to a gentle simmer and place the sole in the warm liquid. Cover and poach for about 5-6 minutes or until cooked through.

4 Lift the sole out of the sauce and place on a warm serving dish. Pour the sauce over and garnish with the grated lime rind, shredded lemon grass and a little lime juice. Serve immediately.

Trout with Coriander Masala

PREPARATION TIME:
25 MINUTES, PLUS MARINATING

COOKING TIME: 20 MINUTES

FREEZING: NOT SUITABLE

335 CALS PER SERVING

SERVES 2

1 onion

2 garlic cloves

2.5 cm (1 inch) piece root ginger

1 green chilli

4 large tomatoes

15 ml (1 tbsp) coriander seeds

5 ml (1 tsp) ground turmeric

5 ml (1 tsp) fenugreek seeds

45 ml (3 tbsp) chopped fresh coriander

juice of 2 limes

30 ml (2 tbsp) sunflower oil

15 ml (1 tbsp) garam masala

salt

2 whole trout, each about 250-275 g (9-10 oz), cleaned, or 4 trout fillets

lime wedges, to garnish

1 Peel and chop the onion. Peel the garlic and ginger. Deseed the chilli. Finely chop the tomatoes.

2 Put the onion, garlic, ginger, chilli, coriander seeds, turmeric, fenugreek seeds, chopped coriander and lime juice in a blender or food processor and blend until well mixed.

3 Heat the oil in a frying pan, add the spice paste and cook, stirring, for 8-10 minutes.

4 Add the tomatoes, garam masala, and salt to taste, and continue cooking for a further 5 minutes, until the mixture has reduced and thickened slightly. Leave to cool.

5 Using a sharp knife, make deep cuts on either side of the fish, in a criss-cross pattern. Lay the fish in a non-metallic dish, then spread the spice mixture over each side, rubbing it well into the cuts. Cover and refrigerate for 1 hour.

6 Remove the fish from the marinade and place in the grill pan, not on the wire rack, as it may stick. Grill the fish for about 10 minutes on each side or until firm to the touch. Serve at once, garnished with lime wedges.

Steamed Sea Bass with Coconut and Mango

PREPARATION TIME:
20 MINUTES, PLUS MARINATING

COOKING TIME: 25 MINUTES

FREEZING: NOT SUITABLE

385 CALS PER SERVING

SERVES 4

Illustrated opposite

1 sea bass, about 900 g (2 lb), scaled and gutted
225 g (8 oz) Savoy cabbage
4 kaffir lime leaves
2 lemon grass stalks
4 star anise
1 small firm mango
coriander sprigs and lime wedges, to garnish

SPICE PASTE
3 shallots
2 garlic cloves
2.5 cm (1 inch) piece galangal

2-4 dried red chillies
4 coriander roots, scrubbed
15 ml (1 tbsp) tamarind juice
2.5 ml (½ tsp) ground black pepper

COCONUT SAUCE
30 ml (2 tbsp) dried shrimp (optional)
10 ml (2 tsp) hot chilli sauce
30 ml (2 tbsp) Thai fish sauce
30 ml (2 tbsp) rice vinegar
22.5 ml (1½ tbsp) dark muscovado sugar
250 ml (8 fl oz) coconut milk

1 Wash and dry the fish, then using a sharp knife, cut 4 deep slashes in each side of the fish.

2 To make the spice paste, peel and roughly chop the shallots, garlic and galangal; deseed and chop the chillies; roughly chop the coriander roots. Grind to a fairly smooth paste, using a spice grinder or pestle and mortar. Stir in the tamarind juice and pepper. Spread the spice paste inside the cavity and all over the surface of the fish. Place in a non-metallic dish, cover and leave to marinate for at least 4 hours, preferably overnight.

3 Finely shred the cabbage, discarding the core, and arrange in a band down the middle of a large double layer of foil. Sit the fish on top. Lightly bruise the lime leaves, lemon grass and star anise, then place inside the fish cavity. Turn up the sides and ends of the foil but do not seal.

4 To prepare the coconut sauce, mince the dried shrimp if using, with a spice grinder or pestle and mortar. Mix all the sauce ingredients together, then pour over the fish. Seal the foil parcel, place on a baking sheet and bake at 220°C (425°F) Mark 7 for 25 minutes.

5 Remove the parcel from the oven and leave to stand for 5 minutes. Meanwhile, peel and stone the mango, then slice the flesh. Transfer the fish to a warmed serving platter with the cabbage and juices. Arrange the mango on top and garnish with coriander and lime wedges.

Kettle-cooked Sea Bass

PREPARATION TIME: 15 MINUTES

COOKING TIME: 20 MINUTES

FREEZING: NOT SUITABLE

245 CALS PER SERVING

SERVES 8

1.6-1.8 kg (3½-4 lb) sea bass, gutted
1 large bunch spring onions
2 celery stalks
5 cm (2 inch) piece fresh root ginger
oil for brushing
60 ml (4 tbsp) soy sauce
60 ml (4 tbsp) dry sherry
salt and pepper

TO SERVE
30 ml (2 tbsp) vegetable oil
15 ml (1 tbsp) sesame oil
30 ml (2 tbsp) soy sauce
5 ml (1 tsp) caster sugar
8 finely shredded spring onions

1 Wash and dry the fish. With kitchen shears or scissors, cut the tail into a 'V' shape. With a sharp knife, make several deep diagonal slashes on each side of the fish.

2 Finely shred the spring onions and slice the celery; peel the ginger and cut into thin sticks.

3 Pour water under the rack of a fish kettle and place half of the spring onion, celery and ginger on the rack. Brush the outside of the fish lightly with oil, then place over the flavourings on the rack. Sprinkle the remaining spring onions, celery and ginger over the fish, then the soy sauce, sherry, and salt and pepper to taste.

4 Cover the kettle with its lid, bring the water slowly to the boil, then simmer for 20 minutes or until the flesh of the fish is opaque when tested near the bone.

5 To serve, heat the oils in a wok or heavy frying pan, add the soy sauce and sugar and stir well to mix. Add the shredded spring onions and stir to coat.

6 Discard the flavourings from the top of the fish and transfer the fish to a warmed large serving plate. Arrange the freshly cooked spring onion over the fish and drizzle with the cooking liquid.

Green Curry of Fish and Seafood

PREPARATION TIME: 30 MINUTES

COOKING TIME: ABOUT 10 MINUTES

FREEZING: NOT SUITABLE

610-410 CALS PER SERVING

SERVES 4-6

COOK'S NOTE
Whatever you do, don't overcook squid, otherwise it will be tough and live up to its rubbery reputation.

350 g (12 oz) squid
350 g (12 oz) medium raw prawns
450 g (1 lb) firm white fish fillets, such as cod, haddock, halibut, monkfish
15 ml (1 tbsp) oil
45 ml (3 tbsp) Thai green curry paste
1 lemon grass stalk

few kaffir lime leaves, shredded
450 ml (¾ pint) coconut milk
few mussels or clams, cleaned (optional)
30 ml (2 tbsp) Thai fish sauce
squeeze of lime juice
chopped coriander, to garnish

1 Rinse the squid then, holding the body in one hand, firmly pull the tentacles with the other hand. As you do so, the soft contents of the body will come out. Cut the tentacles just in front of the eyes and discard the body contents. Cut the tentacles into small pieces.

2 Squeeze out the plastic-like quill from the body and discard. Rinse the body under cold running water, making sure that it is clean inside. Rub off the fine dark skin, then cut the body into rings or small rectangular pieces.

3 Peel the raw prawns, leaving the small fan-like piece at the end of the tail attached. Using a small sharp knife, make a shallow slit along the outer curve from the tail to the head end and remove the dark intestinal vein. Rinse under cold running water, drain and pat dry.

4 Cut the white fish fillets into large pieces.

5 Heat the oil in a large frying pan, add the curry paste and cook for 2 minutes, stirring all the time. Bruise the lemon grass and add to the pan with the shredded lime leaves. Add the coconut milk and bring to the boil, stirring.

6 Reduce the heat to a simmer, then add the white fish, prawns and squid. Cook for 1-2 minutes until they look opaque. Add the mussels or clams if using, cover with a lid or a baking sheet and simmer for a few minutes until the shells have opened. Discard any closed ones.

7 Flavour with the fish sauce and lime juice and serve immediately, garnished with chopped coriander.

Oriental Seafood Sauté

PREPARATION TIME: 15 MINUTES

COOKING TIME: 15 MINUTES

FREEZING: NOT SUITABLE

230 CALS PER SERVING

SERVES 4

450 g (1 lb) monkfish fillet, skinned
1 red pepper
1 bunch spring onions
1 garlic clove
2.5 cm (1 inch) piece fresh root ginger
275 g (10 oz) trimmed leeks

30 ml (2 tbsp) oil
125 g (4 oz) cooked peeled prawns
15 ml (1 tbsp) hoisin sauce
15 ml (1 tbsp) light soy sauce
15 ml (1 tbsp) dry sherry
pepper

1 Cut the fish into bite-sized pieces. Deseed and roughly chop the pepper; slice the spring onions. Peel and finely chop the garlic and ginger. Roughly slice the trimmed leeks.

2 Heat the oil in a large nonstick frying pan and sauté the monkfish for 2-3 minutes. Remove using a slotted spoon. Sauté the onions, garlic and ginger for 2 minutes or until beginning to soften. Add the leeks and pepper and sauté for a further 10 minutes, stirring, until softened.

3 Return the monkfish to the pan with the prawns, hoisin sauce, soy sauce and sherry. Season with plenty of pepper (the soy sauce is fairly salty). Cook for ½-1 minute, stirring. Serve at once.

Thai Seafood Salad

PREPARATION TIME:
45-50 MINUTES

COOKING TIME: ABOUT 10
MINUTES

FREEZING: NOT SUITABLE

245 CALS PER SERVING

SERVES 4

20 fresh mussels in shells
8 large raw tiger prawns in shells
225 g (8 oz) small squid, cleaned
12 scallops, shelled
2 shallots
1 carrot
10 cm (4 inch) piece cucumber
75 g (3 oz) Chinese cabbage
2 kaffir lime leaves, shredded
30 ml (2 tbsp) chopped fresh coriander

15 ml (1 tbsp) chopped fresh mint
25 g (1 oz) dried grated coconut, toasted

DRESSING
2-3 small red chillies
15 ml (1 tbsp) lime juice
15 ml (1 tbsp) rice vinegar
15 ml (1 tbsp) Thai fish sauce
10 ml (2 tsp) sesame oil
pinch of sugar

1 Scrub the mussels thoroughly under cold running water and remove their beards. Discard any with damaged shells or any that remain opened when sharply tapped. Cut the heads off the prawns and peel away the shells. Make a shallow slit down the back of each prawn and remove the dark intestinal vein; rinse well. Score the body pouches of the squid with a sharp knife, but leave the tentacles whole. Clean the scallops by removing the dark beard-like fringe and tough greyish muscle from the side of the white meat, and separate the white meat from the coral if preferred; slice the white meat into rounds.

2 Place the mussels in a large saucepan with just the water clinging to the shells. Cover with a tight-fitting lid and steam for 4-5 minutes until the shells have opened. Discard any that remain closed. Drain, reserving the poaching liquid, and refresh the mussels under cold running water. Set aside.

3 Return the mussel liquid to the boil. Add the prawns and poach for 3 minutes, then add the squid and scallops and cook for a further 2-3 minutes until all the seafood is cooked. Remove with a slotted spoon and immediately refresh under cold running water. Reserve 30 ml (2 tbsp) of the poaching liquid.

4 Peel and thinly slice the shallots and carrot. Halve, deseed and slice the cucumber. Shred the cabbage. Place the vegetables in a bowl and toss in the seafood, lime leaves, coriander and mint.

5 For the dressing, deseed and finely dice the chillies and mix with the reserved poaching liquid and the rest of the ingredients. Add to the salad, toss well and divide between individual serving plates. Top each salad with toasted grated coconut and serve at once.

Prawns Fried with Greens

PREPARATION TIME: 20 MINUTES

COOKING TIME: ABOUT 10 MINUTES

FREEZING: NOT SUITABLE

195-130 CALS PER SERVING

SERVES 4-6

COOK'S NOTE
If raw prawns are unobtainable, use cooked ones instead. Add with the lime juice; heat through for 1 minute only.

2 garlic cloves

1 lemon grass stalk

2 kaffir lime leaves

2 red shallots, or 1 small red onion

1-2 hot red chillies

4 cm (1½ inch) piece fresh root ginger

15 ml (1 tbsp) coriander seeds

75 g (3 oz) green beans

175 g (6 oz) mangetout

450 g (1 lb) large raw prawns in shells

1 small head of pak choi or Chinese flowering cabbage, or 2-3 baby pak choi

30 ml (2 tbsp) oil

juice of 1 lime, or to taste

30 ml (2 tbsp) Thai fish sauce

1 Peel the garlic and slice thinly. Cut the lemon grass in half and bruise with a rolling pin. Tear the kaffir lime leaves into small pieces. Peel and thinly slice the shallots or onion. Slice the chillies, discarding the seeds if a milder flavour is preferred. Peel the ginger and cut into long, thin shreds. Crush the coriander seeds. Trim the beans and mangetout.

2 Peel the prawns, leaving the tail end attached. Using a small sharp knife, make a shallow slit along the outer curve from the tail to the head end and remove the dark intestinal vein. Rinse under cold running water, drain and pat dry with kitchen paper.

3 Trim the pak choi or Chinese flowering cabbage, removing any discoloured leaves or damaged stems. Leave baby pak choi whole; tear other leaves into manageable pieces.

4 Heat the oil in a wok or large frying pan. Add the garlic, lemon grass, lime leaves, shallots, chillies, ginger and coriander seeds, and stir-fry for 2 minutes. Add the green beans and cook for 2 minutes. Add the prawns, mangetout and pak choi or Chinese flowering cabbage and stir-fry for 2-3 minutes, until the vegetables are cooked but still crisp and the prawns are cooked.

5 Add the lime juice and fish sauce, and heat through for 1 minute. Serve immediately, while the vegetables are crisp.

VARIATION
Replace the prawns with skinned chicken breast fillets, cut into wafer-thin slices. Stir-fry with the beans at stage 4.

Oriental Grilled Prawns

PREPARATION TIME:
20 MINUTES, PLUS MARINATING

COOKING TIME: 10 MINUTES

FREEZING: NOT SUITABLE

75 CALS PER SERVING

SERVES 4

700 g (1½ lb) raw tiger prawns in shells

15 ml (1 tbsp) clear honey

4 lemon wedges and coriander sprigs, to garnish

ORIENTAL SPICE MIX

15 ml (1 tbsp) star anise

5 ml (1 tsp) coriander seeds

5 ml (1 tsp) fennel seeds

5 ml (1 tsp) cloves

5 ml (1 tsp) black peppercorns

2.5 cm (1 inch) piece fresh root ginger

1 garlic clove

1 Make the spice mix. Coarsely grind the star anise, coriander and fennel seeds, cloves and peppercorns in an electric spice grinder or with a pestle and mortar. Peel and grate the ginger; peel and crush the garlic. Add the ginger and garlic to the spices and mix well. Set aside.

2 Peel the prawns, leaving the tail end attached. Using a small sharp knife, make a shallow slit along the outer curve from the tail to the head end and remove the dark intestinal vein. Rinse under cold running water, drain and pat dry with kitchen paper.

3 Thread the prawns onto 8 wooden skewers. Brush with honey and spread with the spice mix. Cover with cling film and leave to marinate for 30 minutes.

4 Cook the prawns under a grill, close to the heat, for about 5 minutes on each side, until cooked. Serve garnished with lemon wedges and coriander.

Thai-style Prawn and Pumpkin Curry

PREPARATION TIME: 20 MINUTES

COOKING TIME: ABOUT 20 MINUTES

FREEZING: NOT SUITABLE

675 CALS PER SERVING

SERVES 4

225 g (8 oz) button onions
225 g (8 oz) squash, such as pumpkin
2.5 cm (1 inch) piece fresh root ginger
30 ml (2 tbsp) oil
30 ml (2 tbsp) Thai red curry paste or Indian mild curry paste
600 ml (1 pint) thin coconut milk

10 ml (2 tsp) sugar
225 g (8 oz) cooked peeled prawns
25 g (1 oz) fresh spinach or basil leaves
juice of 1 lime
225 g (8 oz) broad rice or thread egg noodles
2-3 shredded spring onions, to garnish
chilli sauce to accompany (optional)

1 Peel the button onions and halve if large. Peel and roughly chop the squash. Peel and slice the fresh root ginger. Heat the oil in a wok or large, nonstick frying pan and fry the onions and squash together with the ginger for about 5-7 minutes or until golden brown.

2 Stir in the curry paste, then add the coconut milk and sugar. Bring to the boil then simmer the mixture, uncovered, for 7-10 minutes or until the onions and squash are tender.

3 Off the heat, stir in the prawns and spinach leaves. Add a little fresh lime juice to taste.

4 Cook the noodles according to the packet instructions. Drain well and serve immediately with the curry. Garnish with shreds of spring onion, and accompany with chilli sauce, if wished.

Gingered Prawns with Coconut Rice

PREPARATION TIME:
25 MINUTES, PLUS SOAKING

COOKING TIME: 20-25 MINUTES

FREEZING: NOT SUITABLE

565 CALS PER SERVING

SERVES 4

225 g (8 oz) long-grain rice
25 g (1 oz) butter
3 cardamom pods, bruised
250 ml (8 fl oz) coconut milk
5 ml (1 tsp) sea salt
5 ml (1 tsp) caster sugar
4 kaffir lime leaves, bruised
450 g (1 lb) raw tiger prawns in shells

2 garlic cloves
5 cm (2 inch) piece fresh root ginger
30 ml (2 tbsp) sunflower oil
2.5 ml (½ tsp) dried crushed chilli flakes
1 small papaya
15 g (½ oz) dried grated or shredded coconut, toasted
30 ml (2 tbsp) lime or lemon juice

1 Soak the rice in cold water to cover for 1 hour, then drain well. Melt the butter in a saucepan, add the rice and cardamom pods and stir over a medium heat for 1 minute until all the grains are glossy.

2 Stir in the coconut milk, salt, sugar, lime leaves and 250 ml (8 fl oz) of water. Bring to the boil, lower the heat and simmer gently, uncovered, for 10 minutes. Cover the pan with a layer of foil, then position the lid to ensure a tight seal. Place over a very low heat for 10-12 minutes.

3 Meanwhile, prepare the prawns. Remove the heads and peel away the shells, leaving the tail shell attached. Make a slit down the back of each one and remove the black intestinal vein. Wash well and pat dry; set aside.

4 Peel and finely chop the garlic; peel and thinly shred the ginger. Heat the oil in a wok, add the garlic, ginger and chilli flakes and stir-fry for 1 minute. Add the prawns and stir-fry for a further 5 minutes. Remove the pan from the heat and carefully stir in the cooked coconut rice until evenly combined. Cover and set aside.

5 Peel the papaya, cut in half and discard the seeds. Slice the flesh thinly.

6 Transfer the rice and prawns to a warmed serving plate, arrange the sliced papaya over the top, scatter over the toasted coconut and drizzle with the lime juice. Serve at once.

Prawns with Spinach

PREPARATION TIME: 25 MINUTES

COOKING TIME: 15 MINUTES

FREEZING: NOT SUITABLE

255 CALS PER SERVING

SERVES 4

Illustrated opposite

700 g (1½ lb) large raw prawns in shells
1 onion
1 garlic clove
5 cm (2 inch) piece fresh root ginger
450 g (1 lb) spinach leaves
30 ml (2 tbsp) ghee or oil
10 ml (2 tsp) ground turmeric

5 ml (1 tsp) chilli powder
15 ml (1 tbsp) black mustard seeds
10 ml (2 tsp) ground coriander
large pinch of ground cloves
300 ml (½ pint) coconut milk
salt
15 ml (1 tbsp) lime or lemon juice

1 To prepare the raw prawns, remove the heads, if necessary, then peel off the shell leaving the fan-like piece at the end of the tail attached. Using a small sharp knife, make a shallow slit along the back of each prawn and remove the dark intestinal vein. Rinse the prawns under cold running water. Drain and pat dry with kitchen paper.

2 Peel and slice the onion. Peel and chop the garlic. Peel the ginger and cut into thin strips.

3 Trim the spinach leaves and wash thoroughly; drain well.

4 Heat the ghee or oil in a large frying pan or wok. Add the onion, garlic and ginger and fry, stirring, until softened. Add the spices and cook for 2 minutes, stirring all the time.

5 Add the coconut milk, bring to the boil, then lower the heat and simmer for 5 minutes. Add the prawns and simmer for about 4 minutes or until they just begin to look opaque.

6 Add the spinach; it may be difficult to fit it all in but don't worry, it will reduce down as it cooks in the steam. Cover the pan with a lid or a baking tray and cook for about 3 minutes or until the spinach is wilted.

7 Stir the wilted spinach into the sauce and add the lime or lemon juice. Serve immediately.

COOK'S NOTE
Do not lift the lid while the spinach is cooking, otherwise all the steam will escape.

Prawns Fried with Okra

PREPARATION TIME: 25 MINUTES

COOKING TIME: 10 MINUTES

FREEZING: NOT SUITABLE

300 CALS PER SERVING

SERVES 4

700 g (1½ lb) large raw prawns in shells
450 g (1 lb) fresh okra
2 onions (preferably red)
2 small green chillies
1 garlic clove (optional)
3 medium ripe juicy tomatoes
45 ml (3 tbsp) ghee or oil

10 ml (2 tsp) ground cumin
15 ml (1 tbsp) mustard seeds
salt and pepper
squeeze of lemon juice, to taste
10 ml (2 tsp) garam masala
45 ml (3 tbsp) coarsely grated fresh coconut
or desiccated coconut, toasted

COOK'S NOTE
When trimming okra, snip only a tiny piece from each end. Avoid cutting into the flesh or the okra will become sticky and soggy during cooking.

1 Remove the heads from the prawns if necessary, then shell, leaving the tail end attached. Using a small sharp knife, make a shallow slit along the outer curve from the tail end to the head end and remove the dark intestinal vein. Rinse the prawns under cold running water. Drain and pat dry with kitchen paper.

2 Wash and trim the okra. Peel the onions and cut into thin rings. Slice the chillies, discarding the seeds if a milder flavour is preferred. Peel and slice the garlic, if using. Cut the tomatoes into small wedges.

3 Heat the ghee or oil in a wok or large heavy-based frying pan. Add the onions and cook over a high heat until browned. Add the okra, prawns, chillies, garlic if using, cumin and mustard seeds. Cook over a high heat, shaking the pan constantly, for 5 minutes or until the prawns are bright pink and the okra is softened but not soggy.

4 Add the tomato wedges and salt and pepper to taste. Cook for 1-2 minutes to heat through; the tomatoes should retain their shape. Add a little lemon juice, to taste.

5 Turn the mixture into a serving dish and sprinkle with the garam masala and coconut. Serve immediately.

Prawns and Cucumber in a Spicy Sauce

PREPARATION TIME:
20 MINUTES, PLUS STANDING

COOKING TIME: 30 MINUTES

FREEZING: NOT SUITABLE

450 CALS PER SERVING

SERVES 4

2 medium cucumbers
salt
2 onions
2 garlic cloves
50 g (2 oz) butter
20 ml (4 tsp) plain white flour
10 ml (2 tsp) ground turmeric
5 ml (1 tsp) ground cinnamon
10 ml (2 tsp) sugar

1.25 ml (¼ tsp) ground cloves
750 ml (1¼ pints) coconut milk
300 ml (½ pint) fish stock
15 g (½ oz) fresh root ginger
3-4 green chillies
450 g (1 lb) raw tiger prawns in shells
juice of 1 lime
30 ml (2 tbsp) chopped fresh coriander
coriander sprigs, to garnish

COOK'S NOTE
If raw prawns are difficult to come by, use cooked ones instead. Add them to the sauce and heat through for 2-3 minutes – no longer or they will become rubbery.

1 Cut the cucumbers in half lengthways and remove the seeds, using a teaspoon. Cut into 2.5 cm (1 inch) chunks. Place the cucumber in a colander set over a bowl and sprinkle with salt. Leave for 30 minutes, to allow the salt to extract the excess juices.

2 Peel and slice the onions; peel and chop the garlic. Melt the butter in a pan, add the onions and garlic and cook for about 5 minutes, until softened. Add the flour, turmeric, cinnamon, 5 ml (1 tsp) salt, the sugar and cloves; cook, stirring, for 2 minutes. Add the coconut milk and fish stock, bring to the boil and simmer for 5 minutes.

3 Meanwhile, rinse the cucumber thoroughly under cold running water to remove the salt. Peel the ginger and cut into very thin slices. Halve the chillies, remove the seeds and slice thinly.

4 Add the ginger, chillies and cucumber to the sauce, and continue to cook for a further 10 minutes.

5 Meanwhile, shell the prawns, leaving the tail end attached, if preferred. Using a small sharp knife, make a shallow slit along the back of each prawn and remove the dark intestinal vein. Rinse the prawns under cold running water and pat dry on kitchen paper. Add the prawns to the sauce and cook for a further 5-6 minutes until they turn pink.

6 Just before serving, stir in the lime juice and chopped coriander. Garnish with sprigs of coriander.

Stir-fried King Prawns on Sesame Noodles

PREPARATION TIME: 10 MINUTES

COOKING TIME: 10 MINUTES

FREEZING: NOT SUITABLE

410 CALS PER SERVING

SERVES 4

150 g (5 oz) mangetout
4 spring onions
7.5 cm (3 inch) piece fresh root ginger
10 ml (2 tsp) sesame seeds
5 ml (1 tsp) salt
250 g (9 oz) egg noodles
30 ml (2 tbsp) oil

16 raw king prawns in shells
juice of 1 lime
10 ml (2 tsp) shredded fresh coriander leaves
30 ml (2 tbsp) soy sauce
5 ml (1 tsp) sesame oil
lime wedges, to garnish

1 Top and tail the mangetout. Trim and roughly chop the spring onions. Peel and grate the ginger. Put the sesame seeds in a small, heavy-based pan and shake over a medium heat until they begin to turn golden and develop a toasted aroma. Tip the toasted sesame seeds out on to a saucer.

2 Bring a large pan of water to the boil, add the salt and mangetout and return to the boil. Simmer for 30 seconds, then drop in the egg noodles, turn off the heat and leave to stand for 6 minutes.

3 Meanwhile, heat the oil in a wide frying pan. Add the prawns and cook for 1½-2 minutes each side, scattering on the spring onions and ginger before you turn them. Squeeze on the lime juice and sprinkle on the coriander when the prawns are cooked.

4 Drain the noodles and mangetout and toss in the soy sauce, sesame oil and toasted sesame seeds. Transfer to a heated serving dish or individual plates. Arrange the prawns and spring onions on top and garnish with lime wedges.

Prawn and Glass Noodle Salad

PREPARATION TIME: 15 MINUTES

COOKING TIME: 1 MINUTE

FREEZING: NOT SUITABLE

350 CALS PER SERVING

SERVES 2

50 g (2 oz) glass (or cellophane) noodles
75 g (3 oz) shiitake mushrooms
1 large carrot
1 large courgette
12 large cooked prawns, shelled
15 ml (1 tbsp) toasted sesame seeds
30 ml (2 tbsp) chopped fresh coriander, to garnish

DRESSING
2 garlic cloves
15 ml (1 tbsp) light soy sauce
30 ml (2 tbsp) sugar
15 ml (1 tbsp) wine vinegar
15 ml (1 tbsp) sesame oil
1 red chilli

1 First make the dressing. Peel and crush the garlic and mix with the soy sauce, sugar, wine vinegar and sesame oil in a small bowl. Cut the chilli in half lengthways, remove the seeds, then cut into very fine strips. Mix into the dressing.

2 Cut the noodles into 10 cm (4 inch) lengths. Cook in boiling water for 1 minute or according to packet instructions. Drain thoroughly and refresh under cold running water. Drain again.

3 Trim the mushrooms and slice finely. Add to the dressing and mix thoroughly.

4 Cut the carrot and courgette into fine julienne, or matchstick strips.

5 Place the noodles in a bowl and add the mushrooms with the dressing, the carrot and courgette julienne, and the prawns. Toss the salad well to combine all the ingredients. Sprinkle with the sesame seeds and garnish with chopped coriander to serve.

VARIATIONS
Use other cooked seafood such as squid, mussels or crab meat, instead of prawns.
For a warm salad, do not refresh the cooked noodles with cold water. Simply drain and toss the hot noodles with the other ingredients.

Fruit and Prawn Salad with Chilli Dressing

PREPARATION TIME: 15 MINUTES

COOKING TIME: 2 MINUTES

FREEZING: NOT SUITABLE

240 CALS PER SERVING

SERVES 4

1 firm ripe papaya
1 pink grapefruit
1 small firm ripe mango
1 large firm ripe banana
12 large cooked prawns, or 4 cooked lobster tails
orange rind shreds, to garnish

DRESSING
25 ml (1½ tbsp) lemon juice
15 ml (1 tbsp) rice vinegar
15 ml (1 tbsp) caster sugar
5 ml (1 tsp) dark soy sauce
1.25 ml (¼ tsp) dried crushed red chillies
30 ml (2 tbsp) groundnut oil
pinch of salt

COOK'S NOTE
The best way to test the papaya and mango is by gently squeezing them. There should be a small amount of give, but the fruits should not feel soft.

1 First make the dressing. Place the lemon juice, vinegar, sugar, soy sauce and chillies in a small saucepan and heat gently to dissolve the sugar. Remove from the heat and whisk in the oil and salt. Leave to cool.

2 Prepare the fruits. Peel and halve the papaya, then scoop out the seeds and thinly slice the flesh. Peel the grapefruit, removing all of the white pith, and cut out the segments free from the membranes. Peel and stone the mango, then cut the flesh into slices. Peel and slice the banana.

3 Arrange the fruits on a large serving platter and spoon over the dressing. Peel the prawns or lobster tails, leaving on the tail end shells. Arrange on top of the salad and garnish with orange shreds. Serve immediately.

Mussels with Lemon Grass and Basil

PREPARATION TIME: 10 MINUTES
COOKING TIME: 5 MINUTES
FREEZING: NOT SUITABLE

120-60 CALS PER SERVING
SERVES 2-4

900 g (2 lb) fresh mussels in shells
7.5 cm (3 inch) piece fresh root ginger
2 lemon grass stalks

10 sprigs basil
torn basil leaves, to garnish

1 Scrub the mussels thoroughly under cold running water and pull away any straggly beards. Discard any opened mussels which do not close when tapped firmly. Peel and roughly chop the fresh root ginger. Slice the lemon grass into 7.5 cm (3 inch) pieces and lightly crush.
2 Place all the ingredients in a large saucepan and add enough water to come 1 cm (½ inch) up the sides of the pan.
3 Bring to the boil, cover and steam over a medium heat for about 5 minutes or until the mussels have opened. Discard any which remain closed. Drain and serve, garnished with torn basil leaves.

Thai Mussel Salad with Crispy Vegetables

PREPARATION TIME: 25 MINUTES
COOKING TIME: 8-10 MINUTES
FREEZING: NOT SUITABLE

280 CALS PER SERVING
SERVES 2

1 large carrot
1 large courgette
1 small head of fennel
10 ml (2 tsp) sea salt
48 fresh mussels in shells
oil for deep-frying
few basil or celery leaves, to garnish
50 g (2 oz) frisée (curly endive), to serve
STOCK
1 garlic clove
2.5 cm (1 inch) fresh root ginger

2 kaffir lime leaves
2 lemon grass stalks
2 red chillies
15 ml (1 tbsp) Thai fish sauce
DRESSING
45 ml (3 tbsp) lime juice
25 ml (1 fl oz) rice vinegar
25 g (1 oz) caster sugar
5 ml (1 tsp) dried crushed red chillies
2.5 ml (½ tsp) salt

COOK'S NOTE
If time permits, soak the mussels in a bowl of cold water with a handful of oatmeal added for several hours before cooking to help rid them of any grit.

1 Using a swivel vegetable peeler, pare the carrot, courgette and fennel into thin ribbons. Place in a colander and sprinkle with the salt. Set aside to drain for 30 minutes.
2 Meanwhile, scrub the mussels thoroughly under cold running water and pull away any straggly beards. Discard any opened mussels which do not close when tapped firmly. Set aside.
3 To make the stock, peel and slice the garlic and ginger; bruise the lime leaves, lemon grass stalks and red chillies. Place all the stock ingredients in a saucepan with 150 ml (¼ pint) cold water. Bring to the boil, cover and simmer for 10 minutes, then strain into a clean pan.
4 Add the mussels to the stock, bring to the boil, cover and cook over a high heat for 4-5 minutes or until the shells have opened. Discard any mussels that remain closed. Strain, reserving the liquid and immediately refresh the mussels under cold running water. Drain and set aside.
5 Place 60 ml (4 tbsp) of the reserved mussel liquid in a small pan. Add the dressing ingredients, heat gently to dissolve the sugar, then keep warm.
6 Wash the vegetables to remove the salt and pat dry thoroughly with kitchen paper.
7 Heat a 10 cm (4 inch) depth of oil in a deep saucepan to a temperature of 180°C (350°F) or until a cube of bread dropped in browns in 30 seconds. Deep-fry the vegetables in batches for 1 minute until crisp and golden. Drain on kitchen paper. When all the vegetables are cooked, deep-fry a few basil or celery leaves for the garnish.
8 Divide the frisée between four serving plates, top with the crispy vegetables and sit the mussels on top. Spoon over the warm dressing and serve at once, garnished with the crispy fried herbs.

Mussels in Spiced Coconut Milk

PREPARATION TIME: 20 MINUTES

COOKING TIME: 18 MINUTES

FREEZING: NOT SUITABLE

630-475 CALS PER SERVING

SERVES 3-4

Illustrated opposite

1.8 kg (4 lb) fresh mussels in shells
5 ml (1 tsp) fenugreek seeds
10 ml (2 tsp) cumin seeds
10 ml (2 tsp) coriander seeds
2 onions
4 garlic cloves
2.5 cm (1 inch) piece fresh root ginger
30 ml (2 tbsp) ghee or oil
4 cloves

1 cinnamon stick
3 dried red chillies
4 curry leaves (optional)
45 ml (3 tbsp) lime or lemon juice
600 ml (1 pint) coconut milk
salt
30 ml (2 tbsp) sesame seeds
coarsely grated fresh coconut, to garnish (optional)

1 To prepare the mussels, scrub thoroughly under cold running water and pull away any straggly beards. Discard any opened mussels which do not close when tapped firmly. Set aside.

2 Dry-fry the fenugreek, cumin and coriander seeds in a small heavy-based pan until they begin to release their aroma, shaking the pan frequently. Allow to cool, then crush using a pestle and mortar.

3 Peel and quarter the onions. Peel the garlic. Peel and halve the ginger. Put the onions, garlic and ginger in a blender or food processor with the dry-fried spices. Purée until smooth, adding a little water if necessary to prevent sticking.

4 Heat the ghee or oil in a large heavy-based saucepan or flameproof casserole. Add the onion mixture and fry for about 5 minutes until browned, stirring all the time. Add the cloves, cinnamon, chillies and curry leaves and fry for 2 minutes.

5 Add the lime or lemon juice, coconut milk, salt and 150 ml (¼ pint) water. Bring to the boil, lower heat and simmer for 5 minutes, stirring occasionally.

6 Add the mussels, cover with a tight-fitting lid and cook, shaking the pan occasionally, for 5 minutes or until the mussels have opened. Discard any that do not open.

7 Serve in warmed bowls, sprinkled with sesame seeds and garnished with coconut, if desired.

Crab Salad

PREPARATION TIME: 20 MINUTES

COOKING TIME: 3 MINUTES

FREEZING: NOT SUITABLE

165 CALS PER SERVING

SERVES 6

450 g (1 lb) white crab meat, thawed if frozen
6 spring onions
30 ml (2 tbsp) chopped fresh coriander
15 ml (1 tbsp) chopped fresh chives
pinch of cayenne pepper
2 garlic cloves
2.5 cm (1 inch) piece fresh root ginger
30 ml (2 tbsp) sunflower oil
2 kaffir lime leaves, shredded

2.5 ml (½ tsp) dried crushed chilli flakes
60 ml (4 tbsp) lime juice
15 ml (1 tbsp) sugar
5 ml (1 tsp) shrimp paste (optional)
15 ml (1 tbsp) Thai fish sauce or soy sauce
1-2 heads of radicchio or red chicory
50 g (2 oz) cucumber
25 g (1 oz) bean sprouts
lime wedges and coriander sprigs, to garnish

COOK'S NOTE

If you are lucky enough to obtain fresh cooked crabs you will need two, each about 1.4 kg (3 lb). The dark meat is not included in this dish but it can be frozen for future use.

1 Flake the white crab meat into shreds and place in a bowl. Finely chop the spring onions and add to the crab with the coriander, chives and cayenne pepper. Mix gently, then cover and chill until required.

2 Peel the garlic and ginger and crush together, using a pestle and mortar or spice grinder. Heat the oil in a small pan, add the garlic, ginger, lime leaves and chilli flakes and fry over a gentle heat for 3 minutes until softened but not brown. Add the lime juice, sugar, shrimp paste if using, and the fish or soy sauce. Stir well, then remove from the heat. Leave until cold.

3 Drizzle the cooled dressing over the crab mixture and toss lightly until evenly combined. Arrange the radicchio or chicory leaves on serving plates and spoon in the crab mixture. Thinly slice the cucumber and arrange on top of each serving with the bean sprouts. Garnish with lime wedges and coriander sprigs to serve.

VEGETARIAN DISHES

Indian and Asian cooking offers an abundance of healthy, flavour-filled dishes to add to a vegetarian diet. Mixed vegetables are turned into a delicious-tasting curry with the addition of chillies, fennel seeds and cardamoms, or transformed into a korma with a creamy almond spice sauce. Pulses are an Indian speciality – green lentils cooked with potatoes in a coconut sauce or combined with aubergines and mushrooms are two inspiring ideas drawn from the cuisine. Tofu, a popular Oriental ingredient, is given a new character when grilled and served with a plum sauce or stir-fried with bean sprouts, water chestnuts and broccoli in an oyster sauce. A hearty vegetable pilaf makes an ideal vegetarian meal, as do noodles when mixed with mangetout, red pepper and pak choi and tossed in a lime dressing. The possibilities are endless.

Illustration: Stir-fried Vegetables with Oyster Sauce (recipe page 162)

Cauliflower in Curry Sauce

PREPARATION TIME: 10 MINUTES

COOKING TIME: 20 MINUTES

FREEZING: NOT SUITABLE

260 CALS PER SERVING

SERVES 4

1 large cauliflower
1 small onion
2.5 cm (1 inch) piece fresh root ginger
90 ml (6 tbsp) ghee or oil
5 ml (1 tsp) black mustard seeds
5 ml (1 tsp) cumin seeds
5 ml (1 tsp) salt

5 ml (1 tsp) ground turmeric
3 tomatoes, skinned
1 small green chilli
2.5 ml (½ tsp) sugar
30 ml (2 tbsp) chopped fresh coriander
chapatis (see page 194), to serve

1 Divide the cauliflower into small florets, discarding the green leaves and tough stalks. Wash well and dry on kitchen paper. Peel and finely chop the onion and ginger.

2 Heat the ghee or oil in a heavy-based saucepan or flameproof casserole. Add the mustard seeds and, when they begin to pop, stir in the cumin seeds, onion, ginger, salt and turmeric. Fry for 2-3 minutes, stirring constantly.

3 Add the cauliflower and mix well to coat with the spice mixture. Finely chop the tomatoes and stir into the cauliflower. Deseed and chop the green chilli and stir into the pan with the sugar and half of the chopped coriander. Cover the pan tightly with a lid and cook gently for 15 minutes or until the cauliflower is tender but not mushy.

4 Uncover the pan and boil rapidly for 1-2 minutes to thicken the sauce. Transfer to a warmed serving dish and sprinkle with the remaining chopped coriander. Serve immediately with chapatis.

Green Lentil and Coconut Soup

PREPARATION TIME: 20 MINUTES

COOKING TIME:
ABOUT 40 MINUTES

FREEZING: SUITABLE

555 CALS PER SERVING

SERVES 4

Illustrated opposite

225 g (8 oz) whole green lentils
1 large onion
2 garlic cloves
350 g (12 oz) floury potatoes
50 g (2 oz) creamed coconut
60 ml (4 tbsp) oil
1.25 ml (¼ tsp) ground turmeric

10 ml (2 tsp) ground cumin
750 ml (1¼ pints) vegetable stock
300 ml (½ pint) coconut milk
finely grated rind of 1 lemon
salt and pepper
toasted fresh coconut and coriander sprigs, to garnish

1 Put the lentils into a sieve and wash thoroughly under cold running water. Drain well. Peel and chop the onion. Peel and crush the garlic. Peel and dice the potatoes. Roughly chop the creamed coconut.

2 Heat the oil in a large saucepan. Add the potatoes and fry gently for 5 minutes until beginning to colour. Remove with a slotted spoon and drain on kitchen paper.

3 Add the onion to the pan and fry gently for 10 minutes until soft. Add the garlic, turmeric and cumin and fry for 2-3 minutes. Add the chopped coconut, vegetable stock, coconut milk and lentils and bring to the boil. Reduce the heat, cover with a lid and simmer gently for 20 minutes until the lentils are just tender.

4 Add the potatoes and lemon rind and season with salt and pepper. Cook gently for a further 5 minutes until the potatoes are tender. Serve hot, garnished with toasted coconut and coriander sprigs.

Red Lentils with Aubergine and Mushrooms

PREPARATION TIME: 10 MINUTES

COOKING TIME: ABOUT 45 MINUTES

FREEZING: NOT SUITABLE

218 CALS PER SERVING

SERVES 6

350 g (12 oz) split red lentils
2 garlic cloves
5 ml (1 tsp) ground turmeric
1 aubergine, trimmed
225 g (8 oz) mushrooms
2.5 ml (½ tsp) light muscovado sugar
salt and pepper

15 ml (1 tbsp) sunflower oil
5 ml (1 tsp) cumin seeds
5 ml (1 tsp) black mustard seeds
2.5 ml (½ tsp) fennel seeds
5 ml (1 tsp) garam masala
fresh coriander, to garnish

1 Put the lentils into a sieve and wash thoroughly under cold running water. Drain well.

2 Peel and crush the garlic and put in a large saucepan with the lentils and turmeric. Cover with 1.5 litres (2½ pints) water. Boil rapidly for 10 minutes, lower the heat and simmer for about 15 minutes more.

3 Meanwhile, cut the aubergine into 2.5 cm (1 inch) cubes. Halve the mushrooms. Add the aubergine and mushrooms to the lentils with the sugar and salt and pepper. Continue simmering gently for 15-20 minutes until the vegetables are tender.

4 Heat the oil in a small saucepan and fry the remaining spices for 1 minute or until the mustard seeds begin to pop.

5 Stir the spice mixture into the lentils, cover the pan with a tight-fitting lid and remove from the heat. Leave to stand for 5 minutes for the flavours to develop. Turn into a warmed serving dish and garnish with coriander.

Spiced Mixed Vegetable Pot

PREPARATION TIME: 20 MINUTES

COOKING TIME: ABOUT 1 HOUR

FREEZING: NOT SUITABLE

240 CALS PER SERVING

SERVES 6

5 ml (1 tsp) cumin seeds
15 ml (1 tbsp) coriander seeds
5 ml (1 tsp) mustard seeds
3 onions
450 g (1 lb) carrots
350 g (12 oz) leeks
350 g (12 oz) mooli (white radish)
450 g (1 lb) button mushrooms

2 garlic cloves
25 g (1 oz) fresh root ginger
45 ml (3 tbsp) oil
1.25 ml (¼ tsp) ground turmeric
175 g (6 oz) split red lentils
50 g (2 oz) brown or green lentils
salt and pepper
60 ml (4 tbsp) chopped fresh coriander

1 Crush the cumin, coriander and mustard seeds in a mortar with a pestle.

2 Peel and slice the onions and carrots; slice the leeks. Peel and roughly chop the mooli; halve the mushrooms if large. Peel and crush the garlic. Peel and grate the ginger.

3 Heat the oil in a very large flameproof casserole. Add the onions, carrots, leeks and mooli, and fry for 2-3 minutes, stirring constantly. Add the mushrooms, garlic, ginger, turmeric and crushed spices, and fry for a further 2-3 minutes, stirring.

4 Stir in the lentils with 750 ml (1¼ pints) boiling water. Season with salt and pepper and return to the boil. Cover and cook at 180°C (350°F) Mark 4 for about 45 minutes or until the vegetables and lentils are tender. Stir in the chopped coriander before serving.

Sour Chick Peas with Tomatoes

PREPARATION TIME:
20 MINUTES, PLUS SOAKING

COOKING TIME: 1½ HOURS

FREEZING: SUITABLE

455 CALS PER SERVING

SERVES 4

350 g (12 oz) chick peas
2 large onions
4 garlic cloves
5 cm (2 inch) piece fresh root ginger
15 ml (1 tbsp) cumin seeds
15 ml (1 tbsp) coriander seeds
60 ml (4 tbsp) oil
2.5 ml (½ tsp) dried chilli flakes
finely grated rind and juice of 2 limes

25 ml (5 tsp) tamarind juice
150 ml (¼ pint) vegetable stock
two 400g (14 oz) cans chopped tomatoes
45 ml (3 tbsp) chopped fresh coriander
15 ml (1 tbsp) caster sugar
5 ml (1 tsp) salt
coriander leaves, to garnish
naan bread, to serve

COOK'S NOTE
For a thicker sauce, return
the casserole to the hob
after baking in the oven, and
bubble down for 5 minutes.

1 Cover the chick peas with plenty of cold water and leave to soak overnight. Drain the chick peas and put in a large saucepan. Cover with plenty of water and bring to the boil. Boil rapidly for 10 minutes, then drain.

2 Peel and chop the onions. Peel and crush the garlic. Peel and finely grate the ginger. Lightly crush the cumin and coriander seeds using a pestle and mortar.

3 Heat the oil in large, flameproof casserole dish. Add the onions and fry gently for 5 minutes. Add the chilli, garlic, ginger and crushed seeds and cook for 1 minute. Add the chick peas, lime rind and juice, tamarind juice, vegetable stock and tomatoes and bring to the boil. Cover with a lid and bake at 170°C (325°F) Mark 3 for 1-1¼ hours or until the chick peas are tender and juices are pulpy.

4 Stir in the chopped coriander, sugar and salt and return to the oven for a further 15 minutes. Scatter with coriander leaves and serve hot or cold with naan bread.

Spiced Dal Croquettes

PREPARATION TIME:
15 MINUTES, PLUS SOAKING
AND CHILLING

COOKING TIME: 15 MINUTES

FREEZING: SUITABLE

235 CALS PER SERVING

SERVES 4

225 g (8 oz) moong dal (mung bean)
5 ml (1 tsp) caraway seeds, crushed
2.5 ml (½ tsp) chilli powder
5 ml (1 tsp) garam masala
2.5 ml (½ tsp) ground turmeric

salt and pepper
about 60 ml (4 tbsp) ghee or oil
300 ml (½ pint) natural yogurt
30 ml (2 tbsp) chopped fresh mint

COOK'S NOTE
As the dal are not cooked
before being ground to a
paste, it is essential to soak
them for the full 24 hours or
they will not be soft enough
to grind.

1 Put the dal into a sieve and wash thoroughly under cold running water. Drain well.

2 Put the dal in a bowl and cover with cold water. Leave to soak for 24 hours.

3 Drain the dal, then work in batches in a food processor until ground to a fine paste. Add the spices and 2.5 ml (½ tsp) salt and work again until thoroughly mixed in.

4 Heat a little ghee in a heavy-based frying pan until smoking hot. Add spoonfuls of the croquette mixture and fry for 2-3 minutes on each side until lightly coloured. Remove the croquettes with a slotted spoon, then drain well on kitchen paper while frying the remainder. Add more ghee to the pan as necessary.

5 Put the yogurt in a blender or food processor with the mint and salt and pepper to taste. Work to a thin sauce.

6 Place the hot cakes in a shallow serving dish and pour over the yogurt sauce. Cover the dish and chill for at least 2 hours before serving. Serve chilled.

Skewered Tofu with Spiced Plum Sauce

PREPARATION TIME: 20 MINUTES

COOKING TIME: ABOUT 8
MINUTES

FREEZING: NOT SUITABLE

590 CALS PER SERVING

SERVES 4

Illustrated opposite

450 g (1 lb) firm tofu
2 garlic cloves
1 small red chilli
15 ml (1 tbsp) sesame oil
15 ml (1 tbsp) vegetable oil
5 ml (1 tsp) caster sugar
salt
1 large red pepper
1 large orange pepper

1 lime
15 ml (1 tbsp) sesame seeds

SPICED PLUM SAUCE
2 spring onions
90 ml (6 tbsp) plum sauce
juice of 1 lime
2.5 ml (½ tsp) Chinese five-spice powder

COOK'S NOTES
These skewers are not
suitable for barbecuing.

Ready-made plum sauce is
widely available from
supermarkets.

1 Cut the tofu into 2 cm (¾ inch) chunks and thoroughly drain on kitchen paper.

2 Peel and crush the garlic. Deseed and finely chop the chilli. Mix the garlic and chilli with the oils, sugar and a little salt.

3 Deseed the red and orange peppers and cut the flesh into chunks. Thread the tofu and peppers onto 8 bamboo skewers. Cut the lime into 8 wedges and reserve.

4 Place the skewers on a foil-lined grill rack and brush generously with the garlic and oil mixture. Sprinkle with the sesame seeds and cook under a medium grill for about 8 minutes, until browned, turning very carefully half way through cooking.

5 Meanwhile, trim the spring onions and slice diagonally, as thinly as possible. Place in a small saucepan with the plum sauce, lime juice, five-spice powder and 30 ml (2 tbsp) water. Stir in any leftover garlic and oil mixture and heat through gently for 2 minutes.

6 Serve the skewers at once with the hot sauce and the lime wedges for squeezing over.

Thai Grilled Vegetables

PREPARATION TIME:
20 MINUTES, PLUS MARINATING

COOKING TIME: 25 MINUTES

FREEZING: NOT SUITABLE

350 CALS PER SERVING
SERVES 4

2 small red chillies
15 g (½ oz) fresh root ginger
2 garlic cloves
grated rind and juice of 1 large lime
400 ml (14 fl oz) can coconut milk
5 ml (1 tsp) soft brown sugar
15 ml (1 tbsp) peanut butter

1 lemon grass stalk, about 15 cm (6 inches)
450 g (1 lb) courgettes
1 bunch spring onions
450 g (1 lb) asparagus
125 g (4 oz) rice noodles
red chilli, to garnish

1 To make the marinade, deseed the chillies; peel the ginger; peel and crush the garlic. Place the chillies, ginger and garlic in a blender or food processor with the lime rind and juice, the coconut milk, sugar and peanut butter. Process until smooth. Lightly crush the lemon grass and add to the marinade.

2 Thickly slice the courgettes and spring onions. Trim the asparagus. Place all the vegetables in the marinade, cover and leave in a cool place for at least 1 hour.

3 Remove vegetables from the marinade; discard the lemon grass. Reserve the marinade. Grill or barbecue the vegetables in batches, turning occasionally, for 5-10 minutes until tender.

4 Meanwhile cook the noodles according to the packet instructions and drain.

5 Place the reserved marinade in a small saucepan, bring to the boil and reduce to a syrupy consistency. Toss through the noodles and serve with the vegetables. Garnish with red chilli.

Eggs Fu-yung

PREPARATION TIME: 10 MINUTES

COOKING TIME:
ABOUT 5 MINUTES

FREEZING: NOT SUITABLE

480-240 CALS PER SERVING

SERVES 2-4

8 spring onions
125 g (4 oz) shiitake or oyster mushrooms
125 g (4 oz) canned bamboo shoots
½ green pepper
45 ml (3 tbsp) groundnut or vegetable oil
125 g (4 oz) frozen peas, thawed

6 eggs
salt
2 good pinches chilli powder
15 ml (1 tbsp) light soy sauce
spring onion curls, to garnish

1 Trim and slice the spring onions; slice the mushrooms; drain and chop the bamboo shoots; deseed and dice the green pepper.

2 Heat the oil in a wok or large frying pan, add the spring onions, mushrooms, bamboo shoots, green pepper and peas and stir fry for 2-3 minutes.

3 Beat the eggs, then season with salt and chilli powder. Pour the egg into the pan and continue to cook stirring, until the egg mixture is set.

4 Sprinkle over the soy sauce and stir well. Serve at once, garnished with spring onion curls.

VARIATIONS
Replace the green pepper with 75 g (3 oz) thinly sliced ham or cooked peeled prawns.

Cumin Courgettes with Paneer

PREPARATION TIME:
25 MINUTES, PLUS PRESSING

COOKING TIME: ABOUT 30
MINUTES

FREEZING: CUMIN COURGETTES
ONLY (STAGE 6)

420 CALS PER SERVING

SERVES 6

125 g (4 oz) onion
450 g (1 lb) tomatoes
900 g (2 lb) courgettes
45 ml (3 tbsp) oil
5 ml (1 tsp) ground turmeric
5 ml (1 tsp) chilli powder
10 ml (2 tsp) white cumin seeds

30 ml (2 tbsp) tomato purée
salt and pepper
PANEER
2.3 litres (4 pints) full-fat milk
about 75 ml (5 tbsp) strained lemon juice
oil for frying

1 To make the paneer, bring the milk to the boil in a deep saucepan. As soon as it boils, remove from the heat and add the lemon juice. Stir thoroughly, then return to the heat for about 1 minute; the curds and whey should separate very quickly. Immediately remove the pan from the heat.

2 Line a large sieve or colander with a double thickness of muslin and place over a large bowl. Pour the curds and whey into the muslin and leave until cool enough to handle.

3 Gather up the muslin around the curds and squeeze to remove the excess whey; discard the whey. Place the wrapped curds on a chopping board. Put a small board on top and weight it down with a few large cans or weights. Leave for 3-4 hours until the cheese feels firm.

4 Peel and slice the onion. Remove the skins from the tomatoes and roughly chop. Slice the courgettes into 5 mm (¼ inch) pieces.

5 Heat the oil in a large frying pan and fry the onions until well browned. Add the courgettes with the turmeric, chilli powder and cumin seeds. Fry gently for 2-3 minutes, stirring.

6 Add the tomatoes, tomato purée and 150 ml (¼ pint) water. Season with salt and pepper. Bring to the boil, cover and simmer for 15-20 minutes or until the courgettes are just tender.

7 Meanwhile, remove the muslin from the paneer and cut into 1 cm (½ inch) cubes. Heat 2.5 cm (1 inch) depth of oil in a deep frying pan and fry the paneer cubes a few at a time without stirring until brown. Drain on kitchen paper.

8 Stir the paneer cubes into the courgette mixture and heat gently for 1-2 minutes. Serve.

COOK'S NOTE
If the curds and whey do not separate in stage 1, add another 15 ml (1 tbsp) lemon juice and reheat.

Sesame and Cabbage Rolls

PREPARATION TIME: 25 MINUTES

COOKING TIME: ABOUT 20 MINUTES

FREEZING: SUITABLE (STAGE 4)

170 CALS PER ROLL

MAKES 12-14

Illustrated opposite

50 g (2 oz) dried shiitake mushrooms
450 g (1 lb) cabbage
225 g (8 oz) canned bamboo shoots
1 bunch spring onions
4 garlic cloves
45 ml (3 tbsp) sesame oil
60 ml (4 tbsp) sesame seeds

45 ml (3 tbsp) soy sauce
2.5 ml (½ tsp) caster sugar
two 270 g (10 oz) packs filo pastry
1 egg, beaten
oil for deep-frying
spiced plum sauce (see page 158), to serve

1 Cover the mushrooms with boiling water and leave to soak for 20 minutes. Finely shred the cabbage, discarding the core. Thoroughly drain the bamboo shoots. Trim and chop the spring onions. Peel and crush the garlic.

2 Heat the sesame oil in a large wok or frying pan. Add the garlic and sesame seeds and fry gently until golden brown. Add the cabbage and spring onions and fry, stirring, for 3 minutes.

3 Thoroughly drain and roughly slice the mushrooms. Add to the pan with the bamboo shoots, soy sauce and sugar and stir until evenly combined. Leave to cool.

4 Cut the filo pastry into 18 cm (7 inch) squares. Keep the filo squares covered with a damp tea-towel as you work. Place 1 square of filo on the work surface and cover with a second square. Place a heaped tablespoon of the filling across the centre of one square to within 2.5 cm (1 inch) of the ends. Fold the 2.5 cm (1 inch) ends of pastry over the filling. Brush one unfolded edge of the pastry with a little beaten egg, then roll up to make a thick parcel shape. Shape the remaining pastry and filling in the same way.

5 Heat a 5 cm (2 inch) depth of oil in a deep-fat fryer or large heavy-based saucepan to 180°C (350°F) or until a cube of bread dropped into the oil browns in 30 seconds. Fry a batch of rolls for about 3 minutes or until crisp and golden. Remove with a slotted spoon and drain on kitchen paper; keep warm while frying the remainder.

6 Serve hot with the plum sauce for dipping.

Stir-fried Vegetables with Oyster Sauce

PREPARATION TIME: 30 MINUTES

COOKING TIME: 12-15 MINUTES

FREEZING: NOT SUITABLE

300 CALS PER SERVING

SERVES 4

175 g (6 oz) firm tofu
oil for deep-frying
2 garlic cloves
1 green pepper
225 g (8 oz) broccoli
125 g (4 oz) yard-long beans or French beans
50 g (2 oz) bean sprouts
50 g (2 oz) canned straw mushrooms
125 g (4 oz) canned water chestnuts
30 ml (2 tbsp) oil

30 ml (2 tbsp) chopped fresh coriander, to garnish

SAUCE
100 ml (3½ fl oz) vegetable stock
30 ml (2 tbsp) oyster sauce
15 ml (1 tbsp) light soy sauce
10 ml (2 tsp) clear honey
5 ml (1 tsp) cornflour
pinch of salt

COOK'S NOTE
Canned straw mushrooms are available from larger supermarkets and Oriental food stores. As an alternative use small fresh button mushrooms, adding them to the stir-fry 2 minutes earlier than the bean sprouts.

1 Drain the tofu, dry well on kitchen paper and cut into large cubes. Heat a 10 cm (4 inch) depth of oil in a deep saucepan until it registers 180°C (350°F) on a thermometer or until a cube of bread dropped into the oil browns in 30 seconds. Add the tofu and deep-fry for 1-2 minutes until crisp and golden. Drain on kitchen paper; set aside.

2 Blend all the ingredients for the sauce together and set aside.

3 Peel and thinly slice the garlic; deseed and slice the green pepper. Cut the broccoli into small florets and any stalk into thin slices. Trim the beans and cut into short lengths; wash and dry the bean sprouts; drain the mushrooms and water chestnuts.

4 Heat the 30 ml (2 tbsp) oil in a wok or large frying pan, add the garlic and fry for 1 minute. Remove the garlic and discard. Add the green pepper, broccoli and beans, and stir-fry for 3 minutes. Add the bean sprouts, mushrooms and water chestnuts and stir-fry for 1 minute.

5 Add the tofu together with the sauce and bring to the boil. Simmer covered for 3-4 minutes until the vegetables are tender. Sprinkle with the chopped coriander and serve at once.

Gingered Stir-fried Vegetables

PREPARATION TIME: 15 MINUTES

COOKING TIME: 10 MINUTES

FREEZING: NOT SUITABLE

440-290 CALS PER SERVING

SERVES 4-6

2 garlic cloves
2.5 cm (1 inch) piece fresh root ginger
1-2 red chillies
900 g (2 lb) mixed vegetables
60 ml (4 tbsp) oil
125 g (4 oz) cashew nuts, peanuts or almonds

15 ml (1 tbsp) light soy sauce
15 ml (1 tbsp) dry sherry
5 ml (1 tsp) sugar
5 ml (1 tsp) Chinese five-spice powder (optional)

1 Peel and crush the garlic; peel and slice the ginger; deseed and chop the chillies. Prepare the mixed vegetables as necessary, and cut into thin strips or slices.

2 Heat the oil in a wok or large deep frying pan. Add the garlic, ginger and chillies, and stir-fry for 1-2 minutes. Add the nuts and cook for 2 minutes, stirring all the time. Remove the nuts with a slotted spoon and set aside.

3 Add slower-cooking vegetables to the oil remaining in the wok. Cook over a very high heat for 3-4 minutes, stirring all the time. Add the remaining vegetables and cook for a further 2-3 minutes or until heated through but still very crisp.

4 Add the soy sauce, sherry, sugar and five-spice powder, if using. Cook for a further minute, then transfer to a warmed serving dish. Sprinkle with the nuts and serve immediately.

Mushroom Chow Mein

PREPARATION TIME: 15 MINUTES

COOKING TIME: 10 MINUTES

FREEZING: NOT SUITABLE

380 CALS PER SERVING

SERVES 4

3 garlic cloves
1 large green chilli
350 g (12 oz) mixed mushrooms, such as oyster, brown-cap and field
175 g (6 oz) egg noodles
10 ml (2 tsp) dark soy sauce
20 ml (4 tsp) dry sherry

5 ml (1 tsp) sesame oil
5 ml (1 tsp) cornflour
5 ml (1 tsp) sugar
45 ml (3 tbsp) vegetable oil
salt and pepper
coriander omelette (see page 169), to serve

1 Peel and slice the garlic; deseed and slice the chilli. Slice the mushrooms as necessary.

2 Cook the noodles according to the packet instructions. Rinse thoroughly in cold water and leave to drain.

3 Mix the soy sauce with the sherry, sesame oil, cornflour and sugar.

4 Heat the vegetable oil in a wok or large, nonstick frying pan and fry the garlic and chilli for 2 minutes. Add the mushrooms and fry for 2-3 minutes. Stir in the noodles and the soy sauce mixture and bring to the boil. Bubble for 2-3 minutes, until well combined and piping hot. Season with salt and pepper.

5 Serve garnished with thin slices of cold, rolled-up omelette.

Vegetable Biryani

PREPARATION TIME: 20 MINUTES

COOKING TIME: 45 MINUTES

FREEZING: NOT SUITABLE

485 CALS PER SERVING

SERVES 4

350 g (12 oz) basmati rice
1 large onion
2.5 cm (1 inch) piece fresh root ginger
1-2 garlic cloves
3 carrots
225 g (8 oz) French beans
salt and pepper
50 g (2 oz) ghee or oil
5 ml (1 tsp) ground coriander

10 ml (2 tsp) ground cumin
5 ml (1 tsp) ground turmeric
2.5 ml (½ tsp) chilli powder
225 g (8 oz) small cauliflower florets
5 ml (1 tsp) garam masala
juice of 1 lemon
hard-boiled egg slices and coriander sprigs, to garnish

1 Put the rice in a sieve and rinse under cold running water until the water runs clear.

2 Peel and chop the onion; peel and grate the ginger; peel and crush the garlic; peel and thinly slice the carrots; trim and halve the French beans.

3 Put the rice in a saucepan with 600 ml (1 pint) water and 5 ml (1 tsp) salt. Bring to the boil, then reduce the heat and simmer for 10 minutes or until only just tender.

4 Meanwhile, heat the ghee or oil in a large heavy-based saucepan, add the onion, ginger and garlic and fry gently for 5 minutes or until soft but not coloured. Add the coriander, cumin, turmeric and chilli powder and fry for 2 minutes more, stirring constantly to prevent the spices catching and burning.

5 Remove the rice from the heat and drain. Add 900 ml (1½ pints) water to the onion and spice mixture and season with salt and pepper. Stir well bring to the boil. Add the carrots and beans and simmer for 15 minutes, then add the cauliflower and simmer for a further 10 minutes. Lastly, add the rice. Fold gently to mix and simmer until reheated.

6 Stir the garam masala and lemon juice into the biryani and simmer for a few minutes more to reheat and allow the flavours to develop. Taste and adjust the seasoning, if necessary, then turn into a warmed serving dish. Garnish with egg slices and coriander and serve immediately.

Basmati Vegetable Pilaf

PREPARATION TIME: 20 MINUTES

COOKING TIME: 25-30 MINUTES

FREEZING: NOT SUITABLE

520 CALS PER SERVING

SERVES 4

Illustrated opposite

1 small cauliflower
225 g (8 oz) baby carrots
2 courgettes
175 g (6 oz) patty pans
175 g (6 oz) okra
handful of baby spinach leaves (optional)
1 onion
15 ml (1 tbsp) sunflower oil
5 ml (1 tsp) green cardamom pods, seeds removed and crushed

5 ml (1 tsp) cumin seeds
5 ml (1 tsp) black mustard seeds (optional)
2 long cinnamon sticks
10 ml (2 tsp) garam masala
275 g (10 oz) brown basmati rice
300 ml (½ pint) vegetable stock
150 ml (¼ pint) apple juice
400 g (14 oz) can tomatoes
30 ml (2 tbsp) pumpkin seeds
raita (see page 199), to serve

COOK'S NOTE

If you are following a vegetarian diet, seeds play a very beneficial part, providing useful amounts of the B vitamins. Pumpkin, sunflower, sesame and poppy seeds are readily available from most large supermarkets.

1 Break the cauliflower into small even-sized florets. Scrub the carrots and leave whole, trimming the root and leaving on a tuft of stalk. Cut the courgettes into 2.5 cm (1 inch) chunks. Cut the patty pans in half; trim the okra. Clean the spinach thoroughly, if using.

2 Peel the onion and cut into large chunks. Heat the oil in a large nonstick pan, add the onion and fry gently until soft. Stir in the spices and cook for a few minutes to release the flavours.

3 Wash the basmati rice in a sieve under cold running water; drain well. Add to the pan, stirring well to coat with the oil and spices. Pour in the hot vegetable stock, add the apple juice and the tomatoes with their juice. Bring to the boil and simmer for 10 minutes.

4 Stir in the prepared vegetables, except the spinach. Cover and simmer gently for 15-20 minutes, until just tender but still firm. Add the spinach leaves, if using, and fold in until just wilted.

5 Place the pumpkin seeds on a baking tray and toast under the grill for a few minutes until golden. To serve, stir the pumpkin seeds into the pilaf and accompany with raita.

Eggs with Coconut and Coriander Noodles

PREPARATION TIME: 5 MINUTES

COOKING TIME: 38 MINUTES

FREEZING: NOT SUITABLE

605 CALS PER SERVING

SERVES 6

10 spring onions
2 medium chillies, one red, one green
30 ml (2 tbsp) oil
10 ml (2 tsp) ground turmeric
10 ml (2 tsp) English mustard or mustard powder
two 400 ml (14 fl oz) cans coconut milk
30 ml (2 tbsp) lemon juice
10 ml (2 tsp) sugar

salt and pepper
6 hard-boiled eggs

CORIANDER NOODLES
two 250 g (8 oz) packets medium egg noodles
salt and pepper
15 ml (1 tbsp) sesame oil
60 ml (4 tbsp) chopped fresh coriander

COOK'S NOTE

If you can't find cans of coconut milk, use 120 ml (8 tbsp) coconut milk powder mixed with 900 ml (1½ pints) warm water in its place, then mix 20 ml (4 tsp) cornflour with a little water and stir in after stage 3 to thicken the sauce.

1 Trim and finely slice the spring onions. Deseed and finely slice the chillies.

2 Heat the oil in a saucepan. Gently fry the spring onions until just beginning to soften, then add the chilli, turmeric and mustard. Cook for about 1 minute.

3 Stir in the coconut milk, lemon juice and sugar. Season well, bring to the boil, stirring all the time, then simmer very gently for about 30 minutes, stirring.

4 Add the halved eggs and simmer for a further 5 minutes or until the eggs are completely warmed through.

5 Meanwhile, cook the noodles according to packet instructions, adding a pinch of salt and 10 ml (2 tsp) sesame oil to the water. Drain well, then toss with the remaining sesame oil and chopped coriander. Season to taste.

6 Serve the eggs and sauce on a bed of the coriander noodles.

Chinese Noodles with Roasted Peanuts and Chilli

PREPARATION TIME: 20 MINUTES

COOKING TIME: 15 MINUTES

FREEZING: NOT SUITABLE

350 CALS PER SERVING

SERVES 4

1 red chilli
3 garlic cloves
1 onion
15 ml (1 tbsp) oil
2 pieces stem ginger
125 g (4 oz) raw peanuts, toasted
225 ml (8 fl oz) vegetable stock

30 ml (2 tbsp) light soy sauce
1 bunch spring onions
1 red pepper
100 ml (4 fl oz) yellow bean sauce
225 g (8 oz) thread egg noodles
salt and pepper
small handful of torn coriander, to garnish

1 Deseed and roughly chop the chilli. Peel and roughly chop the garlic. Peel and roughly chop the onion.

2 Heat the oil in a heavy-based frying pan, add the chilli, garlic and onion and fry for about 3-4 minutes.

3 Slice the stem ginger and place in a food processor with half the peanuts, the cooked onion mixture, the stock and soy sauce. Process until well combined.

4 Trim and finely slice the spring onions lengthways, then cut across into 2.5 cm (1 inch) slices. Deseed and roughly dice the red pepper.

5 Place the peanut mixture in a saucepan and add the spring onions, red pepper and yellow bean sauce. Heat gently for 5 minutes.

6 Meanwhile, cook the noodles according to the packet instructions. Drain well and add to the prepared sauce. Heat through gently for 2 minutes, adding salt and pepper to taste. Turn out onto serving plates and serve scattered with the remaining peanuts and the torn coriander.

VARIATION
Add 75 g (3 oz) blanched mangetout with the noodles at stage 6.

Crispy Noodles with Vegetables

PREPARATION TIME: 20 MINUTES

COOKING TIME: ABOUT 10 MINUTES

FREEZING: NOT SUITABLE

390 CALS PER SERVING

SERVES 4

125 g (4 oz) rice vermicelli noodles or rice sticks
oil for deep-frying
2.5 cm (1 inch) piece fresh root ginger
175 g (6 oz) shiitake or button mushrooms
few Chinese leaves
1 red chilli
15 ml (1 tbsp) peanut or vegetable oil
125 g (4 oz) mangetout
75 g (3 oz) bean sprouts

30 ml (2 tbsp) soy sauce
30 ml (2 tbsp) dry sherry
5 ml (1 tsp) sugar

CORIANDER OMELETTE
2 eggs
30 ml (2 tbsp) milk
45 ml (3 tbsp) chopped fresh coriander
salt and pepper
a little oil or butter for frying

COOK'S NOTE
Do not cook too many noodles at a time as they expand on cooking.

1 To make the omelette, put the eggs, milk, coriander and seasoning in a jug and whisk together, using a fork.

2 Heat a little oil or butter in an omelette pan or small frying pan. Pour in the egg mixture and cook over a high heat until it begins to set.

3 Turn the omelette out onto a sheet of nonstick baking parchment and leave to cool. When cool, roll up and cut into thin slices.

4 Break the noodles into lengths, about 7.5 cm (3 inches) long. Heat the oil in a deep-fat fryer to 175°C (345°F), or until a cube of bread browns in 1 minute. Deep-fry a small handful of noodles at a time for about 30 seconds until they swell and puff up. Remove from the pan with a slotted spoon and drain on crumpled kitchen paper.

5 Peel and shred the ginger. Thickly slice the mushrooms. Coarsely shred the Chinese leaves. Slice the chilli, removing the seeds if a milder flavour is preferred.

6 Heat the peanut oil in a wok. Add the mushrooms and ginger and stir-fry over a high heat for 2 minutes. Add the chilli, mangetout, bean sprouts and shredded leaves and stir-fry for 1 minute. Add the soy sauce, sherry and sugar and cook for 1 minute to heat through. Add the noodles to the pan and toss to mix lightly, being careful not to crush them.

7 Turn the vegetables and noodles into a warmed serving bowl and top with the omelette shreds. Serve immediately.

Oriental Tofu and Bean Salad

PREPARATION TIME:
10 MINUTES, PLUS MARINATING AND COOLING

COOKING TIME: 5 MINUTES

FREEZING: NOT SUITABLE

215 CALS PER SERVING

SERVES 4

2.5 cm (1 inch) piece fresh root ginger
30 ml (2 tbsp) dark soy sauce
30 ml (2 tbsp) dry sherry
30 ml (2 tbsp) orange juice
pepper
175 g (6 oz) smoked firm tofu
1 garlic clove

125 g (4 oz) mangetout
4 spring onions
15 ml (1 tbsp) sesame or vegetable oil
½ head Chinese leaves
400 g (14 oz) canned black-eyed beans, drained

1 Peel and finely grate the ginger. Put in a bowl with the soy sauce, sherry, orange juice and pepper to taste and mix well. Cut the tofu into 1 cm (½ inch) cubes and stir it into the mixture. Leave to marinate for 1 hour. Drain the tofu, reserving the marinade.

2 Peel and finely chop the garlic; trim the mangetout; trim and finely slice the spring onions.

3 Heat the oil in large nonstick frying pan. Add the tofu and cook stirring, for 2 minutes. Add the garlic, mangetout and spring onions and stir-fry for a further 2 minutes. Transfer to a bowl and leave to cool.

4 Finely shred the Chinese leaves. Wash and dry and place in a large salad bowl.

5 Rinse and drain the beans and add to the cold tofu mixture with the reserved marinade. Mix together and pile on top of the Chinese leaves. Carefully toss the salad before serving.

Hot and Sour Noodle and Vegetable Salad

PREPARATION TIME:
30 MINUTES, PLUS OPTIONAL
CHILLING

COOKING TIME: 3-4 MINUTES

FREEZING: NOT SUITABLE

345 CALS PER SERVING

SERVES 4

Illustrated opposite

2 carrots
50 g (2 oz) baby sweetcorn
50 g (2 oz) mangetout
50 g (2 oz) broccoli florets
1 small red pepper
125 g (4 oz) Chinese cabbage or pak choi
2 garlic cloves
50 g (2 oz) canned water chestnuts, drained
30 ml (2 tbsp) peanut or sunflower oil
15 ml (1 tbsp) sesame oil
5 ml (1 tsp) dried crushed chilli flakes
5 ml (1 tsp) grated fresh root ginger

75 g (3 oz) rice vermicelli noodles
30 ml (2 tbsp) chopped fresh coriander
25 g (1 oz) raw peanuts, toasted and chopped, to garnish

DRESSING
30 ml (2 tbsp) peanut oil
5 ml (1 tsp) chilli oil
10 ml (2 tsp) caster sugar
30 ml (2 tbsp) lime juice
15 ml (1 tbsp) rice vinegar
15 ml (1 tbsp) Thai fish sauce
salt and pepper

1 Cut the carrots into matchsticks; halve the baby sweetcorn lengthways if large; top and tail the mangetout; cut the broccoli into small florets. Deseed and thinly slice the red pepper; roughly shred the Chinese cabbage or pak choi; peel and crush the garlic; slice the water chestnuts.

2 Place the two oils in a small pan, add the garlic, chilli flakes and ginger and heat until smoking. Strain the oil into a wok or large frying pan. Add the prepared vegetables and stir-fry for 2-3 minutes until just starting to wilt. Immediately remove the pan from the heat.

3 Soak the noodles according to the packet instructions. Meanwhile, whisk all the dressing ingredients together, seasoning with salt and pepper to taste. Strain the cooked noodles and toss with a little of the dressing.

4 Stir the remaining dressing into the vegetables together with the chopped coriander. Arrange the noodles and vegetables on individual serving plates. Scatter over the toasted peanuts and serve at once or chill for up to 1 hour before serving.

Vegetable Salad with Peanut Dressing

PREPARATION TIME: 15 MINUTES

COOKING TIME: 20 MINUTES

FREEZING: NOT SUITABLE

330 CALS PER SERVING

SERVES 6

125 g (4 oz) roasted salted peanuts
125 g (4 oz) shallots or onions
25 g (1 oz) creamed coconut
1 garlic clove
15 ml (1 tbsp) oil
2.5 ml (½ tsp) chilli powder
15 ml (1 tbsp) soft brown sugar
juice of 1 lemon

salt and pepper
125 g (4 oz) cabbage
150 g (5 oz) cucumber
175 g (6 oz) cauliflower
175 g (6 oz) new potatoes
175 g (6 oz) baby carrots
175 g (6 oz) French beans
3 hard-boiled eggs, peeled and quartered

1 Blend the peanuts to a fine powder; peel and finely chop the shallots or onions. Grate the creamed coconut. Peel and crush the garlic.

2 Heat the oil in a frying pan. Add the shallots or onions and garlic and cook, stirring, for 1 minute. Add the chilli powder, sugar and 150 ml (¼ pint) water. Bring to the boil, add the peanuts and simmer for 5 minutes. Stir in the coconut and 10 ml (2 tsp) lemon juice. Cook for 1 minute, adjust the seasoning and set aside.

3 Shred the cabbage. Slice the cucumber. Cut the cauliflower into florets.

4 Cook the potatoes in boiling, salted water until just tender. Drain and cool. Bring a large pan of salted water to the boil and add the cabbage, cauliflower, baby carrots and French beans. Cook for 3 minutes. Drain, refresh in cold water and drain again.

5 Gently reheat the peanut sauce until just below boiling and pour over the vegetables; toss well. Arrange on a platter with the eggs.

ACCOMPANIMENTS

Complete an Indian or Asian spread with the traditional accompaniments on offer in this chapter. Choose from the inspiring range of vegetable side dishes – simple cooking techniques are combined with spicy flavours to create instant stir-fries, delicious spinach dishes, aromatic potato ideas, exotic Indian dals and crisp salads. Rice and noodles are classic accompaniments – try the Chinese favourite, fried rice, or for the perfect complement to a spicy main dish, serve a fragrant coconut rice or noodles tossed in a sesame and coriander dressing. Delicious Indian breads – chapatis, pooris and parathas – provide the ideal foil to curries, while fresh-tasting chutneys and relishes are particularly good with grills and fried delicacies. Raita, a cooling combination of yogurt and cucumber, is a cooling partner to any fiery dish.

Illustration: Spinach Parathas (recipe page 196)

Asparagus and Mangetout with Chinese Lemon Sauce

PREPARATION TIME:
5-10 MINUTES

COOKING TIME: 10 MINUTES

FREEZING: NOT SUITABLE

115 CALS PER SERVING

SERVES 4

Illustrated opposite

1 garlic clove
225 g (8 oz) mangetout
225 g (8 oz) asparagus spears
salt
15 ml (1 tbsp) vegetable oil
5 ml (1 tsp) sesame oil
30 ml (2 tbsp) dry sherry
15 ml (1 tbsp) caster sugar

10 ml (2 tsp) light soy sauce
grated rind and juice of 1 lemon
5 ml (1 tsp) cornflour
15 ml (1 tbsp) toasted sesame seeds, for sprinkling
strips of lemon rind and coriander sprigs, to garnish

1 Peel and crush the garlic clove. Top and tail the mangetout.

2 Cut off the woody part of the asparagus stems and cut the asparagus diagonally into 3 or 4 pieces. Cook in a pan of boiling salted water for about 5 minutes until just tender. Drain well.

3 Heat the oils in a wok or frying pan and fry the mangetout, garlic and asparagus for 2 minutes.

4 In a bowl, mix the sherry with the sugar, soy sauce, lemon rind and juice, cornflour and 75 ml (5 tbsp) water.

5 Stir the mixture into the pan and cook until the sauce thickens and coats the vegetables. Sprinkle with the sesame seeds and garnish with lemon rind and coriander sprigs.

Spicy Mushrooms

PREPARATION TIME: 20 MINUTES

COOKING TIME: 30 MINUTES

FREEZING: NOT SUITABLE

150 CALS PER SERVING

SERVES 6

1 large aubergine, about 350 g (12 oz)
2 large onions
3 garlic cloves
350 g (12 oz) button mushrooms
5 cm (2 inch) piece fresh root ginger
about 60 ml (4 tbsp) oil
10 ml (2 tsp) hot chilli powder

5 ml (1 tsp) ground turmeric
5 ml (1 tsp) garam masala
5 ml (1 tsp) ground cumin
two 400 g (14 oz) cans chopped tomatoes
salt and pepper
225 g (8 oz) frozen peas

1 Cut the aubergine into chunks. Peel and finely slice the onion; peel and crush the garlic. Wipe the mushrooms and halve. Peel and coarsely grate the ginger.

2 Heat about 60 ml (4 tbsp) oil in a large, nonstick frying pan. Fry the aubergine pieces until golden brown, adding more oil if necessary. Remove the aubergine from the pan and drain on kitchen paper. Add a little more oil to the pan if necessary, then add the garlic, onions and ginger. Cook until golden, stirring occasionally. Mix in the spices and cook for 1 minute, stirring all the time.

3 Return the aubergine to the pan with the tomatoes. Adjust the seasoning then bring to the boil, cover and simmer for about 20 minutes or until the aubergines are tender.

4 Stir in the mushrooms and frozen peas and cook for about a further 10 minutes, adding a little water if necessary to thin down slightly. Transfer to a heated serving dish.

Stir-fried Mushrooms with Cashew Nuts

PREPARATION TIME: 10 MINUTES
COOKING TIME: 5 MINUTES
FREEZING: NOT SUITABLE

90 CALS PER SERVING
SERVES 4

225 g (8 oz) brown-cap mushrooms
15 ml (1 tbsp) oil
25 g (1 oz) unsalted cashew nuts
15 ml (1 tbsp) lemon juice

60 ml (4 tbsp) chopped fresh coriander
salt and pepper
15 ml (1 tbsp) single cream (optional)

1 Slice the mushrooms. Heat the oil in a frying pan. Add the nuts and cook over a high heat for 2-3 minutes or until golden. Add the mushrooms and cook for a further 2-3 minutes or until tender, stirring frequently.
2 Stir in the lemon juice, coriander and seasoning and bubble up. Off the heat, stir in the cream. Adjust the seasoning and serve.

Stir-fried Courgettes with Sesame Seeds

PREPARATION TIME: 5 MINUTES
COOKING TIME: 12 MINUTES
FREEZING: NOT SUITABLE

130 CALS PER SERVING
SERVES 6

900 g (2 lb) courgettes
1 spring onion
4 garlic cloves
30 ml (2 tbsp) vegetable oil
2.5 ml (½ tsp) salt

15 ml (1 tbsp) sesame oil
pepper
30 ml (2 tbsp) toasted sesame seeds
banana leaves, to serve (optional)

1 Thinly slice the courgettes; thickly slice the spring onion. Peel and crush the garlic.
2 Heat the vegetable oil in wok. Add the garlic and fry for 2 minutes.
3 Add the courgettes and stir-fry for 7-8 minutes. Stir in the spring onion, salt and sesame oil. Season with pepper. Cook for a further minute, then add the sesame seeds. Stir once and serve hot or cold on a bed of banana leaves.

Stir-fried Bean Sprouts with Peppers and Chillies

PREPARATION TIME: 10 MINUTES
COOKING TIME: 4 MINUTES
FREEZING: NOT SUITABLE

100 CALS PER SERVING
SERVES 4

2 garlic cloves
2.5 cm (1 inch) piece fresh root ginger
6 spring onions
1 red pepper
1 green pepper
2 green chillies

45 ml (3 tbsp) oil
350 g (12 oz) bean sprouts
15 ml (1 tbsp) dark soy sauce
15 ml (1 tbsp) sugar
15 ml (1 tbsp) malt vinegar
a few drops sesame oil (optional)

1 Peel and chop the garlic and ginger. Trim and cut the spring onions into 2.5 cm (1 inch) slices. Deseed and thinly slice the peppers. Deseed and finely chop the chillies.
2 Heat the oil in a wok or large frying pan, add the garlic, ginger, onions, peppers, chillies and bean sprouts and stir-fry over a medium heat for 3 minutes.
3 Add the soy sauce, sugar and vinegar and mix well. Stir-fry the mixture for a further 1 minute.
4 Sprinkle with a few drops of sesame oil, if wished. Transfer the mixture to a hot serving dish and serve at once.

Roasted Peppers with Oriental Dressing

PREPARATION TIME: 10 MINUTES

COOKING TIME: 10-15 MINUTES

FREEZING: NOT SUITABLE

70 CALS PER SERVING

SERVES 4

2 red peppers
1 yellow pepper
1 orange pepper

DRESSING
½ small red chilli
½ small green chilli

15 g (½ oz) piece fresh root ginger
1 small bunch spring onions
60 ml (4 tbsp) soy sauce
juice of 2 lemons
15 ml (1 tbsp) white wine vinegar
30 ml (2 tbsp) clear honey

1 Cut the peppers in half. Place cut-side down on the grill rack and cook under a hot grill for 10-15 minutes or until the skins become blackened and blistered all over. Cover with a clean damp tea-towel and leave to cool. The steam helps to lift the skins.

2 To prepare the dressing, halve, deseed and finely chop the chillies. Peel and finely shred or chop the ginger. Trim and slice the spring onions diagonally.

3 Place all the dressing ingredients in a small bowl and whisk together until thoroughly combined.

4 Remove the skin and seeds from the charred peppers, then cut into thick slices. Spoon the dressing over the peppers to serve.

VARIATION
For a 'less hot' version, omit the red and green chillies from the dressing. Sprinkle a little chopped coriander or parsley over the peppers to serve.

Aubergine in a Hot Sweet and Sour Sauce

PREPARATION TIME: 10 MINUTES

COOKING TIME: 35 MINUTES

FREEZING: NOT SUITABLE

180 CALS PER SERVING

SERVES 4

200 g (7 oz) onion
2.5 cm (1 inch) piece fresh root ginger
2 red chillies
45 ml (3 tbsp) oil
7.5 ml (1½ tsp) cumin seeds
7.5 ml (1½ tsp) coriander seeds
3 cloves

5 cm (2 inch) cinnamon stick
450 g (1 lb) aubergines
15 ml (1 tbsp) paprika
juice of 2 limes
45-60 ml (3-4 tbsp) dark muscovado sugar
5-10 ml (1-2 tsp) salt
whole red chillies, to garnish (optional)

1 Peel and slice the onion; peel and finely chop the root ginger; finely chop the chillies, discarding the seeds if a milder flavour is preferred.

2 Heat the oil in a large wok, add the onion, ginger and chilli and stir-fry until softened, for about 4 minutes. Add the next four spices and cook for 2-3 minutes. Cut the aubergines into 2.5 cm (1 inch) pieces.

3 Add 300 ml (½ pint) water to the wok and reduce the heat. Stir in the paprika, lime juice, sugar and salt with the aubergine. Bring to the boil. Simmer, covered, for about 20 minutes until the aubergine is tender.

4 Uncover and bring to the boil. Bubble for 3-4 minutes until the liquid is thick enough to coat the aubergine pieces. Garnish with whole red chillies if wished.

Aubergine with Yogurt Dressing

PREPARATION TIME:
35 MINUTES, PLUS COOLING
AND CHILLING

COOKING TIME: ABOUT 10
MINUTES

FREEZING: NOT SUITABLE

110 CALS PER SERVING

SERVES 8

700 g (1½ lb) aubergines
salt and pepper
90-120 ml (6-8 tbsp) oil
7.5 ml (1½ tsp) ground cumin
7.5 ml (1½ tsp) ground coriander

1 garlic clove
150 ml (¼ pint) natural yogurt
10 ml (2 tsp) chopped fresh mint or 5 ml (1 tsp) mint sauce
chopped fresh mint, to garnish

1 Thinly slice the aubergines. Place in a colander set over a plate and sprinkle with salt. Leave to degorge the bitter juices for 30 minutes. Rinse under cold running water then pat dry on kitchen paper.

2 Heat 45 ml (3 tbsp) oil in a large frying pan. Add enough aubergine slices to form a single layer and sprinkle with a little of the ground cumin and coriander. Brown the aubergines on both sides and cook for about 2-3 minutes until transparent and tender. Remove from the pan with a slotted spoon and drain on kitchen paper. Repeat with the remaining aubergine slices and spices, adding more oil as necessary. Arrange the cooked aubergine on a flat serving dish and allow to cool.

3 Peel and crush the garlic and mix into the yogurt. Add the mint and pepper to taste. Spoon over the aubergine slices, cover lightly, chill for at least 10-15 minutes before serving. Garnish with chopped fresh mint.

Spinach and Mushroom Bhaji

PREPARATION TIME: 15 MINUTES
COOKING TIME: 45 MINUTES
FREEZING: SUITABLE

120 CALS PER SERVING
SERVES 8

2 garlic cloves
2.5 cm (1 inch) piece fresh root ginger
15 ml (1 tbsp) black mustard seeds
10 ml (2 tsp) coriander seeds
5 ml (1 tsp) cumin seeds
2 large onions
450 g (1 lb) button mushrooms
45 ml (3 tbsp) ghee or oil

10 ml (2 tsp) ground turmeric
5-10 ml (1-2 tsp) chilli powder
400 g (14 oz) canned chopped tomatoes
900 g (2 lb) spinach
salt and pepper
about 60 ml (4 tbsp) toasted shredded coconut, to garnish

COOK'S NOTE
Frozen spinach can be used for this recipe. You will need 450 g (1 lb) frozen leaf spinach, thawed and well drained.

1 Peel and roughly chop the garlic and ginger. Put the mustard, coriander and cumin seeds in a large heavy-based frying pan and dry-fry over moderate heat for 2-3 minutes, stirring all the time. Remove the spices from the pan and crush with the garlic and ginger using a pestle and mortar.

2 Peel and thinly slice the onions; thickly slice the mushrooms. Heat the oil in the pan, add the onions and cook gently, stirring frequently, for about 10 minutes until softened and golden. Add the spice paste, turmeric and chilli powder and cook gently, stirring all the time, for 5 minutes.

3 Add the mushrooms and stir well, then add the tomatoes and bring to the boil, stirring. Simmer for 10 minutes, stirring occasionally.

4 Roughly shred the spinach and add to the pan. Stir well, then season with salt and pepper to taste. Lower the heat, cover and simmer for 15 minutes, stirring frequently to blend in the spinach as it cooks down. Check the seasoning and sprinkle with the coconut to serve.

Fried Masala Potatoes

PREPARATION TIME: 10 MINUTES

COOKING TIME: 30 MINUTES

FREEZING: NOT SUITABLE

515-345 CALS PER SERVING

SERVES 4-6

2 onions
4 garlic cloves
2.5 cm (1 inch) piece fresh root ginger
900 g (2 lb) new potatoes
oil for deep-frying
10 ml (2 tsp) cumin seeds
15 ml (1 tbsp) coriander seeds

7.5 ml (1½ tsp) garam masala
45 ml (3 tbsp) ghee or oil
5 ml (1 tsp) chilli powder
2.5 ml (½ tsp) ground turmeric
10 ml (2 tsp) salt
300 ml (1 pint) natural yogurt
paprika, to garnish

1 Peel and chop the onions, garlic and ginger.

2 Wash the potatoes and scrub clean if necessary. Cut into 2.5 cm (1 inch) pieces. Pat dry with kitchen paper. Heat the oil in a deep-fat fryer to 180°C (350°F) Mark 4 and deep-fry the potatoes in batches for 10 minutes or until golden brown. Remove from the oil and drain on kitchen paper.

3 Place the cumin and coriander seeds in a blender or food processor with the garam masala, ginger, garlic and onions. Purée until smooth, adding a little water if necessary.

4 Heat the ghee or oil in a heavy-based frying pan, add the masala paste and fry gently for about 5 minutes. Add the chilli, turmeric and salt and fry for a further 1 minute.

5 Pour in the yogurt, then add the potatoes. Stir well and cook for another 5 minutes until completely heated through. Serve piping hot, sprinkled with a little paprika.

Chick Peas with Spinach

PREPARATION TIME:
10 MINUTES, PLUS OVERNIGHT
SOAKING FOR DRIED CHICK
PEAS

COOKING TIME: 2½-3¼ HOURS,
OR 15 MINUTES IF USING
CANNED CHICK PEAS

FREEZING: SUITABLE

325-215 CALS PER SERVING

SERVES 4-6

Illustrated opposite

COOK'S NOTE
The cooking time for dried
chick peas will depend on
their 'freshness'. If they have
been stored for a long time
and look shrivelled, they
may take even longer than
3 hours to cook.

225 g (8 oz) dried chick peas, or two 425 g (15 oz) cans
salt and pepper
2.5 cm (1 inch) piece fresh root ginger
3 garlic cloves
4 tomatoes
450 g (1 lb) spinach leaves

handful of fresh coriander
45 ml (3 tbsp) ghee or oil
10 ml (2 tsp) ground coriander
5 ml (1 tsp) ground cumin
10 ml (2 tsp) paprika
coriander sprigs, to garnish

1 Pick over the dried chick peas if using, discarding any small stones or shrivelled peas. Rinse thoroughly in plenty of cold running water, then put into a bowl and add plenty of cold water to cover. Leave to soak overnight.

2 Drain the dried chick peas, put them in a large saucepan with plenty of water and bring to the boil. Lower the heat and simmer gently for 2-3 hours or until tender, adding salt towards the end of the cooking time. Drain well. If using canned chick peas, simply drain and rinse under cold running water.

3 Peel and finely chop the ginger. Peel and crush the garlic. Immerse the tomatoes in boiling water for 30 seconds, then remove and peel away the skins. Finely chop the tomato flesh. Trim and chop the spinach. Tear the fresh coriander.

4 Heat the ghee or oil in a large heavy-based saucepan or casserole. Add the ginger, garlic and spices and cook for 2 minutes, stirring all the time. Add the chick peas and stir to coat in the spice mixture.

5 Add the tomatoes, torn coriander and spinach. Cook for 2 minutes, then cover with a lid and simmer gently for 10 minutes. Season with salt and pepper before serving, garnished with coriander.

VARIATION
Use another pulse in place of the chick peas. Black-eye beans are particularly good; cook as above.

Rice and Dal Pilau

PREPARATION TIME:
ABOUT 15 MINUTES, PLUS
SOAKING

COOKING TIME: 30 MINUTES,
PLUS 10 MINUTES STANDING

FREEZING: SUITABLE

580-385 CALS PER SERVING

SERVES 4-6

Illustrated opposite

50 g (2 oz) chana dal
350 g (12 oz) basmati rice
1 onion
1-2 garlic cloves (optional)
1 hot green chilli, or 2 dried red chillies
60 ml (4 tbsp) ghee or oil
40 g (1½ oz) cashew nuts

10 ml (2 tsp) cumin seeds
4 pieces cassia bark, or 1 cinnamon stick
1 bay leaf
600 ml (1 pint) vegetable stock
5 ml (1 tsp) salt, or to taste
15 ml (1 tbsp) toasted sesame seeds
large pinch of garam masala, to serve

1 Pick over the dal, removing any small stones or green coloured pieces. Wash thoroughly under cold running water, then put in a bowl, cover with cold water and leave to soak for 3 hours.

2 Wash the rice in a sieve under cold running water, then put in a bowl and add plenty of cold water to cover. Leave to soak for 1 hour.

3 Peel and halve the onion, then slice. Peel and thinly slice the garlic. Slice the fresh green chilli, discarding the seeds if a milder flavour is preferred. If using dried chillies, leave whole.

4 Heat the ghee or oil in a large heavy-based saucepan or flameproof casserole. Add the cashew nuts and fry over a high heat until golden brown. Remove from the pan with a slotted spoon and drain on kitchen paper; set aside.

5 Add the onion and garlic to the pan and cook, stirring, until the onion is just tinged with brown. Add the chilli and spices and cook for 1 minute, stirring all the time. Lower the heat slightly. Thoroughly drain the dal and add to the pan. Add the stock and salt.

6 Quickly bring to the boil, stir with a fork, then cover with a tight-fitting lid. Lower the heat and simmer for 10 minutes. Drain the rice and add to the pan; re-cover and cook for a further 10 minutes. Shake the pan occasionally as it cooks, without lifting the lid.

7 Switch off the heat and leave the pan undisturbed for 10 minutes. Turn the rice and dal onto a serving dish and fluff up the grains with a fork. Check the seasoning. Sprinkle with the cashews, sesame seeds and garam masala before serving.

Fried Rice

PREPARATION TIME:
10 MINUTES, PLUS SOAKING
AND CHILLING

COOKING TIME: ABOUT 30
MINUTES

FREEZING: NOT SUITABLE

490 CALS PER SERVING

SERVES 4

350 g (12 oz) long-grain rice
3 Chinese dried mushrooms, or 125 g (4 oz) button mushrooms, sliced
4 spring onions
125 g (4 oz) canned bamboo shoots

30 ml (2 tbsp) oil
125 g (4 oz) bean sprouts
125 g (4 oz) frozen peas
30 ml (2 tbsp) soy sauce
3 eggs, beaten

1 Wash the rice in a sieve under cold running water until the water runs clear. Transfer the rice to a bowl, cover with cold water and leave to soak for 30 minutes.

2 Drain the rice and put in a saucepan. Cover with enough cold water to come 2.5 cm (1 inch) above the rice. Bring to the boil, cover tightly and simmer the rice very gently for 20 minutes. Do not stir.

3 Remove the pan from the heat, leave to cool for 20 minutes, then cover with cling film and chill in the refrigerator for 2-3 hours or overnight.

4 When ready to fry the rice, soak the dried mushrooms, if using, in warm water for about 30 minutes.

5 Drain the mushrooms, squeeze out excess moisture, then cut into thin slivers. Cut the spring onions diagonally into 2.5 cm (1 inch) lengths.

6 Drain the bamboo shoots and cut into 2.5 cm (1 inch) matchstick strips. Heat the oil in a wok or large frying pan over high heat. Add all the vegetables and stir-fry for 2-3 minutes. Add the soy sauce and cook briefly, stirring.

7 Fork up the rice, add to the pan and stir-fry for 2 minutes. Pour in the eggs and continue to stir-fry for 2-3 minutes, or until the egg has scrambled and the rice is heated through.

Fragrant Coconut Rice

PREPARATION TIME: 5 MINUTES

COOKING TIME: 15 MINUTES

FREEZING: NOT SUITABLE

335-225 CALS PER SERVING

SERVES 4-6

25 g (1 oz) creamed coconut
1 lemon grass stalk
350 g (12 oz) basmati rice
salt and pepper
2.5 ml (½ tsp) freshly grated nutmeg

2 cloves
1 cinnamon stick
1 bay leaf
2 slices dried galangal

1 Chop the creamed coconut. Split the lemon grass. Wash the rice in a sieve under cold running water until the water runs clear.

2 Put all the ingredients, except the rice, in a heavy-based saucepan with 600 ml (1 pint) water. Bring slowly to the boil. Add the rice, stir with a fork, then cover and simmer gently for 15 minutes or until all liquid is absorbed and the rice is tender.

3 Leave to stand for 2 minutes before serving.

Pineapple Rice

PREPARATION TIME: 10 MINUTES

COOKING TIME: 20 MINUTES

FREEZING: NOT SUITABLE

150 CALS PER SERVING

SERVES 8

225 g (8 oz) basmati rice
salt and pepper
125 g (4 oz) shallots
2 large red chillies
4 spring onions
125 g (4 oz) fresh or canned pineapple

2 garlic cloves
30 ml (2 tbsp) oil
15 ml (1 tbsp) Thai fish sauce
15 ml (1 tbsp) soy sauce
15 ml (1 tbsp) sugar

1 Rinse the rice under cold running water and drain. Cook the rice in plenty of boiling, salted water for 10 minutes. Drain, rinse well under cold running water, then drain again.

2 Peel and finely chop the shallots; deseed and finely chop the chillies; finely chop the spring onions and pineapple. Mix together and set aside.

3 Peel and crush the garlic. Heat the oil in a large nonstick frying pan, add the garlic and fry for 2-3 minutes. Add the rice, fish sauce, soy sauce and sugar. Cook, stirring, for about 5 minutes or until piping hot. Stir in the pineapple mixture, season with salt and pepper to taste and serve.

Mushroom and Saffron Pilau

PREPARATION TIME: 5 MINUTES, PLUS SOAKING

COOKING TIME: 15-20 MINUTES

FREEZING: NOT SUITABLE

275 CALS PER SERVING

SERVES 6

350 g (12 oz) basmati rice
225 g (8 oz) button mushrooms
60 ml (4 tbls) oil
3 cloves
6 green cardamom pods

1 stick cassia bark or cinnamon
2.5 ml (½ tsp) saffron strands
5 ml (1 tsp) sugar
salt and pepper

1 Wash the rice in several changes of cold water. Place in a bowl, cover with cold water and leave to soak for 30 minutes. Drain and rinse in a sieve under cold running water until the water runs clear.

2 Slice the mushrooms. Heat the oil in large saucepan, add the mushrooms, cloves, cardamom pods, cassia bark or cinnamon, and rice. Cook, stirring, over moderate heat for 1-2 minutes.

3 Add 600 ml (1 pint) water, the saffron, sugar and seasoning. Bring to the boil, stirring. Reduce the heat, cover tightly and cook very gently for 15 minutes, or until all the liquid is absorbed and the rice is tender.

4 Taste and adjust the seasoning. Fluff up the rice with a fork before serving.

Hot Noodles with Sesame Dressing

PREPARATION TIME: 5 MINUTES

COOKING TIME: 5 MINUTES

FREEZING: NOT SUITABLE

320 CALS PER SERVING

SERVES 6

350 g (12 oz) egg noodles
salt and pepper
1 garlic clove
1 small green chilli
45 ml (3 tbsp) toasted sesame seeds

45 ml (3 tbsp) sunflower oil
30 ml (2 tbsp) sesame oil
60 ml (4 tbsp) soy sauce
60 ml (4 tbsp) chopped fresh coriander or parsley

1 Cook the noodles in boiling, salted water according to the packet instructions.

2 Meanwhile, peel and crush the garlic; deseed and finely chop the chilli. Mix the garlic and chilli with the sesame seeds, oils, and soy sauce.

3 Drain the noodles well and toss in the sesame dressing and chopped coriander or parsley. Season to taste and serve immediately.

Special Fried Noodles

PREPARATION TIME: 10 MINUTES

COOKING TIME: 8 MINUTES

FREEZING: NOT SUITABLE

225 CALS PER SERVING

SERVES 6

150 g (5 oz) egg noodles
1 large red chilli
175 g (6 oz) shallots or onions
4 garlic cloves
125 g (4 oz) cabbage
125 g (4 oz) carrots
125 g (4 oz) spring onions

15 ml (1 tbsp) caster sugar
15 ml (1 tbsp) tomato ketchup
15 ml (1 tbsp) soy sauce
30 ml (2 tbsp) oil
225 g (8 oz) large cooked peeled prawns
125 g (4 oz) bean sprouts
salt and pepper

1 Cook the noodles according to the packet instructions, then rinse and drain. Deseed and finely chop the chilli. Peel and finely chop the shallots. Peel and crush the garlic. Very finely slice the cabbage, carrots and spring onions.

2 Make the dressing by mixing together the sugar, tomato ketchup and soy sauce.

3 Heat the oil in a large frying pan over a high heat. Add the chilli, shallots and garlic. Cook, stirring, for 2 minutes or until golden. Stir in the cabbage, carrots and spring onions and cook, stirring, for about 4 minutes. Stir in the noodles, prawns and bean sprouts with the dressing. Toss over a high heat for 1-2 minutes to heat through, then adjust seasoning. Serve immediately.

Prawn and Peanut Noodles

PREPARATION TIME: 10 MINUTES

COOKING TIME: 8 MINUTES

FREEZING: NOT SUITABLE

350-235 CALS PER SERVING

SERVES 4-6

2 spring onions
2 garlic cloves
50 g (2 oz) salted roasted peanuts
125 g (4 oz) medium egg noodles
15 ml (1 tbsp) lemon juice
15 ml (1 tbsp) Thai fish sauce
15 ml (1 tbsp) sugar

2.5 ml (½ tsp) chilli powder
60 ml (4 tbsp) oil
1 egg
50 g (2 oz) bean sprouts
125 g (4 oz) cooked peeled king prawns
30 ml (2 tbsp) chopped fresh coriander
salt and pepper

1 Trim and roughly chop the spring onions. Peel and crush the garlic. Roughly chop the peanuts. Soak the noodles for 4 minutes in boiling water then rinse and drain.

2 Combine the lemon juice, Thai fish sauce, sugar and chilli powder and set aside.

3 Heat the oil in a large, nonstick frying pan. Add the garlic and cook until golden brown. Break in the egg and stir to scramble lightly. Add the noodles and mix well. Add the lemon mixture, stirring all the time. Toss in the spring onions, peanuts, bean sprouts, prawns and coriander. Heat through, season and serve.

Crispy Noodles with Hot Sweet and Sour Sauce

PREPARATION TIME: 10 MINUTES

COOKING TIME:
ABOUT 15 MINUTES

FREEZING: NOT SUITABLE

355 CALS PER SERVING

SERVES 4

125 g (4 oz) rice or egg noodles
oil for deep-frying
frisée leaves, to serve

SAUCE
1 garlic clove
1 cm (½ inch) piece fresh root ginger
6 spring onions
½ red pepper

15 ml (1 tbsp) sliced green chillies in sweetened vinegar
30 ml (2 tbsp) oil
30 ml (2 tbsp) sugar
30 ml (2 tbsp) malt vinegar
30 ml (2 tbsp) tomato ketchup
30 ml (2 tbsp) dark soy sauce
30 ml (2 tbsp) dry sherry
15 ml (1 tbsp) cornflour

1 First make the sauce. Peel and crush the garlic; peel and shred the ginger; trim and slice the spring onions; deseed and finely chop the red pepper; chop the green chillies.

2 Heat the oil in a wok or large frying pan and stir-fry the garlic, ginger, onions and red pepper for 1 minute. Stir in the sugar, vinegar, ketchup, soy sauce and sherry.

3 Blend the cornflour with 120 ml (8 tbsp) water and stir into the pan. Cook for 2 minutes, stirring. Add the chillies, cover and keep warm.

4 Half-fill a wok or deep pan with the oil and heat to 190°C (375°F). Cut the noodles into 6 batches and fry, a batch at a time, very briefly until lightly golden (take care as the hot oil rises up quickly).

5 Drain the noodles on kitchen paper and keep warm while cooking the remainder .

6 Arrange the noodles on a bed of frisée leaves and serve the sauce separately.

Chapatis

PREPARATION TIME:
15 MINUTES, PLUS RESTING

COOKING TIME:
ABOUT 40 MINUTES

FREEZING: SUITABLE

140 CALS PER CHAPATI

MAKES 6

225 g (8 oz) plain wholemeal flour   ghee or melted butter, for brushing

1 Put the flour in a bowl and gradually mix in 150-200 ml (5-7 fl oz) water to form a stiff dough.
2 Turn onto a lightly floured surface and, with floured hands, knead thoroughly for 6-8 minutes until smooth and elastic. Return the dough to the bowl, cover with a damp clean tea-towel and leave to rest for 15 minutes.
3 Heat a griddle or heavy-based frying pan over a low heat until really hot.
4 Meanwhile divide the dough into 6 pieces. With floured hands, take a piece of dough and shape into a smooth ball. Dip the ball of dough in flour to coat, then roll out on a floured surface to a round about 18 cm (7 inches) in diameter.
5 Slap the chapati onto the hot pan. Cook over a low heat and as soon as brown specks appear on the underside, turn it over and repeat on the other side.
6 Turn the chapati over again and, with a clean tea-towel, press down the edges of the chapati to circulate the steam and make the chapati puff up. Cook until the underside is golden brown, then cook the other side in the same way.
7 Brush the chapati with ghee or melted butter. Serve at once or keep warm, wrapped in foil. Continue cooking the remaining chapatis in the same way.

Pooris

PREPARATION TIME:
15 MINUTES, PLUS RESTING

COOKING TIME: ABOUT 10
MINUTES

FREEZING: NOT SUITABLE

200 CALS PER POORI

MAKES 6

Illustrated opposite

COOK'S NOTE
These spectacular puffed-up breads are at their best served straight from the pan while still hot and puffed up. If yours have deflated by the time you serve them, try reviving them by placing under a hot grill for a few seconds.

175 g (6 oz) plain wholemeal flour   oil for deep-frying
5 ml (1 tsp) salt

1 Put the flour and salt in a food processor and process briefly to mix. Measure 150 ml (¼ pint) cold water in a jug. With the machine running, gradually add half of the water through the feeder tube.
2 Now with the machine still running, slowly add enough of the remaining water to make a dough. As soon as the mixture comes together in a ball, stop the machine. You may not need to add all of the water; the amount required depends on the absorbency of the flour.
3 Turn the dough onto a floured surface and knead for 10 minutes until it is smooth, soft and pliable but not sticky. Shape the dough into a ball, cover with cling film and leave to rest at room temperature for 30 minutes.
4 Divide the dough into 6 equal pieces. Cover all except one with cling film. Roll this piece out to a 12 cm (5 inch) circle. Cover with cling film and set aside. Repeat with the remaining dough.
5 Heat the oil in a deep-fat fryer. Test the temperature by dropping in a small cube of bread – it should sizzle immediately on contact with the oil and rise to the surface; remove with a slotted spoon.
6 Carefully slide a poori into the hot oil and press down with the back of a spoon to immerse; it should puff up almost immediately. Turn it over to cook the second side, constantly moving the poori about with the spoon, until it is golden brown. Drain on kitchen paper and keep warm while you cook the remainder. Serve warm.

Spinach Parathas

PREPARATION TIME:
30 MINUTES, PLUS RESTING

COOKING TIME: ABOUT 2 HOURS

FREEZING: SUITABLE

160 CALS PER PARATHA

MAKES 12

175 g (6 oz) plain wholemeal flour
175 g (6 oz) plain white flour
salt and pepper
25 g (1 oz) butter
ghee, butter or vegetable oil, for brushing

FILLING
1 garlic clove
1 red or green chilli
125 g (4 oz) spinach leaves
15 ml (1 tbsp) oil
5 ml (1 tsp) cumin seeds
30 ml (2 tbsp) chopped fresh coriander

COOK'S NOTE
These tasty breads are best served warm from the oven. However, they can be made in advance, then later sprinkled with a little water, wrapped in foil and reheated in a warm oven.

1 Put the flours in a food processor with salt and the butter; work until butter is finely chopped. Measure 300 ml (½ pint) water. With the machine running, pour half the water through the feeder tube and process for 2 minutes.

2 Now with the machine still running, slowly add enough of the remaining water to make a dough. As soon as the mixture comes together in a ball, stop the machine. You may not need to add all of the water; the amount required depends on the absorbency of the flour.

3 Knead the dough on a floured surface for 10 minutes until smooth, soft and pliable, but not sticky. Shape into a ball, cover with cling film and leave to rest for 30 minutes.

4 Meanwhile, make the filling. Peel and crush the garlic. Chop the chilli, discarding the seeds if a milder flavour is preferred. Trim the spinach and chop roughly.

5 Heat the oil in a frying pan, add the chilli and garlic and cook for 2 minutes. Add the cumin seeds and cook for a further 1 minute. Add the spinach and cook until just wilted. Remove from the heat, add the coriander and season with salt and pepper to taste. Leave to cool.

6 Divide the dough into 12 pieces. Cover all but one with cling film. Roll this piece into a 20 cm (8 inch) circle. Using a slotted spoon, place a little spinach mixture in the middle of the circle.

7 Gather up the edges of the dough over the filling and twist to seal. Sprinkle with a little flour, then carefully flatten the ball and roll it out to a 15 cm (6 inch) circle; cover with cling film and set aside. Repeat with the remaining dough and filling.

8 Heat a griddle or heavy-based frying pan until it is very hot. Add 1 paratha, cook over a high heat for 1 minute, then lower the heat and cook more gently for 2 minutes or until small bubbles appear on the surface and the underside is golden brown in patches. Turn the paratha over and cook the second side in the same way.

9 Brush the top with a little melted ghee or butter, turn the paratha again and cook for 1 minute. Brush again, turn and cook for 1 minute or until crisp on the outside and cooked right through. Wrap in foil and keep warm while cooking the remainder. Serve warm.

Lace Pancakes

PREPARATION TIME: 5 MINUTES

COOKING TIME:
ABOUT 1¼ HOURS

FREEZING: SUITABLE

50 CALS PER SERVING

MAKES ABOUT 15

150 g (5 oz) plain white flour
1 egg
300 ml (½ pint) milk and water, mixed

salt and pepper
oil for frying

1 In a food processor, blend the first three ingredients to form a smooth, thin batter. Season with salt and pepper.

2 Lightly oil a nonstick frying pan, dip your fingers into the batter and allow it to run into the pan as you shake your hand.

3 Cook the pancake for 2-3 minutes on one side until golden, then turn it over and cook for a further 2-3 minutes. Repeat this process with the remaining batter. Serve the pancakes warm.

Fresh Coriander Chutney

PREPARATION TIME:
10 MINUTES, PLUS STANDING

COOKING TIME: 5 MINUTES

FREEZING: SUITABLE

85 CALS PER SERVING

SERVES 8

1 onion
1-2 garlic cloves
1-2 green chillies
1 large bunch fresh coriander
30 ml (2 tbsp) ground almonds

45 ml (3 tbsp) lime or lemon juice
45 ml (3 tbsp) oil
10 ml (2 tsp) sugar
salt and pepper

1 Peel and quarter the onion. Peel the garlic. Chop the chillies, discarding the seeds if a milder flavour is preferred. Trim the roots from the coriander if attached, but leave some of the stalks. Wash and thoroughly dry if necessary. Chop roughly.

2 Line a grill pan with foil. Spread the ground almonds on the foil and toast under a medium-hot grill until lightly browned, shaking the pan occasionally so that they brown evenly. Leave to cool.

3 Put the onion, garlic, chillies, coriander and ground almonds in a blender or food processor, together with all of the other ingredients. Process in short bursts until the ingredients are well chopped and evenly mixed, but still retain some texture.

4 Turn into a bowl and leave at room temperature for at least 1 hour to let the flavours develop. Season to taste.

VARIATION

For fresh mint chutney, use a large bunch of fresh mint instead of the coriander. Replace the almonds with sesame seeds. Add a little grated fresh root ginger and a little extra sugar, to taste..

COOK'S NOTE
This chutney will keep in the refrigerator for up to one week.

Fresh Mango Chutney

PREPARATION TIME:
10 MINUTES, PLUS CHILLING

COOKING TIME: NONE

FREEZING: NOT SUITABLE

15 CALS PER 15 ML (1 TBSP)

MAKES ABOUT 225 G (8 OZ)

Illustrated above: bottom left

1 large ripe mango
1 fresh green chilli
juice of 1 lime

1.25 ml (¼ tsp) cayenne pepper
salt

1 Cut the mango either side of (and close to) the stone to make 2 large pieces. Cut the flesh within these pieces into cubes, without breaking the skin.

2 Push the skin inside out to expose the cubes; peel off the skin. Peel the remaining centre section of flesh, still attached to the stone; slice the flesh from the stone

3 Deseed and slice the chilli. Mix the chilli with the mango, lime juice, cayenne and salt. Chill for 1 hour before serving. The chutney will keep for up to 2 days in the refrigerator.

Banana Chutney

PREPARATION TIME:
10 MINUTES, PLUS STORING

COOKING TIME: 1 HOUR

FREEZING: NOT SUITABLE

20 CALS PER 15 ML (1 TBSP)

MAKES ABOUT 1.6 KG (3½ LB)

Illustrated opposite: right

900 g (2 lb) bananas
125 g (4 oz) stoned dates
450 g (1 lb) cooking apples
125 g (4 oz) onions
125 g (4 oz) seedless raisins

5 ml (1 tsp) salt
175 g (6 oz) demerara sugar
15 ml (1 tbsp) ground ginger
2.5 ml (½ tsp) cayenne pepper
300 ml (½ pint) distilled vinegar

1 Peel and slice the bananas and chop the dates. Peel, core and roughly chop the cooking apples. Peel and chop the onions.

2 Place the prepared fruit and onions in a preserving pan and sprinkle with the salt, sugar and spices. Pour in the vinegar and bring gently to the boil. Simmer gently, stirring occasionally, for about 1 hour until no excess liquid remains and the mixture is soft and pulpy.

3 Spoon the chutney into pre-heated sterilized jars, and cover at once with airtight and vinegar-proof tops. Store in a cool, dry, dark place for 2-3 months to mature, before eating.

Fresh Tomato Chutney

PREPARATION TIME:
10 MINUTES, PLUS CHILLING

COOKING TIME: NONE

FREEZING: NOT SUITABLE

10 CALS PER SERVING

SERVES 6

Illustrated opposite: top left

225 g (8 oz) fresh ripe tomatoes
1 onion
1 small green chilli

30 ml (2 tbsp) chopped fresh coriander
15 ml (1 tbsp) white wine vinegar
salt and pepper

1 Roughly chop the tomatoes; peel and finely chop the onion. Deseed and finely chop the green chilli.

2 Mix all the ingredients together, stirring well. Cover and chill.

Raita

PREPARATION TIME:
10 MINUTES, PLUS STANDING

COOKING TIME: NONE

FREEZING: NOT SUITABLE

40-30 CALS PER SERVING

SERVES 4-6

⅛ cucumber
1 garlic clove (optional)
300 ml (½ pint) natural yogurt

45 ml (3 tbsp) chopped fresh mint
salt and pepper
1 hot chilli (optional)

1 Finely chop or grate the cucumber. Peel and crush the garlic if using.

2 Beat the yogurt, then mix in the cucumber and garlic, if using. Add the mint and season with salt and pepper to taste. This makes a cool refreshing raita.

3 For a 'hot' raita, finely chop the chilli (including the seeds for extra heat if wished); stir into the raita.

4 Cover and leave to stand for 30 minutes to let the flavours develop.

VARIATIONS
Add chopped spring onion instead of cucumber
Use chopped fresh coriander instead of mint.
Replace the cucumber with 45 ml (3 tbsp) grated toasted fresh coconut.
Replace the cucumber with 1 chopped banana and a little grated lime rind.

DESSERTS

Fresh fruit is customarily served at the end of many meals in the Far East, but the delicious ideas in this chapter are also perfect for rounding off any aromatic or spicy spread. Bananas coated in crisp sesame-seed toffee or pineapple fritters served with an Oriental sauce are full of contrasting textures and make luscious hot finales. For a rich and filling dessert, choose classic Indian rice pudding, delicately spiced with cardamoms, or on a lighter note serve an unusual Thai baked custard made from moong beans. For a refreshing finish, a fruit salad of melon, papaya, pineapple and mango steeped in a jasmine tea syrup is full of fragrance; for an even cooler finale, the Indian iced dessert, kulfi, or ice cream flavoured with coconut or pistachios are ideal choices.

Illustration: Kulfi (recipe page 216)

Toffee Bananas

PREPARATION TIME: 10 MINUTES

COOKING TIME: ABOUT 20 MINUTES

FREEZING: NOT SUITABLE

360 CALS PER SERVING

SERVES 4

Illustrated opposite

3 firm bananas
45 ml (3 tbsp) plain white flour
7.5 ml (1½ tsp) cornflour
1 egg white
oil for deep-frying
slivers of caramel, to decorate (optional)

SESAME CARAMEL
125 g (4 oz) sugar
30 ml (2 tbsp) sesame seeds

1 Peel the bananas, cut into chunky pieces and dust with a little of the flour. Mix the remaining flour with the cornflour and egg white and stir well to form a paste.

2 Half-fill a deep pan with oil and heat to 180°C (350°F) or until a cube of day-old bread dropped into the hot oil browns in 30 seconds.

3 Dip the banana chunks into the paste and then fry, a few at a time, in the hot oil until golden. Remove with a slotted spoon and drain on kitchen paper and keep warm while cooking the remaining banana chunks in the same way.

4 To make the sesame caramel, place the sugar and 30 ml (2 tbsp) water in a heavy-based saucepan and heat gently until the sugar dissolves, then boil, without stirring, until the mixture is pale straw-coloured. Sprinkle in the sesame seeds and continue cooking briefly until the mixture turns golden.

5 Immediately remove the pan from the heat, add the hot fried banana chunks and stir to coat.

6 Have ready a bowl of iced water and place the hot coated banana chunks into the water to set. Remove at once with a slotted spoon and serve immediately, decorated with slivers of caramel, if using.

Bananas Grilled with Cardamom Butter

PREPARATION TIME: 10 MINUTES

COOKING TIME: 5-8 MINUTES

FREEZING: NOT SUITABLE

280 CALS PER SERVING

SERVES 4

COOK'S NOTE
The buttery syrup which exudes during cooking can be spooned from the lined grill pan back over the bananas when you serve them.

4 large bananas, rinsed
2-3 cardamom pods
50 g (2 oz) soft dark brown sugar

50 g (2 oz) butter, at room temperature
vanilla, coffee or chocolate ice cream, to serve (optional)

1 Line the grill pan with foil, then replace the grill rack. Slit each banana skin along its length and cut the skin back a little at each end so that you can open it out slightly.

2 Break open the cardamom pods and empty the seeds into a mortar. Crush them with a pestle, adding half of the sugar in the latter stages of crushing.

3 Beat the butter and cardamom-flavoured sugar together, then push some of the mixture along the slit in each banana.

4 Place the bananas open-side up on the grill rack and cook under a medium-hot grill for 3-5 minutes until the butter melts into them and the flesh begins to soften. Sprinkle the remaining sugar on top and flash back under the grill until the bananas are softened and the topping is caramelised.

5 Serve the bananas hot in their skins, with ice cream, if wished.

VARIATIONS
Other spices, such as cinnamon or ginger, can ring the changes on cardamom, or you could use vanilla sugar.

Coconut Banana Fritters

PREPARATION TIME: ABOUT
10 MINUTES, PLUS RESTING

COOKING TIME: ABOUT 10
MINUTES

FREEZING: NOT SUITABLE

465-310 CALS PER SERVING

SERVES 4-6

1 egg, separated
15 ml (1 tbsp) sunflower oil
100 ml (3 ½ fl oz) coconut milk
50 g (2 oz) plain white flour
15 g (½ oz) desiccated coconut
25 g (1 oz) sugar

5 ml (1 tsp) ground mixed spice
4 large bananas
oil for deep-frying
icing sugar and ground cinnamon, for dusting
(optional)

1 Place the egg yolk in a large bowl with the oil, coconut milk, flour, coconut, sugar and mixed spice. Beat well, using a wooden spoon, to form a smooth batter. Cover and set aside for 30 minutes.

2 Peel and slice the bananas into 5 cm (2 inch) lengths. Whisk the egg white until stiff, then carefully fold into the batter until evenly combined.

3 Heat a 10 cm (4 inch) depth of oil in a deep saucepan until it registers 180°C (350°F) on a thermometer or until a cube of bread dropped into the oil browns in 30 seconds. Deep-fry the banana pieces a few at a time. Dip them into the batter to coat, then deep-fry in the hot oil for 2-3 minutes until crisp and golden.

4 Drain the fritters on kitchen paper and keep hot while cooking the remainder. Dust with icing sugar mixed with a little ground cinnamon and serve the fritters hot, accompanied by a scoop of vanilla ice cream if wished.

VARIATIONS
Replace the banana with cored and thickly sliced apples, or thickly sliced peaches and nectarines.
Other spices and flavourings can be added to the batter. Try adding a little grated orange rind, or replace the mixed spice with cinnamon.

Pineapple Fritters

PREPARATION TIME: 30 MINUTES

COOKING TIME: ABOUT 10 MINUTES

FREEZING: NOT SUITABLE

230-155 CALS PER SERVING

SERVES 4-6

1 large ripe pineapple
oil for deep-frying
pineapple slices and lemon rind strips, to garnish

PAPAYA SAUCE
450 g (1 lb) papaya
25 ml (1½ tbsp) caster sugar

BATTER
50 g (2 oz) plain white flour
pinch of salt
finely grated rind of ½ lemon
1 egg, separated
5 ml (1 tsp) sunflower oil

1 Peel and core the pineapple, then slice into 1 cm (½ inch) thick rings. Cut each ring into three or four pieces. Pat dry on kitchen paper.

2 To make the papaya sauce, deseed the papaya, then peel and slice the flesh. Place in a blender or food processor and blend until smooth. Stir in the sugar and pour into a sauce-boat or bowl. Set aside.

3 To make the batter, sift together the flour and salt into a bowl. Stir in the lemon rind and make a well in the centre. Place the egg yolk and 60 ml (4 tbsp) water in the well and gradually incorporate the flour mixture, adding enough extra water to produce the consistency of single cream.

4 Whisk the egg white in a separate bowl until holding stiff peaks, then fold into the batter with the sunflower oil.

5 Heat the oil in a deep-fat fryer to 190°C (375°F). Spear 6 pieces of pineapple onto a skewer and dip them into the batter to coat, then drop the pieces into the hot oil. Fry for 3-4 minutes until puffed, golden and crisp. Drain and keep warm while cooking the remainder. Garnish with pineapple slices and lemon rind and serve at once with papaya sauce.

Coconut and Lime-scented Fruits

PREPARATION TIME: 15 MINUTES

COOKING TIME: 9 MINUTES

FREEZING: NOT SUITABLE

320 CALS PER SERVING

SERVES 6

1 small mango
1 small papaya
2 or 3 slices fresh pineapple
125 g (4 oz) kumquats
125 g (4 oz) sugar

juice of 3 limes
400 ml (14 fl oz) coconut milk
1 banana
lime slices, to decorate

1 Cut the mango across either side of the stone, then cut the flesh onto large slices and peel off the skin. Chop the flesh surrounding the stone. Halve the papaya, scoop out and discard the seeds, then peel and roughly chop the flesh. Peel, core and quarter the pineapple slices. Quarter the kumquats.

2 In a large frying pan place the sugar, 75 ml (5 tbsp) lime juice and the coconut milk. Bring to the boil and bubble for 5 minutes. Add the mango and papaya and poach in the syrup for 1 minute.

3 Drain the fruits reserving the syrup; place the fruits in a serving bowl. Return the syrup to the pan and simmer the kumquats in the syrup for 3 minutes. Add the pineapple, kumquats and syrup to the mango and papaya.

4 Roughly chop the banana and stir into the fruits. Decorate with lime slices.

Exotic Fresh Fruit Salad

PREPARATION TIME:
20 MINUTES, PLUS INFUSING

COOKING TIME: 5-6 MINUTES

FREEZING: NOT SUITABLE

150 CALS PER SERVING

SERVES 4

Illustrated opposite

225 g (8 oz) wedge watermelon
225 g (8 oz) wedge galia or ogen melon
1 small papaya
1 small mango
125 g (4 oz) fresh pineapple slices
2 small bananas
finely shredded lime rind (optional), to decorate

JASMINE SYRUP
1 jasmine tea bag
2 strips lime peel
30 ml (2 tbsp) lime juice
25 g (1 oz) sugar

1 First make the syrup. Put the tea bag in a small bowl, pour on 150 ml (¼ pint) boiling water and leave to stand for 10 minutes. Discard the tea bag and pour the tea into a small saucepan. Add the lime peel, lime juice and sugar and heat gently, stirring until the sugar is dissolved. Simmer gently for 5 minutes, remove from the heat and leave to go cold.

2 Prepare the fruit. Scoop out the seeds from both melon wedges and carefully cut the flesh away from the skin. Slice the flesh and place in a large bowl.

3 Halve the papaya, scoop out and discard the seeds, then peel and slice the flesh. Cut the mango across either side of the stone, then cut the flesh into pieces and peel off the skin. Chop the flesh surrounding the stone. Core and quarter the pineapple slices. Peel and slice the bananas. Combine all the fruits together in a bowl.

4 Pour over the cold tea syrup and leave to marinate for 10 minutes before serving. Decorate with shredded lime rind if wished.

VARIATIONS
Other teas, including fruit-flavoured infusions, can be substituted for the Jasmine tea – simply choose your favourite.

Hot Mango and Banana Salad

PREPARATION TIME: 10 MINUTES

COOKING TIME: 5 MINUTES

FREEZING: NOT SUITABLE

199 CALS PER SERVING

SERVES 4

2 large oranges
2 firm but ripe mangoes, about 700 g (1½ lb) total weight
4 small bananas

25 g (1 oz) very low-fat spread
5 ml (1 tsp) soft light brown sugar
30 ml (2 tbsp) rum
30 ml (2 tbsp) lemon or lime juice

1 Coarsely grate the rind and squeeze the juice of 1 orange. Peel the other one with a serrated knife and slice thickly. Cut the mango across either side of the stone, then cut the flesh into large pieces and peel off the skin. Remove any flesh from around the stone and cut all the flesh into bite-sized pieces. Peel and thickly slice the bananas.

2 Melt the low-fat spread in a large, nonstick frying pan. Add 5 ml (1 tsp) sugar with the mango and banana and cook for about 2-3 minutes or until just beginning to soften.

3 Pour in the rum, all of the fruit juice and the orange slices. Bring to the boil then serve immediately, decorated with the grated orange rind.

Fragrant Melon and Lychee Salad

PREPARATION TIME:
10 MINUTES, PLUS CHILLING

COOKING TIME: 2 MINUTES

FREEZING: NOT SUITABLE

150-100 CALS PER SERVING

SERVES 4-6

COOK'S NOTE
For a decorative touch,
serve the salad in a melon
bowl. To make the bowl,
cut a slice off the top of the
whole melon, remove the
seeds, then scoop out the
flesh with a melon baller.

1 ripe honeydew or cantaloupe melon
12 fresh lychees or canned drained lychees
1 Asian pear
15 ml (1 tbsp) lemon juice
8 Chinese gooseberries or physalis
a few sliced strawberries (optional)
a few Chinese gooseberries or physalis, to
decorate

SYRUP
40 g (1½ oz) sugar
75 ml (3 fl oz) orange juice
30 ml (2 tbsp) stem ginger syrup
2 pieces of stem ginger, cut into fine slivers

1 To make the syrup, put 75 ml (3 fl oz) water and the sugar into a saucepan and bring to the boil, stirring. Simmer for 2 minutes, then remove from the heat and stir in the orange juice, ginger syrup and stem ginger. Leave to cool.
2 Cut the melon into quarters, remove the seeds, then cut the flesh into neat slices.
3 Peel the fresh lychees and remove the stones. Peel, core and slice the pear and drizzle with the lemon juice. Remove the outer casings of the Chinese gooseberries.
4 Mix all the fruit in a salad bowl or arrange on individual plates. Pour the cooled syrup over the fruit. Serve chilled, decorated with Chinese gooseberries.

Pineapple and Lemon Grass Salad

PREPARATION TIME:
10 MINUTES, PLUS COOLING

COOKING TIME: 15 MINUTES

FREEZING: NOT SUITABLE

210 CALS PER SERVING

SERVES 4

4 ready-made brandy snap biscuits or
baskets
1 pineapple
3 limes

2 lemon grass stalks
75 g (3 oz) caster sugar
toasted coconut shavings, to decorate

1 Place 2 brandy snap biscuits or baskets on a baking sheet and put in the oven at 200°C (400°F) Mark 6 for 5 minutes or until they melt flat. Cool for 2 minutes, then ease off with a palette knife. Pinch into folds from the centre with the finger and thumb and leave to cool. Repeat this melting and folding process with the remaining brandy snap biscuits or baskets.
2 Peel, core and slice the pineapple. Peel and segment 3 limes.
3 Finely chop the lemon grass and place in a heavy-based saucepan with 75 g (3 oz) caster sugar and 300 ml (½ pint) water. Stir over gentle heat to dissolve the sugar, then increase the heat, bring to the boil and simmer for 5 minutes to make a sugar syrup.
4 Remove the pan from the heat and place the pineapple and lime segments in the syrup. Set aside until warm.
5 To serve, divide the pineapple salad between individual plates, top with the brandy snap shapes and decorate with toasted coconut shavings.

Fresh Fruit Jelly with Poached Kumquats

PREPARATION TIME:
20 MINUTES, PLUS SETTING

COOKING TIME: 18 MINUTES

FREEZING: NOT SUITABLE

140 CALS PER SERVING

SERVES 6

juice of 4 large lemons
30 ml (2 tbsp) powdered gelatine
900 ml (1½ pints) tropical fruit juice or apple and mango juice

POACHED KUMQUATS
225 g (8 oz) kumquats
300 ml (½ pint) orange juice
45 ml (3 tbsp) sugar

1 Mix the lemon juice with the gelatine. Leave to stand for 5 minutes or until it is sponge-like in texture, then place over a pan of gently simmering water until the mixture clears and liquefies. Stir into the tropical juice.

2 Rinse out six 200 ml (7 fl oz) or one 1.1 litre (2 pint) jelly mould(s) but do not dry. Pour in the fruit liquid, cover and place in the refrigerator to set for at least 5 hours.

3 Meanwhile, make the poached kumquats. Halve each kumquat, discarding any pips. Place in a saucepan with the orange juice and sugar, bring slowly to the boil then simmer for about 15 minutes or until the kumquats are tender.

4 Remove the kumquats from the saucepan using slotted spoons and set aside. Bubble down the orange juice until only about 90 ml (6 tbsp) juice remains. Pour over the kumquats and cool. Cover and refrigerate until required.

5 To serve the jelly, dip the whole jelly very quickly in hot water, pour off any water that has gathered on the top of the jelly, then invert onto a serving plate and shake the mould hard; remove the mould carefully. Serve with the poached kumquats.

COOK'S NOTE
If you don't have any small jelly moulds, use small tumblers or egg cups.

Coconut Crème Brûlée

PREPARATION TIME:
30 MINUTES, PLUS CHILLING

COOKING TIME:
ABOUT 1½ HOURS

FREEZING: SUITABLE (STAGE 3)

250 CALS PER SERVING

SERVES 8

75 g (3 oz) creamed coconut
600 ml (1 pint) milk
3 whole eggs, plus 3 egg yolks
150 ml (¼ pint) single cream
30 ml (2 tbsp) caster sugar

1 small mango
2 or 3 slices fresh or canned pineapple
1 banana
juice of ½ lemon
90 ml (6 tbsp) demerara sugar

1 Grate the creamed coconut and place in a saucepan with the milk. Warm through gently until the coconut has dissolved.

2 Whisk the eggs and yolks until evenly blended. Continue to whisk, adding the coconut milk, cream and caster sugar.

3 Strain the mixture into a shallow 1.1 litre (2 pint) ovenproof dish. Place in a roasting tin and pour in enough warm water to come halfway up the sides of the dish. Cook, uncovered, at 170°C (325°F) Mark 3 for 1½ hours or until just set. Cool, cover and chill overnight until firm.

4 Cut the mango across either side of the stone, then cut the flesh into pieces and peel off the skin. Chop the flesh surrounding the stone. Core and chop the pineapple slices. Peel and roughly chop the banana, then toss in lemon juice.

5 Cover the coconut custard with a layer of fruit. Sprinkle with the demerara sugar and place under a medium-hot grill until golden. Serve warm or at room temperature.

Baked Saffron Yogurt

PREPARATION TIME:
10 MINUTES, PLUS INFUSING
AND CHILLING

COOKING TIME:
ABOUT 30 MINUTES

FREEZING: NOT SUITABLE

250 CALS PER SERVING

SERVES 8

300 ml (½ pint) milk
pinch of saffron strands
6 green cardamoms
2 whole eggs, plus 2 egg yolks

400 g (14 oz) can condensed milk
300 ml (½ pint) natural yogurt
mango slices, to decorate

1 Bring the milk, saffron and cardamoms to the boil. Remove from the heat, cover and infuse for 10-15 minutes.

2 Put the eggs, egg yolks, condensed milk and yogurt in a bowl and beat together.

3 Strain the milk into the egg mixture, stirring gently to mix. Divide between 8 ramekin dishes in a roasting tin. Add hot water to come halfway up the sides. Bake in the oven at 180°C (350°F) Mark 4 for about 30 minutes or until firm to the touch.

4 Cool the baked yogurt desserts completely, then chill for at least 2 hours before serving.

5 To serve, run a blunt-edged knife around the edge of each yogurt, then turn out onto individual dishes. Decorate with mango slices.

Almond Sweetmeat

PREPARATION TIME: 5 MINUTES, PLUS COOLING

COOKING TIME: ABOUT 50 MINUTES

FREEZING: SUITABLE

130 CALS PER SERVING

MAKES 24

15 ml (1 tbsp) ghee or melted butter
900 ml (1½ pints) milk
225 g (8 oz) sugar

225 g (8 oz) ground almonds or pistachios
1.25 ml (¼ tsp) almond essence
24 whole blanched almonds, to decorate

1 Grease a 28 x 18 cm (11 x 7 inch) rectangular tin with a little of the ghee or butter. Set aside. Pour the milk into a large, heavy-based saucepan and bring to the boil. Boil rapidly for about 20-30 minutes, stirring occasionally, until reduced to the thickness of double cream. Strain the milk and return to a clean saucepan.

2 Add the sugar, stir well and simmer for 10 minutes. Add the ground nuts and cook for a further 10 minutes, stirring all the time. Do not let the mixture catch or burn.

3 Stir in the remaining ghee or butter and cook, stirring all the time, until the mixture begins to come away from the sides of the pan, then remove the pan from the heat and stir in the almond essence.

4 Pour the mixture into the prepared tin and spread flat with a spatula. Leave to cool for 25 minutes.

5 Cut into 24 diamonds, then press one almond into each diamond. Leave to cool and harden completely before serving.

COOK'S NOTE
For the best flavour, grind the nuts yourself rather than buying them ready-ground.

211

Sweet Indian Rice Pudding

PREPARATION TIME: 5 MINUTES,
PLUS STANDING

COOKING TIME: 55 MINUTES

FREEZING: NOT SUITABLE

525-790 CALS PER SERVING

SERVES 4-6

COOK'S NOTE
Make sure that you use
green cardamoms for this
dish, rather than black ones.
Green cardamoms have a
fine delicate aroma and
taste, whereas black
cardamoms are stronger in
flavour and coarser in
texture – more suited to
savoury dishes.

175 g (6 oz) long-grain rice
2.5 ml (½ tsp) salt
125 g (4 oz) sugar
2.5 cm (1 inch) stick cinnamon
120 ml (8 tbsp) ghee or butter
seeds of 4 green cardamoms

1.25 ml (¼ tsp) grated nutmeg
pinch of saffron strands
125 g (4 oz) flaked blanched almonds
125 g (4 oz) raisins
50 g (2 oz) desiccated coconut

1 Bring a large saucepan of water to the boil. Add the rice and salt and bring back to the boil. Stir once, then simmer, uncovered, for 10 minutes.
2 Meanwhile, put the sugar and cinnamon stick in a separate heavy-based saucepan. Add 300 ml (½ pint) water and heat gently until the sugar has dissolved. Bring to the boil, then boil rapidly for 1 minute. Remove from the heat.
3 Drain the rice. Heat the ghee or butter in a flameproof casserole, add the rice, cardamoms and nutmeg and cook gently, stirring, for 1-2 minutes until the rice glistens.
4 Add the sugar syrup (with the cinnamon stick) to the rice and stir gently to mix. Sprinkle in the saffron and stir again.
5 Cover tightly with a lid and cook in the oven at 180°C (350°F) Mark 4 for 40 minutes. Discard the cinnamon stick and cover the casserole tightly again. Leave to stand for 5 minutes, then stir in the nuts, raisins and coconut. Spoon into individual dishes and serve immediately.

Baked Moong Bean Custard

PREPARATION TIME: 10 MINUTES

COOKING TIME: 1¼ HOURS

FREEZING: NOT SUITABLE

170 CALS PER SERVING

SERVES 8

Illustrated opposite

COOK'S NOTE
Split mung beans are the
hulled seeds of the mung
bean (often called moong
bean). They are pale yellow
in colour and are available
from Indian and ethnic
stores, as well as healthfood
shops and some
supermarkets.

140 g (4½ oz) split mung beans
150 ml (¼ pint) coconut milk
1 egg, beaten
125 g (4 oz) caster sugar
25 g (1 oz) rice flour
2.5 ml (½ tsp) ground cinnamon

pinch of grated nutmeg
15 g (½ oz) dried grated or shredded coconut
125 g (4 oz) strawberries, hulled
icing sugar, for dusting
a little single cream, to serve (optional)

1 Wash the beans under cold running water until the water runs clear. Place in a saucepan and pour in enough water to cover the beans by 5 cm (2 inches). Bring slowly to the boil, cover and simmer over a low heat for 30-35 minutes until completely soft. Drain off any excess water and press the beans through a sieve to form a smooth paste. Set aside to cool.
2 Grease and line a 20 cm (8 inch) cake tin. Transfer the bean purée to a large bowl and beat in the coconut milk, egg, sugar, rice flour and spices. Pour into the prepared tin and scatter the coconut over the surface.
3 Bake in the centre of the oven at 190°C (375°F) Mark 5 for 45 minutes until pale golden and firm in the centre. Leave in the tin to cool slightly. Meanwhile halve or slice the strawberries.
4 Carefully remove the warm custard cake from its tin and transfer to a serving plate. Top with the strawberries and dust with icing sugar. Serve cut into wedges, accompanied by pouring cream if wished.

Sweet Carrot Pudding

PREPARATION TIME: 5 MINUTES

COOKING TIME: 2 HOURS 40 MINUTES

FREEZING: NOT SUITABLE

410-620 CALS PER SERVING

SERVES 4-6

450 g (1 lb) carrots
750 ml (1¼ pints) milk
150 ml (¼ pint) single cream
75 g (3 oz) sugar
15 ml (1 tbsp) treacle
45 ml (3 tbsp) ghee or melted butter

125 g (4 oz) ground almonds
seeds of 6 green cardamoms, crushed
25 g (1 oz) sultanas
chopped pistachios and raw carrot shapes, to decorate

1 Peel and coarsely grate the carrots, then put into a large, heavy-based saucepan. Pour in the milk and cream and bring to the boil, stirring constantly.

2 Simmer gently, stirring occasionally to prevent any sticking, for at least 2 hours until the milk has evaporated and the mixture is greatly reduced.

3 Stir in the sugar and treacle, then simmer for a further 30 minutes, stirring occasionally to prevent sticking.

4 Add the ghee or melted butter, ground almonds, crushed cardamom seeds and sultanas. Cook, stirring, for another 5-10 minutes until the mixture begins to look oily on the surface. Transfer to a serving dish and decorate with the pistachio nuts and carrot shapes. Serve hot or cold.

Gulab Jamun

PREPARATION TIME: 15 MINUTES

COOKING TIME: 25 MINUTES

FREEZING: NOT SUITABLE

425-638 CALS PER SERVING

SERVES 4-6

225 g (8 oz) sugar
6 green cardamoms
175 g (6 oz) dried skimmed milk with vegetable fat
10 ml (2 tsp) baking powder

50 g (2 oz) self-raising flour
15 ml (1 tbsp) semolina
about 150 ml (¼ pint) milk
oil for deep-frying
rose water (optional)

1 Put the sugar in a saucepan with 450 ml (¾ pint) water. Bring slowly to the boil, stirring to dissolve the sugar. Lightly crush the cardamoms and add to the pan. Boil rapidly for 4 minutes. Remove from the heat, cover and set aside.

2 In a bowl, mix together the dried milk, baking powder, flour, semolina and enough milk to mix to a stiff dough rather like shortcrust pastry.

3 Turn out onto a board and knead the dough until smooth, then divide into 24 pieces. Keep covered with cling film to prevent the dough drying out.

4 Roll each piece of dough into a completely smooth ball. Meanwhile, heat the oil in a deep-fat fryer to 170°C (325°F).

5 Deep-fry the dough pieces in batches for 2-3 minutes until golden brown on all sides, turning them with a slotted spoon to ensure even browning. They must not fry too quickly as they have to cook all the way through before becoming too brown on the outside.

6 Remove them from the oil with a slotted spoon and drain on kitchen paper while frying the remainder.

7 While still hot, transfer to a serving dish. Pour over the warm syrup and sprinkle with rose water, if liked. Serve warm or cold.

Mango Pancakes

PREPARATION TIME:
15 MINUTES, PLUS STANDING

COOKING TIME: 15 MINUTES

FREEZING: PANCAKES SUITABLE

105 CALS PER PANCAKE

MAKES 8-12 PANCAKES

125 g (4 oz) plain white flour
pinch of salt
1 egg
300 ml (½ pint) semi-skimmed milk
2 large mangoes
6 passion fruit
10 ml (2 tsp) arrowroot

150 ml (¼ pint) pineapple juice
juice of ½ lime
30 ml (2 tbsp) Malibu (optional)
caster sugar
oil for frying
icing sugar for dusting

1 Blend the flour, salt and egg with the milk in a food processor until smooth. Cover and set aside for 30 minutes.

2 To make the filling, peel and slice the mangoes. Halve the passion fruit and remove the pulp. Mix the arrowroot with 30 ml (2 tbsp) cold water.

3 Place the pineapple juice in a small saucepan and warm gently. Stir in the arrowroot and bring to the boil. Remove from the heat and stir in the passion fruit pulp, lime juice and Malibu, if using. Sweeten to taste and set aside.

4 Lightly brush an 18 cm (7 inch) nonstick pancake pan with oil and heat. When hot, add enough batter to coat the base of the pan thinly, about 45 ml (3 tbsp). Cook for about 3 minutes or until golden, then toss or turn. Cook for a further 1-2 minutes, then transfer to a plate, cover and keep warm. Cook the remaining pancakes in the same way.

5 Fold the pancakes in half, fill with the sliced mango and then fold in half once again. Dust with icing sugar and serve with the warm sauce.

Hot Mango Soufflés with Papaya Sauce

PREPARATION TIME: 55 MINUTES

COOKING TIME: 6-8 MINUTES

FREEZING: SUITABLE BEFORE
BAKING (THAW AT ROOM
TEMPERATURE FOR 2 HOURS
THEN BAKE)

310 CALS PER SERVING

SERVES 6

50 g (2 oz) butter, melted
150 g (5 oz) caster sugar
25 g (1 oz) blanched almonds
2 ripe mangoes, each about 350 g (12 oz)
20 ml (4 tsp) cornflour
30 ml (2 tbsp) orange juice

5 ml (1 tsp) finely grated orange rind
6 egg whites

PAPAYA SAUCE
2-3 papayas
30-45 ml (2-3 tbsp) caster sugar
10-15 ml (2-3 tsp) lemon juice

1 Brush 6 deep ramekins with the butter, then dust with 40 g (1½ oz) of the sugar, tapping out any excess. Chop the almonds coarsely and divide between the ramekins.

2 Peel the mangoes and cut the flesh away from the stones. Purée the mango flesh in a food processor or blender until smooth. Pour the mango purée into a small, heavy-based saucepan and cook over a low heat for 20 minutes, stirring frequently, until reduced to a thick paste.

3 Put the remaining 90 g (3½ oz) sugar in a small heavy-based pan, with 45 ml (3 tbsp) water and dissolve over a low heat, stirring occasionally. Boil rapidly for 2 minutes, then stir the syrup into the mango purée.

4 Blend the cornflour with the orange juice and stir into the mango purée, with the orange rind. Cook, stirring, over medium heat until boiling and thickened. Remove from the heat and cover the surface with dampened greaseproof paper; set aside to cool.

5 Meanwhile, make the papaya sauce. Halve the papayas, scoop out the seeds, then peel. Purée the flesh in a food processor or blender. Add sugar and lemon juice to taste; set aside.

6 Whisk the egg whites in a large bowl until holding soft peaks, then whisk one third into the mango mixture. Carefully fold in the remaining egg whites.

7 Spoon the mixture into the ramekins. Place on a preheated baking sheet and bake at 220°C (425°F) Mark 7 just above the centre of the oven for 6-8 minutes until well risen and golden.

8 Meanwhile, spoon the sauce onto individual plates. When the soufflés are ready, gently unmould onto the sauce and serve at once.

Coconut Ice Cream

PREPARATION TIME:
15 MINUTES, PLUS FREEZING

COOKING TIME: 10 MINUTES

FREEZING: SUITABLE

800 CALS PER SERVING

SERVES 8

Illustrated opposite

275 g (10 oz) sugar
four 450 ml (¾ pint) cans coconut milk

TO DECORATE
few dark red rose petals
few shredded dried red rose petals
freshly grated nutmeg
ground cinnamon

1 Put the sugar and 600 ml (1 pint) water in a heavy-based saucepan and dissolve over a medium heat, stirring occasionally. As soon as it is dissolved, stop stirring, increase the heat and boil rapidly for 10 minutes to make a sugar syrup. Leave to cool completely.
2 Blend the cooled syrup with the coconut milk. Pour into a shallow freezerproof container, cover and freeze for about 3 hours or until partially frozen.
3 Spoon the mixture into a blender or food processor and quickly blend on high speed to break down the ice crystals without letting the ice cream melt. Immediately return to the container, re-cover and freeze again just until mushy. This will probably take another 2 hours.
4 Process again as before. Return to the container, cover tightly and freeze for about 3 hours until firm.
5 Allow to stand at room temperature for 20 minutes before serving. Scoop the ice cream into serving dishes. Scatter with the rose petals, nutmeg and cinnamon.

Kulfi

PREPARATION TIME: 10 MINUTES, PLUS FREEZING

COOKING TIME: 25 MINUTES

FREEZING: SUITABLE

1060 CALS PER SERVING

SERVES 4

COOK'S NOTES
Cook the mixture as rapidly as possible without boiling over. Watch carefully during cooking to ensure it doesn't boil over, or stick to the pan.

In India, Kulfi is traditionally set in special cone-shaped containers. Clean empty yogurt pots are ideal substitutes, or you can use small freezerproof containers, such as ramekins.

450 ml (¾ pint) double cream
400 ml (14 fl oz) can condensed milk
125 g (4 oz) caster sugar
25 g (1 oz) shelled unsalted pistachio nuts

few drops of green food colouring (optional)
few drops of almond essence
40 g (1½ oz) ground almonds
pistachio nuts, to decorate

1 Put the cream, condensed milk and sugar in a large heavy-based, nonstick saucepan and heat gently, stirring all the time, until the sugar is completely dissolved.
2 Bring to the boil, stirring, then reduce the heat until the mixture is boiling steadily. Cook, stirring occasionally, for about 15-20 minutes or until the mixture is thick enough to coat the back of a spoon and reduced to about 600 ml (1 pint); it should be yellow in colour.
3 Meanwhile, finely chop the nuts.
4 When the mixture is cooked, colour it pale green with a few drops of green colouring, if desired. Stir in the almond essence, pistachio nuts and ground almonds. Leave to cool slightly.
5 Divide the mixture between 4 individual moulds, each about 150 ml (¼ pint) capacity. Leave to cool completely.
6 Stand the containers on a baking sheet or plate and place in the freezer for about 4 hours or until frozen.
7 To serve, run a knife around the edge of each kulfi to loosen, then invert onto individual serving plates. Scatter with pistachio nuts and serve immediately.

Cardamom and Pistachio Ice Cream

PREPARATION TIME:
10 MINUTES, PLUS FREEZING

COOKING TIME: 10 MINUTES

FREEZING: SUITABLE

465 CALS PER SERVING

SERVES 6

50 g (2 oz) shelled pistachio nuts
3 litres (5¼ pints) milk
14 cardamom pods

125 g (4 oz) caster sugar
mango, pineapple and papaya, to serve

1 Toast the pistachio nuts under the grill, cool, then roughly chop. Cover and set aside.
2 Place the milk and cardamom pods in a large heavy-based saucepan. Bring to the boil, then simmer vigorously until reduced to 1 litre (1¾ pints). Strain the milk, discarding the cardamom, and stir in the sugar and nuts.
3 Cool quickly and pour into a shallow freezerproof container. Cover and freeze for about 2 hours until partially frozen. Remove from the freezer and beat well to break down any ice crystals. Freeze for several hours until firm. Allow to stand at room temperature for 30 minutes before serving.
4 Serve scoops of the ice cream with sliced mango, pineapple and papaya.

Mandarin Sorbet

PREPARATION TIME:
15 MINUTES, PLUS COOLING
AND FREEZING

COOKING TIME: 1 MINUTE

FREEZING: SUITABLE

170 CALS PER SERVING

SERVES 6

8 mandarins, satsumas or tangerines
2 lemons
a little orange juice

175 g (6 oz) caster sugar
30 ml (2 tbsp) orange liqueur
mandarin or satsuma rind strips, to decorate

1 Peel the mandarins and put in a food processor or blender and process until very finely chopped. Press the mixture through a nylon sieve into a measuring jug.
2 Using a potato peeler, peel off the rind from 1 lemon and reserve. Squeeze the juice from both lemons and strain into the jug. Make up the quantity of juice to 600 ml (1 pint) with orange juice.
3 Place the measured juice, sugar and reserved lemon rind in a pan. Bring to the boil, stirring to dissolve the sugar, and boil for 1 minute. Strain into a bowl and leave to cool.
4 Add the orange liqueur, then pour the mixture into a shallow freezerproof container. Cover, place in the freezer and leave until the mixture is beginning to set about 2.5 cm (1 inch) around the edges – this takes 3-4 hours.
5 Turn the mixture into a bowl, break up with a fork and whisk until smooth. Return to the container, cover and freeze until firm.
6 Place the container of sorbet in the refrigerator for about 20 minutes before serving to soften slightly. Spoon into serving dishes and decorate with mandarin or satsuma rind.

Mango, Ginger and Citrus Sorbet

PREPARATION TIME:
25 MINUTES, PLUS FREEZING

COOKING TIME: 3-4 MINUTES

FREEZING: SUITABLE

140-95 CALS PER SERVING

SERVES 4-6

2 large mangoes, each about 400 g (14 oz)
25 g (1 oz) preserved stem ginger
50 ml (2 fl oz) syrup from the stem ginger jar

50 g (2 oz) caster sugar
finely pared rind and juice of 3 limes

1 Peel the mangoes, using a potato peeler, then cut down either side of the central stone; cut away as much of the remaining flesh as possible. Chop the mango flesh and purée in a blender or food processor until very smooth. Transfer to a bowl and set aside. Finely chop the stem ginger and stir into the purée.

2 Place the ginger syrup in a small saucepan with the sugar, lime rind and juice, and add 75 ml (3 fl oz) water. Heat gently, stirring until the sugar is dissolved. Bring to the boil and simmer for 3 minutes. Remove from the heat and leave to cool.

3 Strain the cooled syrup through a fine sieve into the puréed mango mixture and stir well. Transfer to a freezerproof container and freeze for 2 hours. Remove from the freezer and beat well to break down any ice crystals that may have formed. Return to the freezer for a further 1 hour, then beat again. Repeat once more. Freeze for several hours until firm, or until required.

4 Transfer the sorbet to the refrigerator about 20 minutes before serving to soften slightly. Scoop into individual glass dishes to serve.

VARIATION

Mango Ice Cream: Heat 300 ml (½ pint) double cream with 2 strips lemon rind until boiling. Remove from the heat and leave to infuse for 30 minutes, then strain. Whisk into 3 egg yolks, then heat gently until thickened; do not boil. Cool, then combine with the puréed flesh of 2 large mangoes and 30 ml (2 tbsp) lemon juice. Freeze stirring every hour until firm.

Index

Page numbers in *italic* refer to the illustrations

Special Indian and Asian ingredients can be
obtained by mail order from:
Steamboat Exotic Foods, P.O. Box 452,
Bradford, West Yorkshire, BD4 7TF.
Tel: 01274 693593